SMITTEN

Romantic obsession,
the neuroscience
of limerence,
and how to make
love last

TOM BELLAMY, PhD

ST. MARTIN'S
ESSENTIALS
NEW YORK

The information in this book is not intended to replace the advice of the reader's own physician or other medical professional. You should consult a medical professional in matters relating to health, especially if you have existing medical conditions, and before starting, stopping, or changing the dose of any medication you are taking. Individual readers are solely responsible for their own health-care decisions. The author and the publisher do not accept responsibility for any adverse effects individuals may claim to experience, whether directly or indirectly, from the information contained in this book.

Note: Quotes in the book are from the experiences of limerents who posted public comments on the livingwithlimerence.com website. Comments are attributed by username initials to preserve anonymity.

Published in the United States by St. Martin's Essentials,
an imprint of St. Martin's Publishing Group

EU Representative: Macmillan Publishers Ireland Ltd, 1st Floor,
The Liffey Trust Centre, 117–126 Sheriff Street Upper, Dublin 1, DO1 YC43

SMITTEN. Copyright © 2025 by Tom Bellamy. All rights reserved.
Printed in the United States of America. For information, address
St. Martin's Publishing Group, 120 Broadway, New York, NY 10271.

www.stmartins.com

The Library of Congress Cataloging-in-Publication Data is available upon request.

ISBN 978-1-250-39267-1 (hardcover)
ISBN 978-1-250-39268-8 (ebook)

The publisher of this book does not authorize the use or reproduction of any part of this book in any manner for the purpose of training artificial intelligence technologies or systems. The publisher of this book expressly reserves this book from the Text and Data Mining exception in accordance with Article 4(3) of the European Union Digital Single Market Directive 2019/790.

Our books may be purchased in bulk for specialty retail/wholesale, literacy, corporate/premium, educational, and subscription box use. Please contact MacmillanSpecialMarkets@macmillan.com.

Originally published in the United Kingdom by Watkins,
an imprint of Watkins Media Limited

First U.S. Edition 2025

10 9 8 7 6 5 4 3 2 1

CONTENTS

Introduction: The Discovery of Limerence … 1

Part 1: Understanding Limerence … 9

1. What Is Limerence?
   Love, a crush, or something else? … 10
2. The Phases of Limerence
   From tantalizing glimmer to oppressive obsession … 24
3. The Neuroscience of Limerence
   What today's brain research tells us about infatuation … 34
4. Person Addiction
   Falling into the limerent habit … 47
5. Is Limerence a Mental Illness?
   Am I going crazy? … 61
6. Who Becomes Limerent?
   And how common is it? … 75
7. Why Does Limerence Exist?
   Nature's little joke … 88

Part 2: Understanding Limerent Objects … 99

8. Social and Cultural Forces
   Romeo and Juliet, Beatrice and Dante, … and a thousand high school movies … 100
9. Why Do They Seem So Special?
   Where the glimmer comes from, and how adolescence shapes our romantic lives … 109
10. Why Are Some People So Addictive?
    A rogues' gallery of limerence enablers … 120

11. Dating While Limerent
   Finding the right match   133
12. Social Media
   A limitless database of rumination fodder   144
13. Can't We Just Be Friends?
   Unrequited limerence, forbidden love, and last-ditch bargaining   154
14. Limerence and Long-Term Love
   Life as a limerent   165
15. Limerence and Infidelity
   "I love you but I'm not in love with you"   176

Part 3: Recovering from Limerence   **187**

16. Finding Balance
   Can the ecstatic union last?   188
17. How to Get Rid of Limerence
   First solve the crisis, then figure out why it happened   196
18. Breaking the Limerence Habit
   The psychology of behavioral change   207
19. Getting Over Limerence for a Specific Person
   How to deprogram yourself out of limerence   220
20. Therapy for Limerence
   What works and what doesn't   231
21. Lasting Freedom
   Reshaping your future and moving on   241

About the Author   253
Acknowledgments   254
Notes   256
Index   275

To Teika, of course. Thanks for everything, my love.

INTRODUCTION
THE DISCOVERY OF LIMERENCE

On a long-haul flight from Paris to New York, Professor Dorothy Tennov was testing her friend's patience. An interview with Simone de Beauvoir had drawn the professor to Paris, and on the flight home she was excitedly sharing the findings of her latest psychological research with her friend, Helen Payne. However, this was not a typical case of an academic boring their companion with trivia that could only interest an expert. Dorothy was talking about love.

For several years, Professor Tennov had been quietly working on a side project to her main research. In 1975, she had made a name for herself with a book critiquing psychoanalysis, and a part of that work had involved recording the devastating consequences suffered by patients who fell in love with their therapists. Tennov had been struck by the similarities of the episodes and had begun to investigate further. This had blossomed into broader questions about romantic attachment and the nature of infatuation.

Her research was somewhat clandestine. Then, as now, romantic love was not really considered a fit subject for academic inquiry, but slowly she filled binders with information from hundreds of people suffering through the exquisite agonies of romantic heartache. Tennov's approach to the question of love was to gather information with a magpie-like zeal. Pages filled up with testimonies. Probing questionnaires were used to uncover subconscious triggers, find clues to the psychological basis of infatuation, and identify common experiences that defined the sensation of falling in love. This database of emotional stories was carefully curated and sifted for patterns and core truths.

Tennov also drew widely from the humanities—from Ovid and Plato, Goethe and Stendhal. Marshalling all this material, she tried to make sense of the "madness" of love, to identify the psychological foundations of romantic obsession and to figure out how she could help people recover their emotional balance.

She was making good progress. Her work was converging on a theory that people in love slip into an altered mental state, defined by a rush of euphoric intoxication, a desperate desire for reciprocation from their beloved, and a tendency to idealize this wonderful other person into an impossible model of perfection. This was the insight she was so excited to share, but it was on that flight home from Paris, in conversation with her friend, that she made an unexpected breakthrough.

Bluntly, Helen was bored and frustrated. After listening to Dorothy's enthusiastic monologue with growing impatience, she finally interrupted in exasperation. The range of extravagant emotions that Tennov had described as love were alien to her. Instead, her own love life had been marred by partners who swung through these emotional extremes—their claims of ecstasy and their demands for attention and fear of rejection ruining promising relationships before they got started. As she saw it, the ridiculous, exaggerated version of romance described by Tennov, and portrayed in the media and popular culture, was absurd.

Surprised and abashed, Tennov realized that her work rested on the faulty assumption that everyone's experience of love was essentially the same. That conversation with a valued friend (who had lived a full and rewarding life, with marriages, children, and an active sex life) nudged Tennov into finally recognizing her mistake. She was not compiling a universal description for the sensation of "falling in love"; instead, she had identified a very specific mental state of romantic infatuation that only some people experience. In time, she coined a new word to describe the phenomenon that she was uncovering: *limerence*.

Defining limerence

Tennov published her results in the 1979 book, *Love and Limerence: The Experience of Being in Love*. Since that breakthrough she focused her attention on defining limerence as a phenomenon. It is experienced as a mental state of profound, involuntary, obsessive romantic infatuation with another person (termed the "limerent object"). She compiled a list of symptoms that are characteristic of the condition. Paraphrasing slightly, they are:

- Frequent intrusive thoughts about the limerent object (LO), who is a potential sexual partner
- An acute need for reciprocation of equally strong feeling
- Exaggerated dependency of mood on the LO's actions: elation when sensing reciprocation, devastation when sensing disinterest
- Inability to react limerently to more than one person at a time
- Fleeting relief from unrequited feeling through vivid fantasy about reciprocation from the LO
- Insecurity or shyness when in the presence of the LO, often manifesting in physical discomfort (sweating, stammering, racing heart)
- Intensification of feelings by adversity
- An aching sensation in "the heart" when uncertainty is strong
- A general intensity of feeling that places other concerns in the background
- A remarkable ability to emphasize the positive features of the LO, and minimize, or empathize with, the negative

There are two common reactions to reading that list. The first is, "That's just love—you don't need a special word for that." The second is, "That's not normal—those people are neurotic." This, of course, is Tennov's point: If you fall in love like Dorothy Tennov, thethe first response is more likely; if you fall in love like Helen Payne, then you'd agree with the second response.

That split reaction was also seen in the critical reception to Tennov's book. Some commentators felt that limerence was a powerful new way of understanding romantic attraction, others thought it ridiculous and improbable—describing a mental derangement rather than healthy, mature love. This reaction from the critics fit Tennov's idea that there are two tribes of people who experience the early stages of love in profoundly different ways. While both may get a boost of "new relationship energy," erotic charge, excitement, and attraction, it is the limerents who succumb to the total psychological capture of obsessive, involuntary infatuation that seems so marvelous to them, but so irrational and disproportionate to others.

A new perspective

Dorothy Tennov died in 2007. Limerence remained on the margins of cultural consciousness, making only occasional appearances in psychological research. Mostly, it was overshadowed by other theories of romantic attachment and approaches to the treatment of mood disorders. Despite this relative obscurity, the concept of limerence retained its remarkable explanatory power.

My own discovery of limerence occurred a few years ago, in the midst of a personal crisis. Like Tennov, I had always assumed that the experience of "falling in love" was a human universal, and I hadn't really given it much thought over the course of my life—right up until it became a problem. It turns out that experiencing unwanted limerence for the first time forces some serious self-analysis.

Reading *Love and Limerence* was a revelation, not just because it described the phenomenon of romantic infatuation so astutely, but because—as an academic neuroscientist—I immediately saw how contemporary neuroscience could explain the altered mental state of limerence. We've accumulated an additional half-century of knowledge since Tennov began her work, and know more about the neural mechanisms that control euphoria, reward, motivation, obsession, and addiction. Collectively, these mechanisms can explain the behavioral observations that she made, and the symptoms that limerents encounter.

That half-century of progress has also given us a second big advance. Tennov had to painstakingly gather individual testimony in a pre-internet world, but nowadays we can effortlessly connect with countless other romantic fools online. As my own understanding of limerence developed, I did what any normal person in the modern world would do: I started a blog. This was partly to exorcise my own insistent thoughts, but it was also an opportunity to enthuse about this little-known theory that explained so much about the trials we visit upon ourselves in the name of love.

Over time, that blog has grown into a community of fellow travelers, many of them finding the Living with Limerence site to seek shelter from the emotional storm of obsessive infatuation, and share their stories. Some of those stories are comic, some are tragic—from people who regret the tattoos they hoped would impress their limerent objects, to those who have pined away for decades on secret, unrequited love. Limerence can upend otherwise stable lives, and those effects aren't limited to the limerents themselves, of course. We also hear from their families—men whose wives have emptied the family savings account and sent all the money to an online scammer they're infatuated with, and women whose husbands have transformed from a devoted partner and father into a dismissive and cruel adulterer.

Making sense of limerence

The goal of this book is to explain the phenomenon of limerence—both for those who are currently riding the emotional rollercoaster and for those who have never experienced it themselves (but have perhaps grappled with the perplexing behavior of an apparently irrational lover). It is organized into three parts: understanding limerence, understanding limerent objects, and recovering from limerence—examining what happens in the brain of a limerent, why they become obsessed with certain people, and how they can break out of the psychological trap.

Limerence arises from hard-wired neural systems that were refined over evolutionary history, which are then programmed by our own experiences of growing up in a complex social environment. Cultural pressures shape our response to the experience, and determine how we make sense of the emotional onslaught. All of those factors are important for understanding what happens when we are bewitched by an irresistibly attractive person. What makes them so appealing is an important part of the story too.

Together, the evidence suggests that the best way to understand limerence is as **addiction to another person.** That perspective explains why being with them is so intoxicating, why almost all waking thoughts are dominated by them, and how limerence progresses from a natural high to an exhausting craving that makes it difficult to concentrate on everyday tasks. It also enables us to find practical solutions for how to manage it when it becomes intolerable.

The highs are so high but there is always a crash. Always pain afterward. I just want to feel normal again but can't untangle myself. —JD

You can learn a lot about yourself from how you fall in love, and who you fall in love with.

ARE YOU A LIMERENT? A SELF-TEST QUESTIONNAIRE

These questions are designed to identify the common experiences felt by limerents during periods of romantic infatuation. Answer the following true or false questions for yourself, using your best judgment about whether you *have ever* had these experiences during your own romantic attachments to other people:

1. I become nervous and excited when I am with them—my heart races, and I feel jittery and clumsy.
2. When they are happy and friendly toward me, I feel exhilarated and "high."
3. When they are cold toward me, I am anxious and feel panicked.

4. The whole world seems brighter and more colorful since I met them.
5. I am more energetic and optimistic since I met them.
6. I sometimes crave solitude so that I can spend time fantasizing about them.
7. Being with them is the most desirable thing in my world.
8. They are an extraordinary person, and I like the fact that I can see this while others cannot.
9. I frequently worry about whether they like me as much as I hope.
10. When I am anxious, I can calm myself by remembering a happy encounter with them.
11. I often mentally rehearse conversations I might have with them.
12. I feel compelled to share intimate secrets with them.
13. I compulsively check their social media to try and feel closer to them.
14. I am not romantically interested in anyone else since I met them.
15. My feelings for them are much more powerful than any other interests in my life.
16. I really want them to feel the same way about me as I do about them.
17. I often find it hard to concentrate on what I am doing because I am distracted by thoughts about them.
18. Most romantic movies and songs make me think of them now.
19. I sometimes feel (or like to pretend) that they are with me in spirit even though we are apart.
20. When I have a new experience, I immediately wonder what they would think about it.
21. Their possessions and the places they have been to have special significance for me.
22. I sometimes cannot stop thinking about them, even if I want to.

23. I feel embarrassed by the strength of my crush, and instinctively keep it secret.
24. I sometimes neglect my responsibilities to get more contact with them.
25. I feel intense jealousy or overwhelming anxiety if they flirt with someone else.

Scoring

If you answered "true" to fifteen or more of these questions, it is highly likely that you are a limerent. These statements are based on Tennov's list of symptoms, and were refined by polling visitors to the Living with Limerence website about their own experiences. The quiz is not a psychological diagnosis, but it is a good way to find out whether you feel affinity for the limerence tribe.

PART 1
UNDERSTANDING LIMERENCE

CHAPTER 1
WHAT IS LIMERENCE?

Love, a crush, or something else?

Limerence feels amazing. There are few experiences to match the emotional and physical high caused by the euphoria of limerence. It's a whole-body overload of exhilaration.

Limerence also feels awful. It can wring you out, plunge you into despair, shred your nerves, and leave you feeling unable to regulate your emotions or find peace.

Any attempt to explain limerence needs to capture this range of contradictory emotions. Dorothy Tennov's approach was to gather testimony and search for common experiences that distil the features of limerent infatuation down to its essential elements. That remains a very powerful way of understanding and defining the phenomenon:[1]

> *I once ended an afternoon talking with him, so high that my fingertips were tingling. Literally! I was so overcome by the emotions of being with him that my whole body was hyped up and I had pins and needles in my fingers.* —BT

> *When she's around I don't know how to behave, nor what to say. It's a mixture of uncertainty, fear of rejection, and joy from feeling she's in the same room. Oh, my. It's killing me almost!* —LP

> *It's like my world has been in gray my whole life and now it's suddenly in color. I feel this crazy mixture of shame, euphoria, humiliation, bliss, guilt, anxiety, loss, yearning. I feel like I'm going crazy. I want it to stop and I don't want it to stop.* —CA

WHAT IS LIMERENCE?

Over the course of this summer, the feeling I now know as limerence has been building. I've been irritable, depressed, withdrawn from my family, and derive no pleasure from activities I usually enjoy. When I text her, I am on edge until she replies and when she doesn't, I'm destroyed. I can soothe myself by remembering our moments together and fantasizing how she will reciprocate. —F

I'm just obsessed. I can't turn the thoughts off, I can't escape from the downs, and I keep chasing the highs even though I know I always crash after. I just want her more than anything I've ever wanted before.... Everything about her is perfect. —JD

Limerence is an overwhelming feeling of elation and excitement triggered by the presence of this remarkable other person. When you are with them, it feels like you are walking on air. They cause a surge of giddy euphoria that is intoxicating. The prospect of forming a romantic bond with them offers the promise of "the ecstatic union" described by Simone de Beauvoir.[2] Your whole body feels supercharged—your thoughts fizz and pop, you are more optimistic, your heart races and flutters, you tingle with excitement and energy. You feel invincible.

Unfortunately, that state of bliss is fragile. It's like riding a wave, and inevitably, the wave breaks. The overarousal of their company becomes exhausting. It becomes hard to focus on anything else—your concentration is shot, and you come to realize that the whole world is full of reminders of them. Worst of all are the times when they seem cold to you. Your heart, that used to flutter like a butterfly, now hammers and aches. Shame and anxiety shiver through you. Desperately, you cling to memories of times when they were kind or attentive or flirtatious—using happy memories like anchors to stabilize your mood and soothe the pain of rejection.

This emotional volatility is a symptom of limerence, and it is largely involuntary. Your mood seesaws back and forth, seemingly out of control. Your thoughts and feelings are at the complete mercy of this person who has entered your life and upended it: your limerent object.

There's just something about them

Limerence is an obsession focused on another person. They become the center of your life. They seem to have an extraordinary romantic potency that seduces and bewitches you, and draws you irresistibly toward them. The attraction is so strong it feels uncanny. If you are in the same room as them, you are hyperaware of their presence—woe betide any other poor soul who tries to engage you in conversation when *they* hover on the periphery of your awareness.

> *I was having lunch with a friend, when I realized I'd not heard what she'd said for ages, because he had come into the lunchroom like a massive presence that I was hyperaware of. Seriously, it was like the sun beating down on me just sensing him at the table behind me. —TC*

Everything about them becomes capitalized. It's not just a coffee cup, it's Their Coffee Cup, or Jacket, or Car.

Psychologists call this phenomenon *salience bias*—things associated with them jump out of the drab background and command your attention.[3] Their emotional significance to you amplifies your awareness of them. That reality means, of course, that limerents are also ill-equipped at judging their limerent objects accurately.

Tennov used the term "limerent object" quite deliberately to reflect this distortion. At first sight, it appears objectionable—these are people, not objects! They deserve due respect, not dehumanization simply because they have become the focus of someone else's infatuation. That's true, but limerents do not, in actual fact, respond to their limerent object as a fully rounded human being. They idealize them, idolize them, attribute imaginary motives to them, and project their own desires and hopes onto the blank screen of the fantasy figure living in their head. The term "limerent object" (LO) captures the important fact that limerents *do* engage in objectification. It has psychological significance, so I will continue to use it.

Ultimately, all this idealization—this urge to only see the best in LOs—is part of a desperate desire to believe that something remarkable is happening between the two of you. Naturally, most limerents conclude that their LO must be extraordinary to generate such a strong romantic response. Bad habits are ignored or explained away ("they're only rude to the waiter because they care so much about us having a nice date"), flaws are minimized and virtues amplified. Everything about them becomes enchanting. The romantic promise of such a paragon is limitless, and that leads to the central concern of all limerents: *Do they like me too?*

Reciprocation of romantic feeling is the most desirable thing in a limerent's world. Generally speaking, it isn't enough for the limerent to passively appreciate the merits of their LO; there is a strong impulse to express their overwhelming feelings, seek a positive response, and form a romantic bond. We're not talking admiration for a muse here; we're talking a fully consummated love affair.

The desire for reciprocation rapidly becomes the main preoccupation of life, and that means that rumination and reverie become a central part of the limerence experience. The LO not only captures your attention when you are with them but your daydreams are filled with them. Sometimes these are pleasant fantasies—them reciprocating your feelings and declaring themselves, or sexy fantasies about what you might get up to together once reciprocation has been secured. Other times, the reverie is more grounded. Hours can be spent reviewing previous encounters with the LO, running over what they said, what you said, and what you might have done differently. In the intensive search for signs of reciprocation, you analyze body language and unspoken words with a dedication that would impress a forensic scientist. Yet more hours are spent in rehearsal—imagining future conversations in which you might engineer a confession from them, or subtly hint at your high regard in the hope it will stimulate a response. Although, not too blatantly of course, just in case you risk exposing yourself to the icy stab of rejection.

An extraordinary amount of mental time and energy can be devoted to limerent reverie. At its peak, limerents can report nearly all their waking time being dominated by thoughts of the LO, and a fair portion of their dreams too. Daydreams are used for mood regulation, when a small secondary hit of bliss can be wrung from a happy fantasy to stave off the longing for a while.

This complete capture of the limerent's internal world by the LO leads to the next defining feature of the limerence experience: it feels uncanny. It is not hard to understand why some limerents feel enchanted by their LO, as though they have been struck by a love spell or Cupid's arrow. Limerence is so enthralling it can feel supernatural, numinous.

> *I can't explain what it is about him, but it just feels so right when I'm with him, like we are connected somehow. I know it sounds a bit ridiculous, but it really is like we are soulmates. —FS*

For many limerents, the emotional overload of the LO's company can feel like a transcendent, quasi-spiritual experience. It feels as though a powerful external force has overtaken you, transported you, and upended the world. Ideas that "this was meant to be," or that "this is a power greater than either of us," are reflections of the fact that limerence can feel as though it originates outside us and overwhelms our self-control. People talk about feeling a connection to the divine when in love—for limerents, this fits the ecstasy experienced just by being with their LO. For limerents of a spiritual tendency, the "rightness" of feelings for their LO can be reinforced by this sense of cosmic connectedness—maybe even seen as an indicator that God validates their love. Even for atheist limerents, the sense of a supernatural connection can be a powerfully heady experience.

Limerence, sex, and love

The intense, but unstable, emotional connection of limerence also helps to distinguish it from other romantic drives, such as lust or the longer-term affectional bonding of committed love.

The interrelations of limerence, sex, and love are complex. For most limerents, sexual desire for the LO is an important part of the experience, and many limerents report a striking increase in libido when in a state of limerence. While this springs from the arousal caused by the LO, it can cause a general increase in sexual receptiveness and interest.

I don't know what it is about him, but I've never felt sexier. —J

It sounds awful, but my sex life with my wife is better than it has ever been, because I just feel much more turned on all the time [since I met my LO]. —BB

This erotic charge is common, but it is not the driving force of limerence. The desire for romantic attachment is the strongest craving; the fact that it would lead, naturally and pleasingly, to sex, is a secondary concern.

In fact, that higher-level drive can also add complicating factors to the sexual pursuit of an LO. The intense hope and expectation associated with limerent desire can be counterproductive when it comes to sexual connection. Some limerents report disastrous sexual encounters with their LOs; the high stakes of the situation lead to performance anxiety, insecurity, and clumsiness. Ironically, rather than the culmination of desire, a bad sexual experience with an LO can throw a metaphorical bucket of cold water over the limerence, extinguishing the fire. It can be the disappointment that finally breaks through the idealization.

When I had sex with my LO it pretty much ended my limerence, as it was perfunctory and completely lacking any emotional connection. —A

Limerents certainly lust after their LOs, but sex cannot be the whole story. Many people can stir sexual desire in us (as the size of the erotica and pornography industries prove), but limerence is the most limited of special interests. Only one person can turn it on—or, at least, one person at a time. Similarly, sexual fantasy and limerent fantasy are also fundamentally different in character. There are many ways to trigger sexual arousal, and a wide range of imagined scenarios that can titillate us—even scenarios that we would never want to experience in real life (given all the weird, wild complexity of human sexuality). Limerent fantasies are much more specific, and much more focused, with a single objective—achieving blissful communion with the LO.

Perhaps the strongest evidence that limerence and sex are only indirectly connected is the existence of asexual limerents. When Tennov first identified and defined limerence, she was limited in the size of the pool of interviewees that she could draw from, and she reported a near universal connection between limerence and sex. With the almost limitless access to the wide, rich world of human diversity that the internet offers, we now have an advantage. I have heard from many people who have all the features of limerence—intrusive, obsessive thoughts, delirious euphoria, desperate desire for attachment—in the absence of sexual desire. In some cases, this is because the limerent object is not a good sexual match, in other cases, because sexual desire is outside of the normal experience.

> *It was an entirely independent romantic desire. There were never any sexual components to my fantasies—the closest I got was cuddling! My end goal wasn't intimacy, but rather emotional reciprocation. As for libido, I noticed little difference (my libido is pretty nonexistent to begin with). —BE*

If limerence can exist independently of erotic desire, is it more about a deeper and more meaningful form of love? Again, the relationship between limerence and love is slippery to define. They are obviously connected, obviously elements of the same romantic impulse, but there are also clear distinctions between limerence and "classic love."

Part of the difficulty with trying to resolve these distinctions is that the word "love" is itself so contentious and imprecise. It means different things to different people. The ancient Greeks defined seven types of love, ranging from playful *ludus* (what we might call "friends with benefits") to profound *agape* (spiritual, selfless love). Limerence has been described by Victor De Munck as "a particular carving up of the semantic domain of love," in recognition of the disputes that arise from the fuzziness of love as an umbrella term.[4]

To avoid getting bogged down in those semantics, my definition of "classic love" is: mutual sexual attraction, reciprocal concern for each other's well-being and happiness, and the close, intimate connection of a pair bond. That kind of love takes time. It builds slowly through the reinforcement of emotional and physical intimacy. It's not feasible that genuine bonding of this sort could occur during the first exuberant burst of limerent feelings—there simply hasn't been enough time for an authentic bond to develop.

Limerence is better understood as a desperate *urge to bond*. The overwhelming attraction to the LO is so profound that you hunger for more intimacy, more connection, more attachment. Limerence is greedy and needy, not selfless or unconditional, and during the period of uncertainty limerence can also be jealous and angry. Limerence is the compulsion to form a bond, the urgent rush to secure reciprocation and exclusivity, not the loving connection that grows from mutual care and cultivation of an intimate bond.

Limerence can transform into classic love, but it is far from certain that the desired transition will occur successfully. Stable, happy relationships can emerge from connections that begin in limerence, but the long-term bonds of affection take time to develop, depend on factors that are only loosely related to limerence, and need to last after the limerence has dissipated. Love may come later. Limerence is the altered mental state of euphoria and mania that takes hold while you are trying to first establish that connection.

How limerence begins

These distinctions between limerence, love, and lust also help to illustrate how limerence begins. There are a lot of attractive people in the world. Over the course of a lifetime most limerents will meet many people who could become sexual or romantic partners, and yet they don't become limerent for them all. A very particular set of circumstances needs to occur for attraction to turn into a sustained and disruptive mental state of infatuation. Three key conditions appear to be critical to the development of limerence.

The first is what might be called a psychological match to a specific limerent object—there is something special about certain people that causes a "glimmer" of limerent connection. The second factor is hope—hope that they are attracted to you too, and that there is at least some prospect of reciprocation. If it can be established early on that the LO is not romantically interested at all, then hope dies. Conversely, if the LO is interested and a relationship begins, then the limerence that has been kindled can be quickly satisfied through reciprocation and consummation—and discharged before it becomes too debilitating. The final factor is uncertainty.

For a full-blown bout of obsessive, involuntary limerence, there needs to be some adversity. The uncertainty of not quite knowing how the LO feels about you, or not being able to act on your feelings, promotes the shift from excited intoxication to life-altering obsession.

These three factors work together to really get you in trouble.

The glimmer

Limerents are sensitive to particular individuals. Not everyone can be a limerent object for them. It's a highly personal thing, but there is a kind of volatile synergy with some people that inflames limerent desire, and this is usually recognized at a subconscious level soon after meeting them. It could be their appearance, their mannerisms, their personality quirks, their scent, their confidence—some idiosyncratic combination of traits makes them especially romantically potent. I suspect this is the same elusive "spark" that is missing from a disappointing date—the magic charisma that we only sometimes find in others, and struggle to define or articulate clearly. A compelling frisson of excitement.

It seems there is a blueprint deeply integrated into each limerent's psyche that the subconscious mind is able to rapidly access, and if it spots a match, it kindles the limerent glimmer. That leads to full-body physiological arousal: dilated pupils, racing heart, sweaty palms, and an exhilarating nervous energy. This is not simply the butterflies you might feel when meeting someone especially beautiful or powerful or famous, though. This is different. The limerent glimmer feels more personal, more significant, and more charged with emotional power—as though the atmosphere has suddenly electrified.

Most limerents are able to detect the glimmer quickly, and sense romantic potential soon after meeting the right kind of person, but sometimes it can take longer to fully ignite. It could be that someone who you previously considered a friend slowly becomes more alluring, more interesting, more emotionally significant. Something shifts in your relationship, and you find yourself becoming nervous and excited around them. Regardless of the speed, the symptoms are the same; once the glimmer has started, arousal is heightened whenever they are around.

Just what it is about this other person that connects so deeply with us is an interesting question that is covered later in this book (see Chapter 9), but the key point is this: only a certain fraction of the attractive people we meet are a match for our "limerence blueprint" and capable of causing the glimmer.

Hope

Once you've sensed the glimmer, the next thing your limerent brain tries to determine is the possibility of reciprocation. You become hyperaware of the body language and emotional state of your potential LO. Each interaction is analyzed for meaning. Signs of hoped-for reciprocation accelerate the development of limerence, whereas clear disinterest or hostility can slam on the brakes. More simply, if the signs of reciprocation are very good—your LO flirts with you, gives signals of being stimulated themselves, and starts fiddling with their hair or laughing at your flimsy jokes—that in itself can be a powerful limerence aphrodisiac. It's elating to think that someone fancies you too, and it often makes them seem more attractive in turn.

Whether there are good grounds for hope is subjective, of course, and this is probably the aspect of limerence where there is the greatest variation among individuals about how much evidence is needed for the limerence to progress. At the extreme end we have delusion, where completely neutral or even negative responses from the LO can be distorted into signs of reciprocation (for the truly pathological, think *Enduring Love* by Ian McEwan, which describes erotomania).

This point highlights another common concern about limerence—how it relates to darker forms of obsessive love. Obsession can lead to stalking, coercive control, and other abusive behaviors that seem to fit into the category of disordered love, but these are actually symptoms of psychiatric conditions that are distinct from limerence. Abusive manifestations of obsession are linked to personality disorders that result in mismanaged anger and desire for relationship control, not runaway infatuation.[5] The potential for interplay between limerence and mental illness is covered in more detail in Chapter 5, but in most cases limerence does not lead to such bleak outcomes.

Most limerents aren't delusional or disordered, but they can be overly optimistic. Small gestures of friendliness can be magnified by wishful thinking, whereas signs of disinterest or distaste can be explained away as blunders or misunderstandings on your part.

The strength of hope will also depend on how much contact is possible with the LO. It is perfectly feasible to become infatuated with fantasy figures—celebrities being the obvious example—where reciprocation is wildly implausible. A beau ideal can trigger the giddy buzz of romantic excitement, but there is no real hope of consummation, and this sort of crush rarely progresses much further than a thrilling, but safely imaginary, personal fantasy.

Next on the scale of connection would be feeling the glimmer for people who the limerent only briefly interacts with in daily life: receptionists, fellow commuters, baristas, and so forth. Some communication occurs—maybe mutual smiles of recognition, or a few exchanged pleasantries or brief conversations—but at a superficial level. For some people, this can be enough hope to trigger progression to limerence, but more commonly such limited contact would mean a short-lived crush that fades for lack of reinforcement.

For most limerents, the transition from a manageable crush to the mania of limerence needs an LO who is a more regular part of their lives. Here there is a chance to get to know them at a deeper level, with more opportunities to try and find out how they feel about you. This is the scenario where the LO is a friend, coworker, fellow student, neighbor, or similar, and the hope of developing a romantic connection can seem more credible than for an occasional acquaintance.

> *The key difference between a crush and limerence, to me, is the level of attraction and ability to get over it. I am very attracted to a crush. I am overwhelmingly attracted to an LO. A crush I get over pretty quickly. An LO takes a chunk of my psyche!* —M

The last big factor in determining hope is how the LO responds to any romantic hints (or overtures) that the limerent makes. If both the limerent and LO are straightforward and confident people then the matter can be settled quickly, and hope will either be fulfilled or decisively squashed. Unfortunately, life is rarely so tidy. Even if the limerent does openly declare their feelings, it is likely that their LO would behave the way most people do when caught by surprise—with clumsy befuddlement.

If the LO is flattered by the limerent's feelings, they may demur more delicately than with a simple "No"—perhaps expressing affection, but not enough for romance. Maybe they are sympathetic to the limerent's situation, and so let them down gently by suggesting that external barriers exist to thwart success ("I'm dating someone else, and it's serious"). Perhaps they value the friendship of the limerent and do not want to lose that connection. Finally, it is also possible that the limerent object is a person of dubious character, who enjoys this romantic attention, and actively cultivates the infatuation of the limerent for their own gratification. Such people can deliberately generate false hope to keep the limerent hooked.

All of these possible complications link hope to the third major factor for developing limerence: uncertainty.

Uncertainty

You've felt the glimmer with a potential new LO, you have enough hints of interest from them to give you hope, but now you have to decide whether to take action or wait for more feedback. If, for some reason, there is an obstacle to the free expression of mutual feeling, it acts as rocket fuel for limerence. Either consummation or direct rejection can lead to the cooling of limerent feelings, but uncertainty inflames them.

Uncertainty can come in many forms. One common situation is a limerent object who gives mixed messages.

> *He would have these deep conversations with me but then cold shoulder me the next time we met.* —AJ

That kind of uncertainty can intensify the obsession. It will increase the urge to analyze interactions with the LO, to fantasize about possible scenarios and to plan ways to try and cajole them into revealing their feelings. Uncertainty makes it more likely that an LO will occupy your mind and become an enigma to fixate on. Ambiguous signals cause insecurity in the limerent, making them more likely to ruminate over their behavior and their strategy and, generally, keep guessing about the state of their relationship with the LO.

Another cause of uncertainty is the presence of external barriers that mean you cannot act. The most common, of course, is that one or both of you are already in a committed relationship. Social, moral, personal, and practical barriers prevent you from declaring or consummating your romantic feelings. Another barrier could be literal distance; if you are unable to connect with them except through electronic means. Or a language barrier. Or a religious barrier. Or a hostile family. Barriers, though, are probably best seen as a different category from simple uncertainty, because the impediment to consummation is imposed upon you. You could be mutually limerent with your LO, but the barriers make you unable to act. Unfortunately, matters can get even more tangled.

Divorce can occur. So can extramarital affairs. Aside from death, there is really no such thing as an insurmountable barrier to limerence. Consequently, there is enough uncertainty bound up in social barriers that there is always a possibility that the limerence could be consummated, because even if your moral character insists that you would never betray a partner, the possibility exists that you could. All of this feeds the reverie, mixing yet more big emotions into the already tumultuous stew.

The killer combo of glimmer, hope, and uncertainty reliably leads to the development of limerence. A spark with the limerent object, a hint of romantic interest from them and some complications in the circumstances under which the initial dance of attraction occurs, determine how completely you fall under the spell. While those three factors are necessary for limerence, they are not the whole story. Part of the explanation for the sometimes contradictory features of limerence is that it is a progressive condition. Your state of mind changes as your connection to the LO deepens. Limerence evolves over time, passing through a series of phases that lead ultimately to a state of total mental capture.

Limerence is an altered state of mind. It starts with euphoria, but if you stay in it too long, it can become toxic.

CHAPTER 2
THE PHASES OF LIMERENCE

From tantalizing glimmer to oppressive obsession

Limerence has a direction to it, a kind of irresistible momentum. It starts well—as a highly pleasurable state that seems to be all upside, and with little incentive for the limerent to question what's going on. Unwittingly, though, they succumb to obsessive infatuation in subtle stages that are hardly noticeable. Commonly, bewildered limerents look backward after being thoroughly caught in the grip of romantic monomania and wonder "How did I get here?" The answer, of course, is one step at a time.

Inevitably, trying to identify the specific steps is somewhat artificial. There will be numerous tipping points, and lots of variation in the individual details, but there are key milestones along the way that help to identify how far the limerent is on their journey to romantic calamity. As the limerence progresses, there are clear indications that the mental state of the limerent has shifted in a noticeable and noteworthy way. The length of time spent in each of these phases varies between people, and there are confounding factors that influence each person's response to the cues that drive progression through the phases. Not least is the weird, combustible alchemy that occurs between the psychological vulnerabilities of the limerent and the behavior of the limerent object (LO).

Despite these caveats, there is value in marking out the key phases of limerence. If nothing else, it allows us to understand how the changing psychological experience of limerence relates to what is going on in the brain. This also helps us understand what can be

Divorce can occur. So can extramarital affairs. Aside from death, there is really no such thing as an insurmountable barrier to limerence. Consequently, there is enough uncertainty bound up in social barriers that there is always a possibility that the limerence could be consummated, because even if your moral character insists that you would never betray a partner, the possibility exists that you could. All of this feeds the reverie, mixing yet more big emotions into the already tumultuous stew.

The killer combo of glimmer, hope, and uncertainty reliably leads to the development of limerence. A spark with the limerent object, a hint of romantic interest from them and some complications in the circumstances under which the initial dance of attraction occurs, determine how completely you fall under the spell. While those three factors are necessary for limerence, they are not the whole story. Part of the explanation for the sometimes contradictory features of limerence is that it is a progressive condition. Your state of mind changes as your connection to the LO deepens. Limerence evolves over time, passing through a series of phases that lead ultimately to a state of total mental capture.

Limerence is an altered state of mind. It starts with euphoria, but if you stay in it too long, it can become toxic.

CHAPTER 2
THE PHASES OF LIMERENCE

From tantalizing glimmer to oppressive obsession

Limerence has a direction to it, a kind of irresistible momentum. It starts well—as a highly pleasurable state that seems to be all upside, and with little incentive for the limerent to question what's going on. Unwittingly, though, they succumb to obsessive infatuation in subtle stages that are hardly noticeable. Commonly, bewildered limerents look backward after being thoroughly caught in the grip of romantic monomania and wonder "How did I get here?" The answer, of course, is one step at a time.

Inevitably, trying to identify the specific steps is somewhat artificial. There will be numerous tipping points, and lots of variation in the individual details, but there are key milestones along the way that help to identify how far the limerent is on their journey to romantic calamity. As the limerence progresses, there are clear indications that the mental state of the limerent has shifted in a noticeable and noteworthy way. The length of time spent in each of these phases varies between people, and there are confounding factors that influence each person's response to the cues that drive progression through the phases. Not least is the weird, combustible alchemy that occurs between the psychological vulnerabilities of the limerent and the behavior of the limerent object (LO).

Despite these caveats, there is value in marking out the key phases of limerence. If nothing else, it allows us to understand how the changing psychological experience of limerence relates to what is going on in the brain. This also helps us understand what can be done to slow or reverse the progression. There are several chances to stop—or maybe jump off—the limerence train, before it crashes.

1. Initiation

The first phase is the most decisive for whether limerence will become established, and the easiest opportunity to stop it beforehand. This is the period immediately after meeting someone new—"first contact" if you like. Often this is not a conscious realization, you just respond to them at an emotional level. They are appealing in some indefinable way, something about them excites you and naturally and effortlessly you warm to them. They *attract* you, in the broadest sense of the word. Not only are they romantically appealing, but you feel yourself drawn to them and fascinated by their fairy glamor.

The glimmer is often followed by some tentative attempt to assess their response to you. Again, I should emphasize that this is all largely unconscious—just the normal, instinctive behavior you'd expect after meeting someone you like. This might manifest as showing particular attention to the potential LO, seeking their company and conversation, possibly even some flirtation to gauge how open they are to banter. You are likely to be happy and open, telegraphing interest through all the subtle cues of body language, demeanor, and behavioral signs that reveal you are entranced.

Once this general attraction has kindled, it often leads to a more active attempt to establish whether they are attracted to you too. Testing the water to see if it's warm. This tends to involve deliberate flirting, and perhaps some overt displays of romantic interest. This is a period where expectation is high, and you start seeking signs of reciprocation. It's also likely to be the period in which social media searches begin: friend requests, following them on X, liking Instas—a bit of low-key "stalking" to remind yourself of their appeal. Maybe, they might even mention you . . .

If there is sufficient reason to suspect some mutual feeling from them, the limerence ignites. In contrast, if the flirting fails—if the potential LO is obviously not interested (or even hostile)—then the glimmer can fade and die. That is the first exit point, the first opportunity to disembark from the limerence locomotive before the fires are stoked.

Assuming there has been enough cause for optimism (and to be clear this could be largely in the imagination of the limerent rather than the intent of the LO), then matters progress. The limerent is encouraged, and mentally repositions the LO into a distinct category from ordinary friends and acquaintances. The glimmer sparkles ever brighter. The LO becomes a focus of intense interest—a reward to be sought. Being around them feels good. Life seems pregnant with opportunity and the promise of romantic adventure. You start to see them as someone very special.

2. Euphoria

The second phase of limerence is the really good one. This is when the emotions connected with the LO are overwhelmingly positive. This is the "shivers of excitement" stage.

The preceding initiation phase advances to the point where you are seeing the LO as a romantic focus, and this second phase marks an escalation in the strength of desire. Being with them makes you feel elated. Your time together is intensely rewarding and so, naturally enough, you seek more of it. That becomes a positive feedback loop—the more exposure to them you get, the better you feel. After a while, your mood shifts into a state of general optimism and excitement; of heightened alertness and mental energy.

The highs during this stage are fantastic. Having a good interaction with the LO—say spending time flirting and chatting and getting to know them and starting to bond—causes euphoria. Exquisite intoxication.

> *Think Cupid, instead of shooting an arrow, tossing a meteorite at my heart. That's how it felt. Super intense euphoria.... Never in my life did I once think I could ever feel for another human being like I do for LO. —MJ*

Oh, that energy that makes you "turbocharged!" It's pleasurable one feels on cloud nine! It lasted for a few weeks, maybe a month and a half. The world smiled at me and I smiled back at it. . . . No, there was no ambivalence during the onset of limerence, there was no room for it. Everything was colorful and beautiful, I felt super joyful. —N

Being with them, or daydreaming about them, supercharges your mood, making you nervy and excitable. You feel the limerence in your body as a state of arousal that makes you feel more vital and upbeat and potent. More alive.

This is also the phase in which idealization is in full flow and you are resistant to any negative thoughts about the LO. Their opinions and behavior delight you. You become their champion, finding flattering justifications for any uncouth or objectionable habits and inventing some backstory to explain why they are how they are, and what might be missing from their life. Often, by extraordinary coincidence, this happens to be something you can supply.

The limerence fantasies begin. Imagining a world in which you can be together. Planning for the next opportunity to astound them with your appeal. If you are already in a committed monogamous relationship, then this is also the phase of willful self-delusion: "We're just friends. It's not going anywhere. I can handle it." Almost nothing can burst the bubble of bliss.

It is not an entirely smooth period though. Jealousy is a risk whenever someone else expresses interest in the LO, amplified a hundred times if the LO shows interest in someone else. Anxiety grips you after a negative encounter—when they seem to be cold to you, or disdainful and dismissive. Overall, though, this is the most hopeful period of limerence, when it is early enough for novelty to delight you, and before reality has had a chance to spoil your fantasies and dreams.

Predictably, the euphoria phase is the hardest to break out of. This is the stage in which the metaphorical locomotive is accelerating fast and building steam. You are steeped in an emotional brew that feels warm and invigorating and good, and the most enjoyable pastime imaginable is constructing a delightful fantasy world with your LO at the center of it. Your motivation to stop the train and get off is basically nil.

Despite all this positive reinforcement, full-blown limerence is still not inevitable at this stage. If both you and your LO are single, and you are sufficiently confident and purposeful, you can declare yourself and discover whether you are in for romantic consummation. If successful, the euphoria will last through the honeymoon stage of the new relationship, and then ebb away naturally as proper bonding takes over (or the relationship breaks down).

Alternatively, the hope of this euphoria phase can be smothered by undeniable evidence from the LO that they are not interested in romance. (The comedown will be rough.) Finally, some limerents who are not free to act on their feelings have the self-control to de-escalate from the euphoric highs before the damage done to their other relationships and commitments is too severe.

Most commonly, though, the mix of hope and uncertainty proves sufficiently combustible to drive the limerence engine on into the next phase—the point at which obsession definitively sets in.

3. Psychological fixation

Life becomes all about them. You lose interest in other goals and pursuits. You move from experiencing pleasure when you are with them, to feeling antsy and restless when you are away from them. Seeking contact is the most powerful drive in your life—nothing matters more (at least on an emotional level, even if you manage to maintain your other responsibilities on autopilot).

Life is reorganized around the active pursuit of the LO. Hours might be sunk into studying their social media feeds, searching for crumbs of hope that they are thinking of you, or devising new ideas about how to connect and get closer to them.

This phase is when you begin to change. Friends and family may notice your personality is different—maybe because of increased energy and optimism, but more likely because you are easily distracted, impatient, and difficult to engage with, unless it relates to your primary goal. In the most extreme cases, you start to pick up the mannerisms and opinions of the LO, and drop their name into every conversation. With crushing predictability, everything that happens to you makes you think of an anecdote about your LO.

People can begin to notice. Gossip may start, or teasing, or accusations. This phase is also the point at which the limerent instinctively begins to conceal the depth of their feelings. Many limerents feel ashamed of their infatuation—they sense that the feelings they have for their LO are wildly disproportionate, embarrassing in their ardour. A key tipping point in this phase is the first moment of deceit. The first time you lie about your feelings, your conduct, or your beliefs, to conceal the depth of your regard for the LO. Psychologically, that is a powerful and important moment.

The psychological fixation stage also disrupts life in more concrete ways. You find it hard to concentrate on other tasks, because you like nothing more than immersing yourself in reverie about them. Inevitably, study, work, and domestic responsibilities begin to suffer neglect. The *salience bias* ramps up, and you start to notice everything about them, perhaps change your daily routine to increase exposure to them. New hobbies—that they coincidentally enjoy—catch your attention. Places connected to them become attractive destinations.

> *I spent this morning on Google Street View wandering around the city where he went on holiday last year. [...] I want to feel connected to him and inhabit the same space.* —TD

New experiences and pursuits are passed through the "what would my LO think about this?" filter. Your opinions become more fluid. You open your mind to their political and religious beliefs, even if they are at odds with your previous views.

This is also the phase when uncertainty torments you. Your whole focus is on securing reciprocation so you become hypersensitive to any setbacks. Overanalysis of the LO's behavior, comments, motivations, and mood occupies your mind and keeps them central to your attention. Your emotions become less stable and more dependent on what feedback you are getting from the LO. Although there are still moments of giddy excitement, you may also start to feel a little washed out and queasy.

This phase of limerence is when the locomotive is running at full throttle, but the engine is starting to show signs of overheating. This is also, typically, the point at which many limerents realize that they have a problem. Not only are they obsessed, but they also encounter powerful emotional resistance whenever they attempt to slow the progression of the limerence, or reverse course.

> *I cannot bring myself to stop because the good feelings outweigh the bad. I know it can't go on forever and there is likely some emotional fallout—but I want to delay that fallout just for a little bit... so I can continue to experience what I am experiencing. I physically cannot bring myself to go "no contact." It feels like trying to jump off something when you really don't want to. —LH*

That degree of fixation is hard to undo. When your whole world is focused on one obsessive goal, it is no small thing to stop, review, and establish a more balanced perspective—especially when it feels like ecstatic love is within your grasp. Nevertheless, it is still possible to apply the brakes at this stage. The realization that infatuation has moved from exciting thrill to damaging obsession is enough for some limerents to wake up to the seriousness of their situation and take action to reverse the mental conditioning they've accidentally put themselves through. Unfortunately, the combination of uncertainty and single-minded determination can instead lead into the next phase, when limerence takes a decided turn into the dark.

4. Desperation

This is the phase where the runaway locomotive derails. When the psychological fixation has persisted for long enough, the limerent can become trapped in a sort of mental limbo—spinning their wheels constantly, but not moving forward, or getting closer to the hoped-for reciprocation.

There can be many causes for getting trapped in this limbo state. For example, an LO who will not commit, but will also not let you go. Or insecurity that stops you from disclosing, leading to a terrible tension between fear of rejection if you declare yourself, and fear of giving up too soon. Social barriers that mean you cannot act on your feelings, but you also can't bear the thought of being without them. A limerent affair that has been carried on in secret and is now souring. A doomed attempt to try and stay friends with the LO, in the hope that you'll be able to somehow swallow down those overwhelming passions and suppress them without coming to harm. Whatever the cause, staying trapped in this state of uncertainty for too long triggers the desperation phase, when limerence causes serious psychological distress.

The old daydreams of future bliss turn into intrusive thoughts that cannot be turned off. The obsession becomes involuntary. You are no longer seeking happy highs, you are assailed by anxiety about losing contact with someone who no longer even makes you feel all that good. Your mood is destabilized, swinging between mania and depression, all against a background craving that feels unhealthy. You can still have spikes of hope and optimism, but negative emotions come to dominate your life.

This phase can also be characterized by erratic behavior. In a last-ditch attempt to finally secure reciprocation, the limerent can escalate their risk-taking—being more overt in their romantic overtures or more insistent in pushing at boundaries to force a resolution to the awful limbo of not knowing how the LO feels. More destructive still, the limerent can flip into feelings of resentment and anger about the LO's behavior, feeling entitled to satisfaction or "closure" about the relationship—even if the magnitude and significance of the connection is one-sided and based on the fantasies built up in their head.

The desperation phase is awful. It's the crash that comes from abusing the limerence drug for too long. It's the phase in which the cost of maintaining a state of heightened arousal and frustration for too long comes due. It is also the point at which those limerents who have had a hidden affair with their LO come to face the destructive consequences of their deceit. The illicit vibes give way to suffocating regret.

For most limerents, the desperation phase is when the costs of carrying on outweigh the costs of withdrawal. It's the point where they know they have to take action and start the painful process of weaning themselves off the limerent craving. Like an addict hitting rock bottom, they know they have to get clean, and recover their mental equilibrium.

Unfortunately, that is not trivial.

5. Recovery

The final phase of limerence is when the monomania subsides at last. You begin to recover perspective, and start to see the LO as an actual, real person again, with flaws and everything. To force my locomotive metaphor all the way to the terminus: Recovery is when the wreckage of the train has cooled, and you bring in the cranes, clear up the mess, and start to rebuild.

Sometimes this comes naturally. If the desperation phase was not too severe, or if you have managed to maintain discipline and taken steps to withdraw after the psychological fixation stage, the limerence will slowly run down through lack of fuel. It may take weeks, it may take months, but it will come eventually, as long as you take deliberate action to work toward recovery. Occasionally, it can happen surprisingly abruptly, when something the LO says or does is so objectionable that it hits a metaphorical off switch on the limerence.

More commonly, it is a slow and steady grind.

The strong feelings I had for my LO are fading. I still like him very much but he doesn't light up my life the same way as he used to. I am beginning to see him as an ordinary human being. —R

There are, though, ways to speed up recovery. Understanding what limerence is, and the changes it causes in our neurochemistry and psychology, is an important first step (which we'll discuss in Chapter 3). That knowledge provides strategies to counteract limerence, to turn down the volume on the craving and to recover some emotional stability. Winning some relief from the mania liberates you to begin the deep work of identifying your own psychological vulnerabilities, and how they determine the kinds of people that you become limerent for and how to resist their charms in the future (if you wish to).

How long does limerence last?

About as long as a piece of string. Ho, ho.

The standard answer for how long limerence lasts is between eighteen months and three years.[1] This estimate comes from Tennov's survey of several hundred subjects who were carefully interviewed. On the Living with Limerence site, episodes have been reported to range from a couple of (very emotionally intense) weeks, to more than forty years. The fundamental truth is that time taken for limerence to pass through these various phases to recovery depends on a complex set of factors. Your behavior. Your LO's behavior. The presence of barriers. How much time you spend with the LO. Whether you became sexually intimate. Your personal psychological history, from an early age right up until you met the LO. Limerence can be more likely if you are sad, or lonely, or grieving or bored. There is an unpredictable alchemy that depends on where you are in your life, and where your LO is in theirs, and the circumstances under which you meet.

This is not a cause for defeatism, though. The factors that promote limerence and the factors that reverse limerence are explicable. You are not helpless—even if it can feel like that in the depths of a limerence episode. The first step to taking control is to recognize a central truth about limerence: Despite the apparent wondrous majesty of the limerent object, and their uncanny ability to push your romantic buttons, limerence is happening in your head.

CHAPTER 3
THE NEUROSCIENCE OF LIMERENCE

What today's brain research tells us about infatuation

When Dorothy Tennov first outlined the symptoms of limerence, she conceptualized it as an altered state of mind. The lovestruck people she interviewed felt themselves to be inhabiting a new mode of being—they were decisively *in* love. Being in the state of limerence overlaid all aspects of their daily lives, dominated their thoughts and feelings, and directed their motivation toward the central goal of securing reciprocation from their limerent object.

> *It was like living in a dream or a piece of music or a perpetual rainstorm that never let up. The flow of images and colors and emotions/sensations just never stopped. —S*

Tennov noted that the nature of that self-reported mental state had certain predictable and consistent features in all the limerents she interviewed. She sought to understand the psychological basis of limerence by analyzing the behaviors and beliefs that characterized this altered state.

> *I see limerence as a normal and ordinary feature of the human species, and my approach to its study is basically that of the ethologist who observes animals in natural settings and analyzes the behavior from an evolutionary perspective.*
> *—Dorothy Tennov*[1]

She concluded that limerence was best understood as a definable emotional state that susceptible people could slip into under the right (or maybe wrong) conditions. In her later work, she went further, asserting that limerence is a universal state, experienced in essentially the same way by people from widely diverse cultural backgrounds, personalities, ages, and life histories. She drew an analogy to human universals such as greed, hate, or lust—traits that emerge from fundamental, instinctive drives, under the control of identifiable neural circuits.[2]

> *Limerence will eventually be objectively detectable physiologically and seen as the universal innate on-off mechanism.*
> —Dorothy Tennov[3]

For Tennov, and for the many people who self-identify as limerents, it is a persistent condition that lasts, for good or ill, for months or years. While there are obviously day-to-day variations in the intensity of the ardour, and momentary shifts in the level of preoccupation, there remains a consistent, ongoing feeling of being in love. As Tennov put it: *"The algorithm is either operative or not."*[4]

These are strong claims. They rest on the notion that human brains evolved mechanisms for switching into a relatively stable cognitive mode that produces a romantic obsession so intense it overwhelms all other concerns. How good is the evidence that such a state exists?

How neuroscience works

It's an interesting aspect of academic life that people ostensibly working on the same scientific problem can approach it from dramatically different perspectives. The field of neuroscience is no exception to this principle, and I sometimes ruminate on how it is that researchers find their way into understanding the brain at a particular level of analysis. I've cultivated a theory that confronted with a problem of such intimidating difficulty as a brain, aspiring neuroscientists narrow their focus until they reach a level of detail that they are comfortable with—a level that balances practicalities with their own skillset, but has enough explanatory power to satisfy their curiosity.

Tennov started and stopped at the uppermost level of analysis—human behavior. She was clearly fascinated by the way that people acted and used this as a way to try to understand what was going on in their heads. Others focus deeper, moving into neuroanatomy and defining subregions of the brain that seem to regulate particular behaviors—this is the land of exotic names and connectivity diagrams (e.g., the *ventral tegmental area* of the brain projects to the *nucleus accumbens* and the *prefrontal cortex*). Others go deeper still, investigating the individual cells and molecules that compose the brain (this is the land of neurotransmitters and synapses, where I have always worked).

The basic functional unit of the brain is the "neuron," a specialized cell that conducts electrical impulses. Neurons are connected to one another in networks, where chemical transmitters are released at tiny junctions between the cells known as synapses, relaying signals from neuron to neuron. This simple arrangement leads to a computational network of staggering complexity—billions of neurons signaling continuously through trillions of synapses. This computational perspective leads to the most refined researchers of all—the mathematicians who view the brain as essentially a complex input-output device for carrying out information processing. They deal in equations, rather than cells and tissues.

I mention this tendency toward specialization not as a critique of academic partisanship, but to highlight the difficulty in explaining limerent behavior in terms of neuroscience. To give a comprehensive answer to the question of what's going on in the brain during limerence, we would need to cover all levels of analysis from molecules to behavior—a formidable task. The best we can manage at the moment is to draw from the highlights of each of these neuroscience disciplines, and build up a picture of how the phenomenon of limerence maps onto current knowledge of how the brain works. So, what are the mechanisms by which meeting a dazzling person can lead to dizzying infatuation?

How brains work

Brains, at a fundamental level, are a system of systems. Throughout evolutionary history, brains have become more complex by adding new structures and systems to the existing architecture. For simple and ancient organisms, a rudimentary sensory system that linked detection of movement to an escape reflex could offer a huge survival advantage. Similarly, a way of sensing food (or a mate) and moving toward it, would make it more likely that the striving creature would live long enough to have offspring. These simple sensory reflexes evolved into more refined and sophisticated neural systems that were optimized in the crucible of a lethally competitive world to carry out key behaviors—avoiding danger, seeking reward, learning, feeding, reproduction. They are still with us.

As our forebears evolved over the eons, gaining larger and more complex brains, additional functionality was achieved by expanding some structures or layering new circuits on top of these basic systems. From the spinal cord to the brainstem to the basal ganglia to the thalamus to the cerebral cortex, more and more systems and structures that carried out ever more demanding computational tasks were developed. Simple pain perception and withdrawal reflexes can occur in milliseconds within the spinal cord, but the recognition of discomfort and learning to avoid sources of pain happens in the brainstem and basal ganglia. At the highest level, understanding the context of the pain, and making choices about how to react (such as voluntarily tolerating it for future benefit), requires the cortex.

This sequential view of brain evolution gave rise to the popular idea that we have a primitive "lizard brain" lurking within us.[5] The fundamental systems that guide instinctive behaviors in reptiles still exist in the deeper structures of the human brain, utilizing the same neurotransmitters, circuits, and feedback loops. It is a useful simplification to conceptually separate the deep "animal" drives that originate in these subcortical systems from the executive functions of the cortex—the sense-making part of the brain that is so well-developed in humans. It fits our everyday experience too—

we often feel an emotional compulsion to do things before we've had a chance to actually think about them. It really does feel as though we have urgent, subconscious drives that are impulsive and chaotic and need to be regulated by our calmer, rational selves.

It has a pleasing orderliness to it, this idea. A hierarchy in the brain that allows evolution to be literally seen in the layers of the tissues. Ancient, primitive brainstem at the bottom; more sophisticated but still habitual systems just above in the basal ganglia and limbic system; and the large, swollen, convoluted cortical layer at the very top—the most modern part of the brain. It's a neat and useful framework, but it also misses an important part of the story.

While it is true that the higher brain structures were built on top of the lower structures, they were also integrated into them to an astonishing degree. The feature of the human brain that really distinguishes it from other animals is not the size alone (whales have much larger brains, for example), but the *connectivity*. As the new structures evolved, they were wired into the old structures through anatomical infiltration and functional integration. There is a stupefying complexity to neuroanatomy. The cortex may be king, sitting atop the behavioral hierarchy, but it receives inputs from all the lower centers and sends signals back down to them. There is constant communication back and forth, up and down, between higher and lower brain centers. While we have a metaphorical "lizard brain," with basic systems for pleasure, fear, hunger, sleep, anger, and much more, it is integrated into numerous other systems that can modify or be modified by it.

Since the brain is a system of systems, we need to understand the basic functionality of each system to understand behavior, but we also need to know how they work together and change each other. When it comes to understanding the basis of the altered state of mind that defines limerence in terms of neuroscience, we need to identify the subcortical neural systems that drive the urgent, compulsive behavior, but also how they work together with the higher cortical regions to make sense of the experience and make decisions.

As a starting point, we can be guided by the personal testimonies of people going through limerence as a psychological, emotional, and embodied experience. From the common symptoms described by limerents in the midst of a romantic obsession, there are three key neural systems that feature in a limerent episode: the arousal, reward, and bonding systems.

Arousal

Limerence causes a spectacular boost in energy and excitement. The first flush of limerent exhilaration transforms our mental and physical selves. Our mood lifts, thoughts race, and life becomes vibrant and full of promise. Optimism overwhelms worries, jokes become hilarious, music seems more emotionally resonant and profound. As well as these effects on the mind, the body responds too. Many limerents report a sort of generalized increase in vitality, which is amplified even further when they are with their object of infatuation—their hearts race, breathing gets shallow, blushes break out, and they feel jittery, tingly, and delirious.

In the later phases of limerence, if consummation has been thwarted, this intensity of experience changes character. The boost of nervous energy remains, but it feels as though it has become deranged or misdirected. Instead of euphoria, there is heightened anxiety; racing thoughts become intrusive rather than invigorating, and the supercharged body response becomes exhausting rather than exhilarating. There is still a greater overall intensity of sensation, but it has soured into fretfulness and yearning.

These symptoms—both positive and negative—can all be explained by the neural circuits that regulate *arousal*.

At its simplest, arousal is defined by wakefulness. There are several well-defined brainstem circuits collectively known as the *ascending reticular activating system* that regulate the sleep-wake transition—a complex, interconnected set of "nuclei" (where thousands of neurons are clustered together) that use a wide range of neurotransmitters and project to a wide range of brain regions. This provides a sort of global signal that shifts our mental state between deep sleep, dreaming, and wakefulness. For the case of limerence, while the experience may well influence the quality and duration of sleep (and the content of your dreams), the important aspects of arousal take place when you are awake.

Arousal can progress beyond consciousness, into increasing levels of alertness and excitement. During limerence, we commonly feel not just aroused, but overaroused. We are pushed into a state of racing thoughts, with high attention and vigilance. This process involves a subsystem of the arousal networks centered on a brain region known as the locus coeruleus, which is packed full of neurons that produce the neurotransmitter noradrenaline. When these are activated, noradrenaline is released into other brain regions, causing excitation of these regions and improved cognitive performance—in terms of attentiveness, focus, and quickness of thought.

Another subsystem, operating through the *hypothalamus*, carries the message of arousal out of the brain and into the rest of the body via the *sympathetic nervous system*. These neurons connect to almost all the organs of the body, and activation leads to the classic symptoms of nervous excitement—rapid heartbeat, shallow breathing, dilated pupils, sweaty palms. Again, the sympathetic nervous system uses noradrenaline as its key neurotransmitter, along with the release of adrenaline into the bloodstream from the adrenal glands. This physiological arousal is commonly known as the "fight or flight" response, but it is not just experienced in response to danger—any imperative situation that requires urgent attention will cause it. The thrill of excitement or the stab of fear.

Finally, the arousal of limerence is usually also accompanied by sexual desire. Multiple brain regions integrate sensory stimuli (sight, smell, sound, touch) that indicate erotic opportunity, while the prefrontal cortex adds context. Both psychological and physical desire kindles. The hypothalamus engages yet another system of neurons that cause increased blood flow to the genitals and —ahem—readies the relevant organs for action. Desire excites the mind and lust stirs the loins.

The arousal system is a mechanism for getting you hyped up, and it doesn't really matter if that's due to excitement, trepidation, fear, stress, or lust—the same arousal circuits will produce the same cognitive and physical enhancements. How you ultimately interpret the experience depends on the concurrent activity in other neural systems, overlaid by the executive authority of the cortex. Limerent objects are overarousing in a truly comprehensive sense.

Reward

If there's one thing that can be said for early limerence, it's that it really makes you feel good. At a purely emotional and physical level, euphoria is extremely rewarding. Whether it's ultimately useful to your broader life goals, or helps you achieve your dreams, is immaterial to the neural systems that recognize an exciting potential mate, prompt you to interact with them, and flood your brain with bliss when it seems like they might like you too.

The reward system is another fundamental neural mechanism that is central to the experience of limerence. A cluster of neurons in the *ventral tegmental area* of the brainstem release the neurotransmitter dopamine into several key regions in the *striatum* involved in the regulation of emotion and the learning of associations between stimuli and reward. They also project further into the executive regions of the prefrontal cortex, which allows us to make sense of the reward that we are experiencing.

The idea of a "dopamine high" has become something of a cliché in popular culture. It's a rather hackneyed device in journalism to declare—archly—that a particular source of pleasure "lights up" the same area of the brain as cocaine. Or sex. Or chocolate. While that's not wrong, it's a bit banal, because *everything* rewarding works through this same fundamental neural system. It is the mechanism for recognizing pleasurable stimuli, and learning how they were obtained. Even the most primitive animals need a system for recognizing rewards (tasty food, comfortable environments, attractive mates), learning how to secure them and then seeking more of them in the future. It's critical to survival and reproduction to be able to distinguish nice from nasty in a complex, changeable, and dangerous world.

Limerence is uniquely rewarding. Euphoria is hard to come by in everyday life, and so it's easy to understand why the experience is so extraordinarily desirable. It doesn't take long to learn that a positive interaction with a limerent object makes you feel joyfully high, but the functions of the reward system are more subtle, interesting, and significant than simply recognizing a source of bliss.

Dopamine—despite its popular reputation—is not itself the cause of pleasure. It is actually more important for motivation than for gratification. Dopamine is essential for *reward-seeking*—it's the push that gets you moving, the urge to secure pleasure, the force that kindles desire, the impulse that goads you into action. We'll drill down deeper into the subtleties in the next chapter (it's worth it, they're fascinating), but the actual computational role of dopamine in the brain is as a "reward prediction error" signal.[6] If you get a reward you didn't expect, dopamine is released in a burst of activity. If you see a cue in the environment that you've learned is linked to reward, dopamine is released to motivate you into action. Finally, if you were expecting a reward but didn't get it, dopamine decreases.

The reward system, therefore, has multiple overlapping roles in limerence. It fires up when we first experience that thrilling "glimmer" of recognition that we've met someone super desirable, it motivates us to continue to seek contact with them for the emotional buzz we experience, it ingrains that reward-seeking behavior as a habit, and it causes the discomfort we experience when things are going poorly with our LO—when the expected rewards fail, and we feel rejected or foolish.

There's one last feature of the reward system that's also a key part of the puzzle—emotional rewards can have different characters. There is a distinction between euphoric giddiness and contented serenity. To understand why, we need to discuss a third major neural system that's relevant to limerence.

Bonding

Tennov noted in her definition of limerence that sexual desire was usually present, but secondary—the main goal of limerence is reciprocation of a profound, intense, unique, mutual affection.

> *Limerence is a desire for more than sex, and a desire in which the sexual act may represent the symbol of its highest achievement: reciprocation. Reciprocation expressed through physical union creates the ecstatic and blissful condition called*

"the greatest happiness" and the most profound glorification of the achievement of limerent aims.—Dorothy Tennov[7]

The transcendent feelings of a spiritual, cosmic, magical connection to their limerent object that many limerents report are not easily explained by the thrill of arousal or the euphoria of reward. They map more closely onto another neural system: bonding. This is where the hormones come in.

There are two major hormones—or "neuropeptides"—that are involved in bonding, and they also help illustrate an important problem in making sense of how our basic neurochemistry relates to complex behaviors like falling in love. The hormones are oxytocin and vasopressin, and the problem is that they have been exploited by evolution for several profoundly different roles in the body.

Oxytocin is quite well-known in popular culture, and it has been termed the "cuddle hormone," or "love hormone," but the rough translation of the hormone's name reveals its primary physiological role—"sudden childbirth." At the last stages of pregnancy, pulses of oxytocin are released from the pituitary gland into the blood, to initiate labor.[8] Throughout delivery, oxytocin continues to drive uterine contractions, with yet more being released after birth to protect against postpartum bleeding. Oxytocin is also released in response to skin-to-skin contact between mother and child, and by the nipple stimulation caused by latching and nursing. It triggers milk release—the so called "let down" reflex.

Vasopressin is less well-known, but its primary role in physiology is in the regulation of kidney function and water reabsorption.[9] This can also influence blood pressure, which is again reflected in the etymology—vasopressin roughly translates to "blood vessel constrictor." It is also released from the pituitary into the blood, to be carried around the body in the bloodstream.

At first sight, it isn't obvious why these hormones should also influence bonding, but it is a common feature of biology that an already existing system that evolved to serve one specific purpose can be nudged and adapted into carrying out a new function. This seems to be what happened in romantic attachment—the same neuropeptides that regulate labor and water balance were repurposed into mechanisms for emotional regulation. As well as the neurons that extend to the pituitary gland and release oxytocin and vasopressin into the blood, there is another set of neurons within the hypothalamus that extend back into the brain—releasing the neuropeptides directly into the reward and arousal centers of the basal ganglia.[10]

Oxytocin illustrates this principle beautifully. As well as the physical process of initiating milk supply, the oxytocin released from skin contact and latching is thought to be the neurochemical basis of the overwhelming feeling of love and connection between mother and child.[11] Oxytocin is essential for both the mechanistic aspects of childbirth, and for the process of maternal bonding. The physical stimuli of cuddling, gentle touch, and skin contact promote emotional stabilization and mood regulation in both mother and child, and are essential to the development of trust and stable attachment to caregivers in childhood.

While best characterized in childhood bonding, the effects of oxytocin on mood and emotional connection continue into adulthood. Hence its popular reputation as a love hormone. In laboratory tests, oxytocin administered as a nasal spray increased the trust between strangers in a game of chance, and it caused an increase in the pleasure felt from gentle touch and social interactions.[12] For social animals, oxytocin seems to be a common mechanism for promoting prosocial behavior and for the feelings of distress and discomfort at being excluded from the group.

This fundamental system of linking mood regulation to interpersonal intimacy goes beyond social attachment—it's also involved in sexual behavior. In addition to the intimate touch and skin-to-skin contact inherent in sexual congress, and the obvious pleasurable reward of erotic gratification, a discernible burst of oxytocin is released during orgasm.[13] Oxytocin, it seems, is an essential part of the dreamy flush of postcoital contentment.

How oxytocin and vasopressin achieve these wide-ranging effects on mood is still a matter of debate. One of the issues is that the majority of information that we have about how the neuropeptides regulate bonding comes from a peculiar but fascinating natural case study in monogamy: the humble prairie vole, *Microtus ochrogaster*.

Forgive me one last diversion. Monogamous mating is rare in mammals.[14] The formation of a stable bond between individual males and females is unusual, and sexual monogamy rarer still. The prairie vole is peculiar in that the species show remarkably stable pair bonds that last beyond a single mating season or litter. These bonds even last beyond death, with surviving members of the dyad refusing new mates. Such a striking exception to the normal rules of mating caught the attention of behavioral researchers, especially because even closely related vole species do not have the same tendency to monogamy. Obviously, they started interfering with the faithful little critters. What they found was remarkable.

First, compared to nonmonogamous vole species, prairie voles had surprisingly high densities of oxytocin and vasopressin receptors in the dopamine-rich reward centers of the brain. Second, blocking these neuropeptide receptors during mating dramatically impaired bonding. Third, injecting the neuropeptides directly into the prairie voles' brains could cause pairs to bond without the need to mate. Finally, there was a surprisingly clear-cut sex difference in the bonding mechanism—oxytocin was required in females, vasopressin in males. Vasopressin also had the secondary effect of promoting mate guarding and aggression in males.[15]

Collectively, these prairie vole studies lead to a generalized theory of pair bonding: the combined activation of reward systems and bonding systems during mating leads to a specific mate being powerfully imprinted as the dominant source of reward. The combination of dopamine and neuropeptides together gives a uniquely synergistic reward, linked unwaveringly to the mating partner. It creates a bond strong enough to last a lifetime.

It's easy to get excited and apply this knowledge directly to limerence. The parallel seems so inviting—the neuropeptide bonding system anchors the delirious highs of romantic reward to a particular individual—but caution is needed. It is still not clear how readily the mechanisms uncovered in prairie voles translate to human bonding, although there is some suggestive preliminary evidence. Other primate species have similar anatomical variation in neuropeptide receptor density that seems to correlate with their preference for monogamy, and humans are notable among primates for our social monogamy.[16] The neurons where the genes for oxytocin receptors are active in humans also overlap the brain regions involved in reward and emotional states.[17] More research is clearly needed, but it is also difficult to do. After all, we can't just dissect the brains of limerents to see whether they have unusually high levels of neuropeptide receptors in their reward centers.

Despite this uncertainty about the molecular details, it's not hard to see how the bonding system has multidimensional impacts on limerence. It underpins attachment, emotional security, trust, care, and connection. It makes intimacy more rewarding. It connects sex to affection, triggers jealousy and protectiveness, but most profoundly, it cements the association between a particular person and an immersive, ecstatic, numinous feeling of cosmic connection.

The combined effects of the arousal, reward, and bonding systems cause the extraordinary experience of early limerence. The neuroscience makes sense—the intrinsic drives work together and reinforce each other, rapidly escalating into the nervous excitement and euphoric intoxication of romantic infatuation, carrying us into that altered state of mind that Tennov defined so carefully. But, if that state of delirious bliss was all that limerence involved, then we'd hardly have cause for complaint (except, perhaps, due to exhaustion). Unfortunately, limerence can change. If the hyperaroused state lasts for too long, and reciprocation remains uncertain, it transitions from thrilling to debilitating.

Clearly, the neuroscience underlying limerence can't just be about the thrills. It must also change and adapt. The neural systems we've defined can't simply be busily motoring along in the same way if the emotional experience of limerence changes so profoundly with time. To explain this shift, we have to review what happens in these circuits when limerence progresses, and transforms from a pleasing reward to an obsessive compulsion.

That's when things go wrong in an interesting way.

CHAPTER 4
PERSON ADDICTION
Falling into the limerent habit

Desire is a curious thing. Some desires are easily satisfied—they pass quickly after they are successfully gratified, and rarely intrude into our consciousness. A lazy afternoon at the beach is a pleasure, but one we only seek occasionally. Other desires are insatiable. For those rewards, the thirst for more persists no matter how much access we get. Even after gratifying such desires, the longing barely fades—or if there is any relief it's short-lived. Indulgence of such desires can lead to an escalation of the hunger, rather than contented satisfaction. This is not always a negative thing—to give and receive love is an example of a desire we never tire of—but insatiable desires are hard to moderate.

At the worst extreme, some desires can develop into such an irresistible craving that they become the primary focus of life, dominating all other concerns. These are the desires that religions warn us about. People battle to resist temptation, instinctively sensing that they are too seductive, too powerful, too encompassing; too deranging or destructive to be safely managed. Such desires can persist even after the reward itself ceases to be pleasurable. This is the realm of addiction.

The strength of desire

Limerence certainly falls into this category. Desire for a limerent object is shockingly powerful. Many limerents describe their experience in terms that are usually associated with drug addiction—feeling high, craving supply, suffering withdrawal.

> *By the time I realized I was in serious trouble my limerence was out of control and it was too late, I was hooked on LO and couldn't let go.* —LA

> *I look for him and crave the feeling that I get when I see him, even as I know that I don't want to go back to all the lying and hiding. . . . I know I don't want him—just the flood of chemicals that he triggers. It can be really discouraging and feel shameful to be this kind of junkie.* —J

This isn't just hyperbole. There is good reason to frame limerence in terms of addiction. The arousal, reward, and bonding systems that produce the ecstatic connection of limerence are also central to the development of addiction. When driven too hard and for too long, these systems adapt and remodel. Reward-seeking becomes unbalanced and difficult to resist. The progression of limerence can be understood as a shift from desiring another person to becoming addicted to them.

It's strange that we have a vulnerability like this built into our brains. How does a neural system that evolved to help us seek good things and avoid bad things go haywire and make us want something with harmful intensity? The answer lies in the subtleties and peculiarities of the reward system, and our old friend dopamine. In particular, there are three important concepts that, taken together, explain the strength and persistence of desires: incentive salience, wanting versus liking, and habituation. Broadly—why we notice things, enjoy them and then get bored of them. These factors help explain why limerence can escalate so dramatically from initial attraction into overweening obsession.

Incentive salience

Incentive salience is the phenomenon of noticing things in the environment that we have learned are rewarding, and thereby recognizing them as desirable.[1] It explains why some cues are attention-grabbing—they seem to jump out of the complex background and demand our attention. If you were to walk into an untidy room with litter everywhere, you'd quickly notice if a handful of sparkling gold coins were scattered among the debris, and likely feel an urge to collect them up as a prize. Dopamine is at the heart of this phenomenon, and it causes the stirrings of motivation that begin after we notice something desirable. As it turns out, like good comedy, the influence of dopamine over incentive salience is all in the timing.

Dopamine release is the mechanism by which the brain tracks rewards, and it works by providing a "reward prediction error."[2] In the simplest case, an unexpected reward (say, discovering some tasty fruit when hungry, or having someone attractive declare their love for you) causes a burst of dopamine release into a part of the basal ganglia known as the striatum—specifically, the *nucleus accumbens*. This is a part of the brain that registers pleasurable rewards. When we are not anticipating a reward, but receive it as a surprise, dopamine is released in a burst of activity that signals this unexpected outcome. The failure to anticipate reward is the first kind of prediction error.

The next stage of reward prediction depends on the fact that the reward system does not operate in isolation. It is integrated into other brain regions, most notably those that lay down memories (the *hippocampus*) and interpret outcomes (the *prefrontal cortex*). When a reward has been experienced enough times, we learn to associate that particular object, person, or set of circumstances with pleasure, and therefore know how and when we can get more. As an example, consider the merits of a good cup of coffee. For those who have learned the association, drinking a cup will give predictable gratification. The aroma of coffee brewing reliably provokes desire.

For this reward-prediction scenario, there is an interesting and important shift in the timing of dopamine release.[3] Instead of simply registering surprise, the dopamine system begins to take the initiative. It becomes attuned to cues or triggers in the environment that we've learned are associated with rewards, and dopamine is released in anticipation of securing the prize. The reason I start desiring coffee in the morning when I arrive at my desk is because my cup is next to the keyboard, the kettle is plugged in beside it, and I habitually start my day with a stimulating hit of caffeine. All these cues are reminders of a source of reward, and that causes the release of dopamine in anticipation of pleasure, which motivates me into taking action.

(To give an impression of how effective this system is, I just stopped writing to brew coffee, as the craving was beginning to nag at me enough to spoil my concentration.)

Dopamine release operates as a motivating impulse. Instead of registering an unexpected reward, dopamine is released to stimulate us to *seek* reward. Because of the learned association, cues in the environment subconsciously trigger reward-seeking behavior. If this motivated pursuit results in us successfully securing the reward, a curious thing happens to our dopamine levels: nothing. The burst of dopamine that triggers motivation simply subsides. If the *expected* reward is secured, then no prediction error has occurred, and no additional dopamine is released.

Alternatively, if the expected reward doesn't occur—for example if I've carelessly brewed my coffee too strong—then there is a change in the reward circuits. The dopamine neurons stop firing. That pause in dopamine release signals a failure in reward arrival, a new kind of prediction error. This final point highlights another important subtlety in the dopamine reward system: it's always on. The neurons that release dopamine into the striatum are firing at a baseline rate—ticking away constantly to release a regular, low-level supply of dopamine, known as the "tonic" level. Unexpected rewards cause short-lived bursts of release that are superimposed on top of this baseline (the "phasic" dopamine release), whereas failed rewards decrease the tonic rate of firing. In a way, the reward system works a bit like cruise control in a car—it maintains a fixed steady speed (your basic level of motivation), but you can always hit the accelerator or brake to deal with changing conditions.

The reward system therefore operates as a multifunctional mechanism that allows us to detect rewards, learn to anticipate rewards, recognize cues in the environment that are linked to rewards, motivate action to seek the reward, and assess the success of our predictions. Quite clever, really.

Unfortunately, it has a few imperfections.

Wanting versus liking

The first interesting wrinkle that needs to be considered is the fact that dopamine does not directly cause the sensation of pleasure. Dopamine is a relay system that integrates all the sensory inputs that denote reward, and activates the desire to seek more, but it isn't needed in itself to experience the joyful thrill of bliss.

A recent advance in our understanding of reward-seeking behavior is the fact that wanting and liking are distinct phenomena. Feeling pleasure and wanting pleasure are separate processes at a neurochemical level.[4] The experience of *wanting* is driven by dopamine. The experience of *liking* seems to be triggered by different neurotransmitters, most likely endorphins and endocannabinoids (the natural equivalents of heroin and cannabis, respectively).

Within the circuits of the reward system, there are tiny subregions known as "hedonic hotspots" that are central to the sensation of experiencing pleasure. Injecting drugs that mimic the "liking" neurotransmitters into these hotspots can greatly amplify the intensity of pleasure.

The discovery of this phenomenon came from watching mice drink sugar water. Sweetness is intrinsically pleasurable, and it's possible to measure this objectively from the expression that animals (and people) make when they are enjoying the sensation. From careful research, the details of these neural centers have been pieced together.[5] It's now becoming clear that the mechanism for experiencing intrinsic pleasure is separate from the reward-seeking systems, which means that wanting something and liking it can become uncoupled. Even with no motivation to seek sugar, you can still experience pleasure from tasting it. Conversely, you can be motivated to seek something that no longer provides intrinsic pleasure because you once learned to want it.

This discovery can explain apparently irrational behavior. For example, why a bitter drink like coffee, which should be aversive, can become an acquired taste that is craved as a stimulant. It explains why someone suffering a fearsome hangover could nevertheless want to get drunk again. It explains why some still seek the affection of a partner who was once loving and attentive but has turned moody and distant, or why you continue to crave contact with a limerent object (LO) who is obviously incompatible. If you've learned to want something enough, liking it becomes almost irrelevant.

As a further curiosity of "liking," the distribution and sensitivity of those tiny, hedonic hotspots can be altered by other factors, such as stress, hunger, or pain. That means that you like things less when you're stressed, but you still want them. In fact—in one of life's little ironies—you'll probably want them more than ever, right when they fail to give the hedonic pleasure you'd hoped would bring relief.

Finally, it turns out that many different sources of pleasure all work through the same hotspots. So, chocolate, orgasms, limerence, and heroin may all depend on the same little bundles of cells to evoke their fundamental sensation of pleasure. Our higher centers in the cortex make sense of the different contexts and meanings of the pleasures, but liking has a simple, fundamental basis in the brain.[6]

Dopamine makes us want things, independently of whether we still like them, but what makes that desire for reward fade away? What makes "wanting" stop?

Habituation, or why desire fades

In terms of neuroscience, the fading of reward is known as "habituation." It's a fundamental feature of neurophysiology, and describes the phenomenon where repeated exposure to a stimulus (either good or bad) leads to a diminished response over time. You get used to things that happen repeatedly. This process allows you to stop wanting things that are easily obtained and stop fearing things that are easily avoided.

If you repeatedly listen to a song that you really like, you'll tire of it. If you eat your favorite meal every day, you'll lose your appetite for it. If you constantly consume erotica, you'll become jaded. Habituation is the mechanism through which exposure to rewards leads to fading pleasure, but the devil is in the details, again. There are some subtleties to the mechanism that can explain the unpredictability of loss of desire.

The process of learning to suppress a response to the rewarding stimulus happens at the level of the reward system—there is a decrease in the size of the dopamine release caused by a particular reward cue once the circuit has become habituated.[7] Habituation is most effective when the rewarding stimulus is weak, encountered frequently, and can be predictably secured. People who own orchards rarely crave apples. In contrast, some stimuli are incredibly powerful, hard to find, and unpredictable. Finding a romantic partner is a high-stakes, low-odds endeavor that many people pursue with single-minded determination.

The habituation process isn't always smooth and straightforward. A long period of foregoing a pleasure can result in the desire returning—you effectively forget that you had grown tired of the reward. Similarly, encountering a stimulus in a new or different context can reignite old desires. Finally, some stimuli are stubborn to habituate and undergo a period of increased desire in the early phase of experiencing them—a process known as sensitization. That means a taste of bliss leads to increasingly urgent reward-seeking that grows in intensity before you ever begin to develop a resistance to its charms.

Putting this all together, habituation teaches us that you don't ever really stop wanting something, it's more that you learn you don't *need to want it* anymore. The brain actively, but provisionally, suppresses the reward systems while in a time of plenty. It's pretty obvious that this is a fairly fragile mechanism for suppressing desire. The scope for relapse is high.

How habits form

These neurochemical details of how reward and pleasure work in the brain might seem like an academic diversion—an intellectual rabbit hole—but they have real-world implications for understanding the apparently irrational behavior of people who have been driven into a state of compulsive, single-minded desire.

There is an understandable, foreseeable progression to the behavior that can be predicted from the rules that govern the underlying neural circuits.

When someone encounters an extremely pleasurable reward for the first time, both the dopamine reward and endorphin "liking" systems will be maxed out. This could be the euphoric bliss of an orgasm, a hit of heroin, the thrill of skydiving, a big win for a gambler, or that romantically potent lingering eye-contact with a new limerent object. Such an experience would be memorable and inflame an intense desire. Inevitably, we will want more.

The early phase of reward learning then begins, where the source of pleasure is sought, experimented with and refined until we feel it's understood—how and when the reward can be secured, what cues are linked to it, and what particular behavior enhances or reduces the chance of reward. We test the boundaries and parameters until we are confident about how to get access to the pleasure again. Then we keep doing it, each time reinforcing this reward-learning mechanism.

Once these associations are learned, dopamine motivates us to repeatedly carry out the behavior that works. This is when environmental cues that remind us of the reward trigger the impulse to seek it. Importantly, once this associative learning process has set in, it becomes largely unconscious. We act before we are even aware of what's happening. It isn't that we spot a cue, think about its significance, decide what the best response should be, and then make a purposeful choice—instead, we spot a cue and our brainstem dumps dopamine into the striatum to impel us into action, faster than our thoughts can catch up.

While seeking a limerent object is a good case study in unconscious motivation, perhaps the best modern example of this phenomenon in practice is the cell phone. We've all learned that the little black rectangle in our pocket is an almost limitless source of stimulation—an infinity pool that can be relied on for a rewarding boost of entertainment and distraction when we're bored or uncomfortable.[8] It's often in our hands and lighting up before we're consciously aware of having summoned it. The web browser icon on my desktop is the same—I've often launched it before I've given any thought to what I was intending to look up. I've just learned, at a very deep, subconscious level that there's good stuff on the other end of that click.

The momentary confusion you feel when you find yourself looking at a screen that you didn't consciously, actively choose to engage with, is a good sign that your "executive brain" has been sidestepped by subcortical associative learning. The reward-seeking behavior has transcended active intent. It has become a habit, and habitual behavior can be very hard to unlearn. Once it's established, a habitual program basically runs on automatic.

The transition to addiction

In most cases, development of a habit is not a problem. Indeed, we have this system built into our brains for a good reason—to simplify and clarify action. We need a motivational drive that urges us to explore the world, discover beneficial things and secure them. Habits may become disruptive or frustrating, but for the most part they are not detrimental to the healthy enjoyment of life. If we apply ourselves, we can use willpower to resist the urge to overindulge in a guilty pleasure, and we can generally moderate our reward-seeking behavior when necessary to meet our responsibilities and prioritize long-term goals over short-term gratification. Some desires are not like that, though. Some desires overwhelm all other concerns, become a source of singular obsession, and feel so compulsive and irresistible that everything else in life is neglected. The habit isn't just running on automatic, it's involuntary.

Addiction is generally defined as a habit of compulsively abusing a substance or engaging in a behavior that has an adverse effect on quality of life. There remains a contentious debate about whether addiction should be treated as a disease or a failure of willpower, but for now we will focus on the neurobiology. Knowing about incentive salience, hedonic hotspots, and the limitations of habituation means we can understand how the reward system can end up in a state of persistent overactivation, where the wanting impulse persists with crippling intensity, untethered from logic or voluntary control.

It's easy enough to understand how drugs of abuse like alcohol, cocaine, or heroin can become addictive, because they literally derange the normal functioning of the neurons in the reward circuits. If you use chemicals to directly overactivate the hedonic hotspots, it's not too surprising that euphoria results. If your drug of choice stops the reward circuits switching off, you get wildly positive feedback on how desirable it is. There is also growing evidence that the use of drugs that disrupt dopamine clearance (such as amphetamines and cocaine) prevent habituation and cause sensitization.[9] The more you take, the more you want—regardless of whether the high proves to be reliable. In the case of substance abuse, addiction results from a measurable, physical disruption of the brain's reward system.[10] There is both physiological and psychological dependence.

The concept of behavioral addiction is more contentious. There was skepticism about whether compulsive behaviors, with only psychological cravings and no external substance that directly interfered with the reward circuits, fell within the same category as substance addictions. For a long time, unhealthy behaviors like excessive gambling, eating, shopping, or gaming were considered failures of impulse control, rather than addictions. Since 1990, the consensus within the field of clinical psychology has moved toward accepting that the compulsion for engaging in certain behaviors has a similar underlying neurobiological mechanism to drug seeking, and so should be described as addiction. The best evidence exists for gambling addiction, which is now formally listed in the *Diagnostic and Statistical Manual of Mental Disorders* from the American Psychiatric Association under "Substance-related and addictive disorders."[11]

Gambling addiction is a very useful case study for understanding how the properties of the "wanting" system can be coaxed into a hyperactive state. Gambling companies understand the power of reward, habit, and the unconscious desire that is driving our behavior. If you were to design a game that would maximize the chance of hyping up the arousal and reward systems, while simultaneously preventing habituation from suppressing desire, you couldn't do much better than the slot machine.

Slot machines have an enticing interface, with lots of user engagement through adding coins, pulling levers, or pressing buttons, combined with lots of highly arousing and stimulating sensory cues—flashing lights, spinning wheels, catchy melodies, and the triumphant, clunking rattle of disgorged coins when you win. Slot machines are fun and rewarding to play, and one of the ways this is achieved is through highly optimized payout algorithms.[12] Sometimes the player gets a sudden, unexpected bonanza that corresponds with a sensory overload of lights and sounds. They're a winner! Heady stuff. Afterward, there tends to be a lull in payouts, but after a finely calculated but uncertain interval, there will be another smaller reward to keep them playing.

One of the most important lessons learned from the study of reward habituation is the power of intermittent reward schedules.[13] This fits beautifully within the framework of dopamine acting as a reward prediction error signal. Rewards that arrive reliably after carrying out a particular behavior habituate quickly, whereas rewards that are unpredictable habituate slowly. If a slot machine paid out a fixed sum every twenty spins, it would cease to be exciting or arousing. In contrast, a slot machine that sometimes pays out huge amounts, often pays out smaller amounts, but also has stretches of nonpayment (with near misses!) keeps the player hooked.

Gamblers at a slot machine are treated to round after round of expectation and disappointment, with dopamine peaking in anticipation of a payout, but then dipping after failures. This is a schedule of reinforcement that the dopamine system just can't adapt to. Its role as an error prediction signal is in overdrive as there is no pattern of reward that can be predictably learned.

Over time, the gambler is also likely to develop superstitions as they try to find some sort of sense-making pattern in the sequence of rewards that arrive intermittently and unpredictably. Their wanting system *sensitizes* (the circuits literally increase in strength), and the futile pursuit of mastery becomes a goal in itself. If their "winning system" succeeds they feel triumphant, but when it fails (as it must in the face of a deliberately unpredictable algorithm) they try to escape the aversive dopamine dip by refining their tactics—always in pursuit of the next triumphant high.

For the many people who do not become addicted to gambling, the inconsistency and unpredictability of payouts eventually leads to frustration and disinterest. But for those who get an exhilarating high from the thrill of a win, the desire for more carries them into the cycle of reinforcing, habitual behavior that is needed to cement a compulsion.

Gambling is the most studied and accredited behavioral addiction, but there is a growing recognition that many other conditions involve compulsive, habitual behavior, in which wanting is exaggerated beyond reason, which would also fit this psychological framework.[14]

Limerence as addiction to another person

For limerence, the relevance of the neuroscience of desire and addiction is self-evident. All the elements are present, everything fits into place.

Limerence begins with that glimmer of romantic excitement—the allure of the LO as an unusually attractive and desirable person. Their presence causes arousal, pleasure, even euphoria. This is a high-impact reward stimulus. If there are hints of the hoped-for reciprocation, and the attachment deepens, bonding kicks in, which makes them even more desirable. You want them. Intensely.

Inexorably, the dopamine system transitions into motivating you to seek limerent reward. Incentive salience goes through the roof—everything about them is important, stimulating, noticeable. Places and items associated with them take on a special significance, and objects jump out of the background (their coat on the back of a chair seems to radiate meaning). All those cues in the environment make you think about them, and because thinking about them is pleasurable in itself, this becomes another source of reinforcement.

Limerent reverie is a secondary source of reward, a way of getting a taste of the pleasure of their company by fantasizing about contact. Limerents spend an inordinate amount of time reminiscing about good times with their LO, planning for new ways to gain contact, rehearsing conversations they might have that will delight and amaze the LO and, most tantalizing of all, cajole them into revealing how they feel about the limerent. Add in the erotic fantasies that many limerents indulge in, and you have a scenario where both external and internal worlds are aligned in the reinforcement of the "wanting" drive of dopamine, focused on the hyper-reward of the LO. With enough of this effortless mental training, the desire to seek contact becomes a deeply engrained habit.

If you are unable to freely bond with your LO, or their behavior is ambiguous, inconsistent, or downright manipulative, you end up in a state of anxious uncertainty. The reward you receive is unpredictable. Your clever strategies for seeking reciprocation sometimes work, but sometimes fail. When you get an unexpected hit, it's elating; when you get a rejection, it's devastating. Just like the gambler trying to make sense of the slot machine, your behavior becomes more erratic and irrational as you try to secure the reward, but your reward prediction circuit is still registering repeated errors: the dopamine drive sensitizes, fails to habituate, and you are left stuck in a state of "wanting" so powerful that you crave them more than anything else.

Once that deep habit becomes established, but satisfaction remains unattainable, limerence can turn sour—the urgent, relentless wanting lasts beyond the point at which you are reliably getting pleasure from their company. This is why we can remain limerent for people who treat us badly and make us feel awful. The neuroscience can explain why this happens—wanting can decouple from liking—but it also illustrates the last major principle of addiction that needs to be understood to make sense of the full gamut of limerence from euphoria to emotional prison: breaking the habit hurts.

Withdrawal pains

For people who abuse drugs, withdrawal pain is a significant barrier to recovery. Early on, the drug of choice will give an unnaturally euphoric thrill as the reward and pleasure centers are forcibly maxed out, but the body fights back. The brain removes the receptors and transporters that are being overstimulated, trying to reestablish normality. In practical terms, this means developing a tolerance for the drug, which the addict usually responds to by taking a higher dose. Eventually—typically after a particularly bad experience—the addict will try to break the habit, and then encounter the pain of withdrawal. Where once they took the drug to feel fantastic, now they have to take it just to feel normal.

This is a critical transition in the progression of an addiction. The impulse driving behavior switches from positive motivation to seek reward to negative motivation to avoid pain. Withdrawal hurts. The craving becomes an insistent, intrusive ache that you seek relief from—a significant change from the previous experience of excitedly seeking a pleasurable reward. Although there is clearly a physical component to this dependence in drug abuse, there is a significant psychological component too. We learn to associate emotional pain and psychological aversion with attempts to withdraw from the addiction. Unfortunately, the only way we know how to pacify that new pain is by indulging the addiction.

Many limerents find themselves in this position. They know that the craving is unhealthy, they know that a relationship with their LO is impossible, they know that they need to stop reinforcing the behavior, but they feel helpless to resist. Attempts to break contact with their LO are harrowing and they suffer a deep sense of loss, regret, and panic that they have missed out on a romantic opportunity that is irreplaceable.

> *It feels like I'm possessed. I can't give up on the memory of how good it used to feel. Even though rationally I want to step away from the feeling because it's causing me so much pain, there's just this sadness about letting go of a beautiful possibility. —K*

Collectively, the scientific evidence and our understanding of the ways that insatiable desire becomes habit, then addiction, add up to a simple, unifying conclusion: limerence is best understood as addiction to another person.

CHAPTER 5
IS LIMERENCE A MENTAL ILLNESS?

Am I going crazy?

The concept of limerence as "person addiction" has a lot of explanatory power. The neuroscience of behavioral addiction fits the progression of limerence neatly, and the parallels are just as striking when it comes to the way that limerents act under the influence of a particularly feverish episode. Bluntly, they behave like addicts.

Instinctively, most limerents conceal the intensity of their feelings, sensing that they are so potent that they aren't safe to share—especially if the limerent is not free to bond with the limerent object (LO). Their intuition is that the truth would alarm others so much that it might jeopardize access to the LO.

> *I didn't want to jinx it by talking about it. Also, a part of me must have been subconsciously afraid that if I spoke of my limerence experience to friends/family, someone would point out the inappropriateness/futility of the attachment and tell me to move on. I wasn't ready for a "reality check." —A*

There is an unmistakably illicit thrill associated with limerent euphoria; it feels intoxicating, salacious, guilty. This instinct to conceal, to keep the habit secret, can also mean becoming more deceptive in general: lying about your intentions, minimizing inappropriate behavior, rationalizing poor choices, neglecting commitments and responsibilities, and prioritizing contact with the LO over everything else in life. The motivation to seek them can be so powerful that it crowds out other thoughts—it can be impossible to concentrate on daily tasks because of relentless intrusive thoughts. Limerents often reorder their lives to increase their supply, changing daily routines to maximize the chance of contact. Ultimately, the obsession can get to the point where constantly seeking them diminishes life, but not seeking them causes unbearable emotional pain. The addict's trap: heads you lose, tails you really lose.

Powerful as it is, there is a problem with this concept of limerence as person addiction that should be confronted. For most people, limerence ends. There comes a point when we are no longer enraptured, no longer seeking contact with our LO, no longer giddy with nerves and hyped with overarousal. We eventually exit the limerent mental state and recover our psychological equilibrium, even if the process takes months or years. That sort of inbuilt recovery doesn't generally happen with other addictions. If limerence can be a sort of temporary addiction, is it useful to view it as a psychological disorder, or is it just the way that a subset of people experience love? Limerence certainly doesn't feel "*normal,*" but is it natural?

This question has very important implications for how to make sense of the limerence experience; how to appropriately respond when you start to feel the first glimmer of limerence, and how to manage and recover from the bad episodes. If limerence is, by definition, a mental health problem then it should be treated as a clinical condition. However, if it is instead a trait that some people just *have*, as an inherent feature of their romantic life, then it should be understood and regulated, but integrated into life in a healthy way. How we react to the discovery that we experience limerence should be based on a clear idea of whether it is an illness to be treated, or a trait to be managed.

What is mental illness?

The starting point for understanding how to view limerence in the context of mental health is to define what is meant by a mental illness or disorder. Unfortunately, this is not simple. For most mental health professionals, the definition is usually something along the lines of "a psychological disturbance that impairs an individual's ability to function in life and is a cause of significant distress." It is a disruption in thinking, emotional regulation, or behavior that is severe enough to fall outside of normal human variation, and so becomes clinically significant.[1]

A more formal definition of mental illness often depends on reference to an authority, such as the World Health Organization's *International Classification of Diseases 11th Revision* (ICD-11), or the American Psychological Society's *Diagnostic and Statistical Manual*.[2] These guides collate mental disorders that are recognized by a plurality of health-care professionals as having diagnosable symptoms, a definable set of causes, and that can be distinguished from other, related conditions. Examples would be schizophrenia, major depressive disorder, or bipolar disorder. Limerence does not appear in any of these clinical texts. It is not recognized as a defined mental health disorder by most health authorities.

Another difficulty in drawing firm conclusions is that a lot of mental health problems have very significant overlap with "normal" psychological functioning. When does a large appetite become an eating disorder? When does high sensitivity become an anxiety disorder? When does low empathy become a personality disorder? Limerence falls within this gray area category of normal experience that can become unbalanced or extreme—after all, romantic desire is a healthy part of human life, and many people develop crushes that are disruptive to life. At what point would it make sense to categorize this as an illness?

A starting point for answering these questions is to compare the features of limerence to more orthodox mental health conditions that are associated with obsessive thoughts, mood instability, impaired judgment, and apparently irrational urges. There are some obvious parallels between limerence and other disorders, and it's worth reviewing them to explore the possibility that limerence correlates with these conditions.

Obsessive compulsive disorder

Obsessive compulsive disorder (OCD) is a condition defined by repetitive, unwanted thoughts that are unpleasant and intrusive, which become linked to the compulsive urge to carry out a repetitive act or mental task that gives temporary relief from the obsession.[3] Well-known examples include repeatedly checking locked doors and windows or washing hands an excessive number of times.

Many of the symptoms of limerence overlap with the symptoms of OCD. There's the obsession, of course, but also the presence of intrusive thoughts, the psychological distress, and the compulsive urge to seek contact with the LO.

Professor Albert Wakin was a colleague of Dorothy Tennov for a short period in the seventies, and is one of the few clinicians who has attempted to refine and update the concept of limerence in recent years. In 2007, he published a conference paper with a graduate student, Duyen Vo, that describes limerence as a cross between OCD and addiction. They conceptualize limerence as necessarily harmful, and distinct from love:

> *In a love relationship, one often experiences initial intense feelings and reactions, and absorption in another person that tend to moderate over time, allowing for a more stable, intimate, trusting and committed relationship to flourish. However, in limerence, said initial feelings and reactions somehow fail to subside, becoming increasingly intense, pervasive and disruptive, ultimately rendering difficulty in controlling one's thoughts, feelings and behaviors.*[4]

Where Tennov saw limerence as a euphoric, ecstatic romantic attachment that could sometimes turn bad, the Wakin-Vo model proposes that the term "limerence" should instead be reserved for the specific cases where the romantic obsession becomes damaging. In the Wakin-Vo model, limerence has close parallels to OCD as it involves essentially negative psychological symptoms: difficulty regulating mood, intrusive thoughts, and habitual, almost ritualistic, behaviors (like compulsively checking their social media, reliving powerful memories, or rehearsing future meetings with the LO).

The behavioral parallels are compelling, but from the perspective of neuroscience there is a problem with this analogy. OCD is characterized by two main features: irrational fears that dominate thoughts and the compulsive urge to carry out rituals that temporarily ease those fears. Classic OCD is based on dysregulated anxiety—fears of contamination, insecurity, or harm. In contrast, limerence begins with an intoxicating joy that morphs into an obsession and then reaches a late stage of anxiety only when the desired pair bond cannot be formed. Even then, the fears and anxiety of the limerent are typically focused on panic at the loss of romantic bliss, rather than fear of personal vulnerability.

Accordingly, the neuroscience of limerence is distinct from OCD. For OCD, the fundamental problem is a failure of the executive centers to override the fear system of the brain. The best evidence suggests that OCD arises from overactivation of an emotional processing circuit in the brain (organized around a loop from the orbitofrontal cortex, striatum, and another region known as the *thalamus*), due to weakened regulatory feedback from the cortex.[5] This circuit signals threat detection, which is usually checked by the executive brain to properly judge the true severity of the threat. Everyone feels discomfort if their hands are dirty, due to fears of contamination, but most people get reliable relief by quickly washing their hands. For people with classic OCD, that sense of relief doesn't arrive. Their hands never feel sufficiently clean. Ritualized washing gives fleeting relief, but the feelings of contamination return quickly. In terms of neurobiology, this problem is quite distinct from the runaway activation of reward centers and desperate cravings of limerence.

Perhaps the best illustration of this distinction is the concept of "relationship obsessive compulsive disorder" (ROCD). This is a form of OCD that centers on anxieties about romantic relationships. Superficially, this seems like a perfect description of limerence, but ROCD is defined by anxieties about the quality and stability of a romantic relationship. The intrusive thoughts take forms like "Do I really want to be with them, or could I find someone better?" or "I know I love them, but why doesn't it feel more special?" or "They say they love me, but what if they're lying?" or "Why am I not happier?" The compulsions that follow are attempts to seek constant reassurances from their partner, to judge their relationship against others, to rate the relative attractiveness of themselves and their partner, and an irresistible urge to confess their doubts.

These are not the concerns of a limerent. No limerent has ever looked at their LO and wondered, "Am I attracted to them enough?"

Bipolar disorder

Another mental health condition that has some striking parallels to limerence is bipolar disorder. Here the commonality is in the presence of wild mood swings from elation and exhilaration to devastation and depression.[6] Problems of mood regulation are undoubtedly a core feature of limerence, but again there are clear distinctions. The most obvious is that the mania and depression of bipolar disorder are not generally anchored onto a specific situation, or a particular person.

The extremes of mood experienced in bipolar disorder are generalized—they affect all aspects of life. The mania is all-inclusive, and characterized by restless energy and enthusiasm, and a broad euphoria that fuels creativity and a sense of invincibility. Similarly, the crash into depression that often follows the manic episode is equally broad. Life seems intolerable—pointless, joyless, hopeless, to the point of suicidal thoughts. In contrast, the romantic mania of limerence is focused on seeking reward from a specific person—their behavior has a direct bearing on the limerent's mood; the highs and lows follow a predictable pattern based on the quality of the limerent's interaction with their LO. The instability of bipolar disorder is less predictable than limerence and usually triggered by other stressors, for example bereavement, trauma, insomnia, or substance abuse. There's no doubt that bipolar disorder involves shifts into altered mental states, but it is not usually caused by romantic drives or focused on a desire for a particular person.

We still don't understand the neuroscience of bipolar disorder well. The best evidence suggests it is a neurodevelopmental disorder, that is, it results from irregularities during the refinement and maturation of the neural circuits that regulate mood. Like several other conditions (schizophrenia being the most notable example), there seems to be a confluence of genetic and environmental factors working together at key moments in brain development that lead to the reward, arousal, and executive systems becoming vulnerable to instabilities.[7] It might be due to viral infection, inflammation, or other forms of early life stress—most likely the unlucky coincidence of several small factors all working together.

Whether such genetic and environmental factors contribute to limerence is unknown, but the mood instabilities of limerence are much more demarcated by the specific circumstances of meeting a particular person who triggers the limerent response than the general instabilities of bipolar disorder.

Erotomania

Another mental health disorder—albeit an unusual and rare one—that is sometimes compared to limerence is erotomania. Also known as de Clérambault's syndrome, erotomania is a disorder defined by the delusional belief that someone, usually of high social status, is infatuated with the sufferer, but bound by circumstances to keep their love secret.[8] The delusional belief can be extraordinarily detailed and elaborate, often involving the perception that the "secret admirer" is sending coded messages to the sufferer through subtle means. A 2006 case study review describes a patient who was convinced that her admirer (who in fact had no meaningful connection to her) was communicating his love through messages hidden in car license plates, and that their secret love affair was so well-known among influential people that the president of the United States was certainly well aware of the situation.[9]

The defining feature of erotomania is the delusional nature of the beliefs. Certainly, limerents can be oversensitive to their limerent object's behavior, reading too much into off-hand or ambiguous comments, but limerence is not usually associated with a complete detachment from reality. Romantic hope makes fools of us all, but erotomania patients take even direct, blunt rejection as evidence of love. The patient who saw messages in license plates also believed that her lover had secretly visited her over many nights, conceived several children with her, but that her parents and other enemies had stolen the babies.

Such pronounced delusions reveal a serious underlying psychiatric issue, and erotomania is sometimes associated with other delusional disorders, particularly paranoid schizophrenia. Sufferers often have grandiose or paranoid beliefs that accompany the romantic delusion, sometimes even including hallucinations. Crucially, the sufferer is convinced that they are justified in their beliefs, that they are founded in a truth that only they can see and that their secret admirer welcomes the attention. Stalking, surveillance, relentless correspondence and other invasions of privacy are not uncommon.[10]

Limerents can often feel like they've lost their mind, but generally it's only meant metaphorically. They feel compelled to act in ways that they know they shouldn't, they are confused by the intensity of their urges and emotions, and are disquieted by their lack of self-control, but they don't actually lose their grip on reality. For sufferers of erotomania, the loss of mind is unfortunately all too real.

Attachment styles

In the late twentieth century, John Bowlby introduced one of the most significant and influential ideas in human social psychology: attachment theory.[11] The concepts of attachment theory first emerged from the study of infant-parent bonding, but soon expanded to cover the impact that early childhood attachment has on adult relationships. Attachment theory is now widely regarded as a foundational concept in psychology, buttressed by good evidence of neurobiological correlates for the differences observed between individuals with different attachment styles.[12] Our early life experiences literally shape the development of our brains.

Broadly, attachment theory posits that the experiences we have when seeking comfort as infants determine our emotional and social responses in adulthood. Children need touch. They urgently seek physical contact with their mother, or a surrogate caregiver, when experiencing pain or discomfort. If that physical reassurance is unavailable or unreliable, then disorders in bonding develop. There are heart-rending examples from both the experimental literature and real-world tragedies that emphasize the point: from infant monkeys clinging to a cloth model of a mother when afraid, to the harrowing accounts of the effects of emotional neglect on Romanian orphans uncovered in the 1980s.[13] Childhood bonding is essential for cognitive, emotional and social development, and disruption of this attachment process has long-lasting effects on an individual's personality.

Adult attachment can be categorized in different ways, and experts differ in their preferred terminology, but the most common (and most straightforward) categorization system for the formation of bonds is to define three primary attachment styles: secure, anxious and avoidant.[14] Helpfully, the terms are pretty self-explanatory.

A secure attachment style is characterized by stable, lasting relationships. People with this attachment style tend to have healthy self-esteem, and expect that their partners will respond in a positive, supportive way if they become emotionally distressed. They are able to express their feelings openly, and generally have a good opinion of their relationships.

In contrast, an anxious attachment style is insecure, characterized by fear of abandonment, and a belief that their partner will respond negatively to evidence of distress. Anxiously attached people are emotionally distraught when relationships end. They can be possessive, and seek a "fantasy bond" rather than a balanced, mutually supportive attachment. Low self-esteem is often the underlying issue that results in this attachment style, arising from unreliable or unpredictable care during childhood.

Avoidant attachment is defined by emotional detachment, and by suspicion or disdain for seeking intimacy as a source of comfort. Avoidants are adept at remaining emotionally disengaged and use this as a strategy to protect themselves from pain. They are dismissive of the importance of relationships, neither seek nor give support to their partners, and take pride in self-sufficiency and independence. This attachment style is thought to arise from overly strict or emotionally distant parenting.

Finally, a fourth attachment style that is sometimes proposed is the disorganized or fearful-avoidant style. People with this style can seek emotional comfort, but then react badly and feel stifled when it is offered. There tends to be a swing between neediness and coldness. A need for intimacy, but a fear of it. This is thought to reflect disordered bonding in childhood, with caregivers that were erratic, self-centered or abusive.

People can usually recognize their own attachment style quite reliably just from these brief descriptions. People with anxious or avoidant attachment styles can sometimes recall formative traumas that affected their self-esteem and emotional development, and how they have influenced romantic bonding experiences. Nowadays, a lot of the "talking therapies" focus on identifying problems with forming healthy attachment, and uncovering the life experiences that may have given rise to those psychological insecurities.

In reviewing the symptoms of limerence, and the experience of the altered mental state of romantic infatuation, an obvious hypothesis presents itself: limerence maps neatly onto the anxious attachment style. The obsessive thoughts, the central importance of uncertainty, the desperate craving for reciprocation—they all point to someone with an insecure attachment and excessive need for reassurance. Much of the popular discourse around limerence identifies it as a pathology of childhood trauma, disordered bonding, and the desire for a curative, corrective, fantasy relationship. I think this is a misdiagnosis.

Limerence as an unusual form of attachment

The primary cause for doubt is that many limerents do not recognize or relate to the description of an anxious attachment style, or recall any meaningful difficulties during childhood that could account for a tendency toward insecure romantic bonding. Similarly, some limerents report a life of aloofness and self-sufficiency (characteristic of avoidant attachments), but suffer agonies of doubt because they cannot escape the emotional need for an LO who they both crave and fear. People who otherwise have secure or avoidant attachment styles in the other important relationships in their lives can nonetheless experience limerence.

> *I think my general attachment style is stable and/or avoidant. ... Limerence makes me an anxious mess, but only in relation to LO. Limerence makes me 'bubbly' when my default setting is "reserved." —S*

> *I had been a secure attacher my whole adult life and my first (and to date only) limerence episode shook my world because it was so out of the ordinary for me to feel that way, to not be able to accept a dead end and move on. Still unable to fully accept it. Limerence overpowers even secure attachment... —R*

Furthermore, limerence is a unique, time-limited and unusual form of attachment. Desire for a limerent object is distinct, both from other romantic relationships, and even from the same relationship on the other side of limerence. For people who end up forming long-term relationships with their limerent object, the affectional bonding that follows the early period of limerence-mania is very different in character from the urgent, hungry and emotionally volatile nature of person addiction.

Finally, and perhaps most persuasively, the relationship between attachment style and limerence has been directly tested.[15] A study on hundreds of psychology students (that comically oversampled population demographic), established the attachment style of the participants and then surveyed them using various questionnaires related to scales of romantic and erotic love. One scale they used was for limerence. The results were mixed.

The first thing to note was that the three main attachment styles (for both men and women) reported limerence traits with similar frequencies. There were some statistically significant differences, but these did not skew toward anxious attachment in a simple way. In fact, the disparities mapped pretty well onto what would be expected by the definitions of the attachment styles. "Anxious" limerents scored slightly higher on those questions that related to preoccupation with the limerent object, whereas "avoidant" limerents scored lower on the questions that related to idealization of their limerent object. Overall, the differences were in the range of about 10 to 20 percent higher scores for anxious versus secure attachments, with avoidants varying inconsistently relative to the two other groups. These results suggest that there is certainly some correlation between limerence and attachment, but the differences are smaller than the overall congruence between the different attachment groups—attachment style biases the experience of limerence, but does not cause it.

People with all attachment styles self-report experiencing the symptoms of limerence. Anxious attachment may worsen the symptoms, but it is not a prerequisite for limerence.

Limerence as a uniquely personal experience

Limerence clearly has some similarities to some well-defined mental health conditions, but it's equally clear that there are profound differences. Analogies can be useful starting points for making sense of a problem, but they lead us astray if we only look at the surface details. Unfortunately, there are lots of different ways that brains can go wrong. Limerence can be distinguished from the best-known, clinically defined disorders; it doesn't fit neatly with any of these conditions and isn't usually a consequence of a pre-existing mental health problem.

A secondary question is whether other conditions might coexist with limerence or give a predisposition for person addiction. Do any mental health disorders make it more likely that the person affected will also experience limerence? That is a harder question to answer, mainly because there is very little research into the prevalence of limerence in the general population, let alone in correlation with other conditions or attachment styles. It is certainly a plausible idea. A number of mental health conditions predispose sufferers to the development of addictions—bipolar disorder is correlated strongly with alcoholism, for example.[16] It's reasonable to speculate that limerence may be more common or more intense in people who are generally prone to mood instability or high sensitivity. Similarly, someone inclined to intrusive thoughts may be more likely to experience intense rumination as an aspect of their limerent experience.

These speculations help clarify an important principle when making sense of our own personal limerence experience. Everyone reacts differently. We are all shaped by our personal histories in many complex, subtle, and interlocking ways. The formative experiences of our lives will determine how we react to the onset of limerence, what it feels like for us, what our own particular vulnerabilities and tendencies will be. The influences that shape us will collectively determine the kind of person we become limerent for, the relative intensity of different limerence symptoms, the ease with which we fall into the state, how quickly we recover, and how avidly we seek it. For people with OCD, bipolar disorder, or anxious attachments, the experience of limerence will be different from people with secure attachments and generally good mental health. The combination of factors could worsen symptoms, as there are many ways that the psychological vulnerabilities of other conditions can intersect with limerence. OCD will increase the tendency to develop mental rituals to manage the pain of separation; anxious attachment will significantly exacerbate the sensitivity to mixed messages and unpredictable behavior from a limerent object.

This is the messy reality of trying to distinguish what is just ordinary variation in human experience from what is definitively a mental health problem. Many emotions are like this—take for example anxiety. Anxiety is clearly a natural response to stress, and while it might feel awful, it has obvious survival value. However, if people are repeatedly or continuously exposed to stress (especially if it is not within their control) they develop anxiety disorders, which come with a host of other chronic health conditions that degrade quality of life. A normal emotional state becomes dysregulated. It stops being useful and becomes harmful.

This is how I see limerence. For most people going through their first episode of limerence, the experience is certainly extraordinary, but it isn't necessarily negative. The euphoria of romantic bliss, the warmth of bonding, the emotional attachment to a romantic partner—these are all natural and healthy manifestations of love, which greatly enrich life. If the attraction is mutual, limerence can lead to formation of a pair bond, ecstatic union, maybe even children—all very positive outcomes. It's in the tipping over into mismanaged person addiction that limerence becomes a cause of distress, and identifying the circumstances that trigger that transition is critical for understanding how limerence goes wrong and how best to recover when it has.

Experiencing limerence is not a symptom of mental illness, a psychological wound, or an emotional failing. For most limerents it is a normal part of the process of falling in love, albeit with a force that has a fierce and alarming power. Whether limerence overpowers our psychological defenses and traps us in a debilitating addiction is determined by our emotional vulnerabilities, which depend in turn on our history, personality, and life circumstances. Who we are, and where we are in life, are the critical factors in determining whether limerence is mainly a blessing or a curse.

This individual perspective raises new questions about the sorts of people who might be most susceptible to runaway person addiction. Is limerence more common for some particular personality types, psychological traits, or demographics? Who populates the limerent tribe?

What kinds of people are particularly susceptible to its ecstatic but perilous power?

CHAPTER 6

WHO BECOMES LIMERENT?

And how common is it?

The idea of two groups—limerents and non-limerents—who experience romantic love in a fundamentally different way leads naturally to the question of how many people are in each tribe. Do limerents outnumber non-limerents, or vice versa? Are there particular kinds of people who are more prone to limerence than others? Unfortunately, answering these questions is not as easy as one might hope.

An obvious starting point would be to look for patterns in the people who visit the Living with Limerence site, but it turns out to be such a broad range of individuals—male, female, young, old, gay, straight, bi, asexual, poly, religious, atheist—that it's hard to think of a demographic group that hasn't been represented at some point. It's life's rich pageant in full splendor. While acknowledging this diversity, there are nonetheless some themes that recur—limerence for a coworker, limerence for a therapist, midlife limerence, limerence in an unhappy marriage, introvert limerents, people pleasers. That might be a clue as to which kind of people need support to manage limerence in their lives.

To move beyond guesswork and intuition, we'd need a more objective strategy for getting good quality data on the prevalence of limerence in the general population. Unfortunately, there are a couple of big problems to overcome: We need a precise definition of what limerence is, and we need an unbiased way to poll people about whether they have experienced it. Hilariously, these are two of the hardest problems to solve in social psychology.[1] Nevertheless, unbowed and undaunted, we are going to tackle them . . . after a quick diversion into analyzing the problems. We'll get there in the end. Promise.

Defining limerence and avoiding bias

Limerence was first described by Dorothy Tennov as a distinct mental state that some people fall into during the early stages of romantic love, and she classified that state according to the common symptoms that many of her interview subjects reported. These symptoms are the basis of the quiz at the beginning of this book (see pages 6–8), and the definition that we use at Living with Limerence. So, by those criteria, limerents are people who have enough of the symptoms to qualify. Easy. Until you ask yourself how many symptoms are enough? Is someone a limerent if they have more than half the symptoms and score more than 50 percent on the quiz? Or should we only define limerents as the real extremists, with scores over 95 percent?

This difficulty is what's known as a thresholding problem. If you set a threshold score for a survey to sort people into two categories, what you've done is actually convert a range of responses into a binary choice. There are times when this is powerful and useful, but it also ignores a lot of the important details that are hidden in the differences between people who have been surveyed. What does it mean to score 75 percent on the limerence quiz? Does that mean you are three-quarters limerent, or does it mean you have three-quarters of the symptoms and therefore qualify as a member of the limerence tribe? Is everyone a bit limerent, or is there genuinely a distinct class of people that experience a definable mental state that other people never encounter?

An alternative approach to defining limerence would be to focus on some specific symptoms as especially representative of the condition. For example, we could use the Wakin-Vo definition of limerence mentioned in the previous chapter, which reserves the term for only those cases where the symptoms are so "intense, pervasive and disruptive" that they result in "difficulty in controlling one's thoughts, feelings and behaviors."[2] Looking over the full range of symptoms in the quiz, some of them focus on those negative experiences (intrusive thoughts, anxiety, etc.). Perhaps then, using this alternative definition, people should have to score high on the negative, life-disrupting traits to qualify as limerents?

Defining limerence is not as simple as it first appears.

The second big problem to overcome is bias. Not just the intrinsic psychological biases that we all have as humans, but the difficulty in finding survey participants who are genuinely representative of the general public. The obvious blunders (like oversampling psychology students) are well understood, but the fact remains that it is extremely difficult to find a truly representative sample of "average people" when conducting survey research.

Fortunately, it's not a hopeless case. We just need to interpret the data we do have carefully.

Is limerence binary or a spectrum?

Researchers have been trying to quantify love for a long time—attempting to put a number on how "in love" somebody is.[3] One of the most widely applied psychometric tests used to measure intensity of love is known as "the passionate love scale." It incorporates questions that correspond closely with the symptoms of limerence—so in principle we could just define limerents as "people who score high on the passionate love scale."

A counterargument against this simplification is that the passionate love scale tests are often carried out on cohorts of people who self-report being "in love" or not being "in love" at the outset. That means they already have an intuitive sense that there is a distinct state that people can easily recognize they are "in" or not. A binary condition.

The quiz at the start of this book (see pages 6–8) has been live on the Living with Limerence website for over two years, and (at the time of writing) has been completed by more than twenty-five thousand people. A useful dataset, undoubtedly, but flawed. The quiz is anonymous, so no demographic data is collected, and it will clearly be biased toward people who are actively searching for an online limerence quiz and find their way to the site. We can make some informed guesses about the likely motives of the participants, but it's just not possible to truly understand the bias in the sample (because it was set up as a service for casual visitors, not a research tool).

Despite these limitations, the results are interesting.[4] The first thing to note is that the lowest score from anyone who has taken the test is 0 percent (i.e., they strongly disagreed with every hallmark of limerence). The highest score is 100 percent, and there are a significant number of people in that category—of the twenty-five thousand-plus who have taken the survey, nearly five hundred people "strongly agreed" with every single question (compared with twenty-three people in the 0 percent group).

The average score is 70 percent. Interestingly, from a statistical perspective, the graph of all results is what's known as a bell-shaped curve.[5] That means that the average score of 70 percent is the peak of the graph, making it the most common individual score too (technically, the statistical mean, median, and mode are essentially the same). That's interesting because it suggests that there aren't two clearly distinct groups of people taking the test, some of whom are limerent and some of whom are non-limerent. We seem to have the broadest possible range of scores, with a peak at 70 percent.

There's more than one way to interpret those results. One is to assume that the selection bias is so strong toward limerents (as only they would find the test), that the results measure the variation in intensity for limerence within the limerent tribe. An alternative interpretation is that the sample is actually a good representation of how the general population relates to limerence and there is a genuine spectrum to the condition. Unfortunately, the limitations inherent in self-selecting online surveys mean it is difficult to know which is the likelier explanation.

There is one last interesting correlation to discuss: In the Wakin-Vo model of limerence as an unhealthy state—where love goes wrong—there should be a population of people who experience the "positive" symptoms of limerence but manage them well and never feel the downsides of person addiction. Limerents would instead be that population who experience negative effects most powerfully. By sorting the questions into positive symptoms (e.g., "The whole world seems brighter and more colorful since I met them") and negative symptoms (e.g., "I sometimes cannot stop thinking about them, even if

I want to") we can test how distinct these two states are. In other words, is there any evidence for *Happy Limerents* who only experience the positive love-rush, or for *Anxious Limerents* who mainly get the anxiety and addiction?

The answer is clear: no. Of all the people who have taken the quiz, only 5 percent "agreed" with the majority of positive symptoms but "disagreed" with the majority of negative symptoms. Similarly, only 5 percent agreed with the negative but disagreed with the positive. Fully 82 percent of participants agreed with both.

It seems that when it comes to limerence it is very rare to have the good without the bad.

The bias problem

There is no way around the fact that questioning people with an anonymous quiz they have discovered by browsing online introduces all kinds of unknown biases into the results. To try to get a less biased estimate of how common limerence is, I adopted a more direct approach.

There are polling firms that allow businesses and researchers to quiz huge populations of individuals, using incentives that encourage them to complete the survey. There are issues—such as how much the promise of payment influences the speed and honesty of their answers—but it is a good way to solve the self-selection problem. One strategy would be to send out my limerence quiz to random people and see how the results compare with the previous data. Instead, I decided to design a new survey that was simpler to take and interpret (increasing the odds that people would complete it rather than run out of patience and abandon it).[6] With the help of the Living with Limerence community I came up with a concise description of limerence, and asked a forced yes/no question:

> *Some psychologists believe that in the early stages of romantic love, people can fall into an altered state of mind that feels very different from everyday life. In this mental state, the lovestruck*

person is overwhelmed by the desire to bond with the person they are infatuated with. Their emotions swing between feeling ecstatic and feeling devastated, depending on whether it seems that their love is returned. Their thoughts are dominated by the other person so much that it is hard to concentrate on other tasks. They crave them so strongly that it almost feels like an addiction.

Do you think you have ever experienced this mental state yourself? (Yes or No)

If the participants answered "Yes" they were prompted with a follow-up question:

Has this experience ever caused you so much emotional distress that it was hard to enjoy life? (Yes or No)

The goal of this survey was to try and directly test Tennov's model of limerence as an altered state of mind, and Wakin-Vo's model of limerence as a mental disorder. The survey was run over two days and gathered answers from 1,500 American and British adults.[7] Demographic data were also collected. The results were as follows:

- Sixty-four percent of participants had experienced the altered mental state as described, 36 percent had not.
- Of those who had experienced it, 50 percent had found it so distressing that it was hard to enjoy life.

Those numbers suggest that Tennov's definition of limerence fits nearly two-thirds of the population at large (when forced into a binary choice), and that about a third of the people who completed the survey had suffered from limerence so badly that it became a life-disrupting affliction. Is it wise to take these raw numbers at face value, though?

Although the random survey approach is certainly less biased than relying on visitors to the Living with Limerence website, there may be different distortions that are not so obvious—such as the kinds of people that fill in surveys for rewards. Fortunately, it was possible to drill down into the data and search for any sign of curious patterns or anomalies. There are some interesting details hidden in the demographics.

Sex and sexuality

It's a long-standing trope in art and philosophy that men and women experience love differently. There is a lot of evidence in biology and evolution for different mating strategies too.[8] If we go with the stereotypes, we might assume that the prevalence of limerence would differ between the sexes, perhaps based around whether the primary motive drive is seed-sowing or infant-nurturing (as we'll see in chapter 7, these sorts of assumptions actually miss the mark).

The survey was completed by 712 male and 786 female participants (two participants self-identified their sex as "other," which presumably reflects a nonbinary identity). Of the men, 67 percent were limerents, compared to 61 percent of the women. Statistical analysis suggests that this small difference is not meaningful—men and women experience limerence to the same extent (and the two nonbinary contributors split evenly too, with one limerent and one non-limerent). This result fits well with Tennov's assumptions, and my own anecdotal experiences hearing from limerents who comment on the site and send me emails—both men and women suffer through the agonies of person addiction. The altered mental state of limerence is something we share, not something that divides us. Men and women can be equally irrational and unstable when they fall in love.

It's nice to have that settled.

A second interesting question is whether limerence is more common among some sexualities than others. When Tennov first published her research in 1979, she did not encounter a single bi-limerent individual—only hetero-limerents or homo-limerents. At the time, she acknowledged that this might be a simple problem of numbers, or a reluctance for subjects to admit to bisexuality in an intolerant age, and it turns out she was right. I've heard from several bi-limerents in the Living with Limerence community:

> *My original LO was female, that was when I was a teenager and lasted acutely for about 6-7 years (and oh, who am I kidding, less acutely for the rest of my life.) Many LOs under the bridge since then, but my current is male with shared archetypal traits with original LO. I identify as bisexual and have happily dated many different types of people from all over the gender spectrum. —Q*

> *Can confirm that bi-limerence is real because I have it. —PL*

> *I am limerent mostly/only for one gender and sexually attracted mostly/only to the other. I wonder how common this is. Yes, this makes life quite complicated. —DL*

Another reason to wonder about sexuality is that there is a growing body of evidence that the experience of limerence among young homosexual men may cause them to engage in risky sexual behavior, to impress a limerent object.[9] This is serious because this demographic group is disproportionately likely to contract HIV by taking such risks. Understanding how limerence affects their decision-making might save them from lifelong repercussions.

In the survey, there was no detectable difference in the prevalence of limerence between heterosexual and homosexual participants. Segregating for gay men versus lesbians also showed no significant differences. However, despite this general similarity, there were a couple of unexpected outcomes.

First, the options available to participants for self-identification were "heterosexual," "homosexual," "bisexual," "other," and "prefer not to say." In contrast to the most recent US census data, the distribution of respondents in our survey was quite evenly spread among these categories: 53 percent identified as heterosexual, while the remaining four categories each scored in the 10 to 15 percent range.[10] Regardless of this disparity between our sample and the census data, a second unexpected outcome was that bisexual participants were disproportionately likely to have experienced limerence, at 71 percent. It's hard to reach any clear conclusions about why this might be, but we can perhaps speculate that people who are generally more open about sexual attraction could also be more open to infatuation. Alternatively, flipping the correlation, perhaps limerents are more likely to be bisexual than non-limerents—if someone is able to feel the glimmer for people of either sex, their libido will follow as person addiction sets in. At this stage, we can only really speculate about a curious and unexpected result.

Personality types

Another potential source of variation in susceptibility for limerence is personality type. There are various ways that people can be neatly sorted by personality traits into different categories or identities. The theoretical framework with the best evidence to date is ranking individuals along what are known as the Big Five personality dimensions: Openness to new experiences, Conscientiousness, Extraversion, Agreeableness, Neuroticism (using the handy acronym, OCEAN).[11] An alternative model for sorting personalities is the Myers-Brigg Type Indicator (MBTI) test.[12] This tool is well established, and has been used in many research and commercial contexts—though not without controversy. For our purposes, it is useful as a starting point to look for correlations with limerence because many people have taken the Myers-Brigg test in their lives and are able to identify their MBTI personality category.

In another self-selecting online poll, the clinical neuroscientist and author Lucy Bain asked limerents to identify their MBTI type.[13] The results were striking. Although all personality types reported limerence, the introvert personality types were highly overrepresented compared to the general population. That's noteworthy because introversion/extraversion is a personality trait that is also incorporated in the much better validated OCEAN framework, and so has explanatory power beyond the contentious theoretical basis of MBTI.

This outcome of introversion correlating with limerence also makes some intuitive sense. The limerent tendency to daydream about their LO, to live in a fantasy world of anticipation and rumination, seems tailored to an introvert personality. Countering that, the experience of finding another person's company energizing, stimulating, and intoxicating could be read as an extrovert trait. Limerents feed off their limerent object's attention, after all.

To try and get to the bottom of this, our online survey group were also asked about their introvert/extrovert personality type. The results were as follows: 61 percent of the introverts were limerents, 71 percent of extroverts. Defying expectations from the earlier poll, it seems that extroverts are more likely to be limerents than introverts.

There are a few possible explanations for this startling discrepancy, but probably the most obvious is that introverts would be more likely to seek help by searching for articles online to understand what they are going through, rather than talking to other people (which would be the extrovert instinct). That would cause a selection bias for introverts in the population who knew their MBTI type and were inclined to complete the online test—another problem with sampling bias rather than a genuine link between limerence and personality type. It really is hard to find reliable data that is representative of the "true" general public.

Age

Another demographic trait that might be relevant to limerence is age. For most people, their first experience of romantic love begins in adolescence. Although it might be dismissed as a teenage crush, the emergence of sexuality during puberty also seems to result in the capacity to enter the altered mental state of limerence. However, one of the reasons that teenage love is disparaged as puppy love might be that many people "grow out" of the tendency to experience crushes, which they interpret as maturing into a more stable and measured approach to love that leaves the wild infatuations of youth behind.

A second period where limerence seems to become an issue is midlife. A lot of the visitors to Living with Limerence are going through what could be called a limerent midlife crisis. It is, by its nature, a destabilizing phase of life. Many extramarital affairs begin in midlife, when people can go through a sort of psychological "second adolescence."[14] Midlifers often experience a sort of panic over lost time—a sense that the prime of their life is slipping away; that it is the last chance to make new choices, find a new partner, and reinvent their lives. Moreover, some limerents report their first ever limerent experience in this psychologically complex phase of life.[15]

> For about two years I've been in a state of what I now know is classic limerence. The problem is, I can't really believe it isn't love, because this is the first time I've ever felt like this despite being in my forties. —R

> [At 38] it's my first Limerence in 14 years [of] marriage. I'm torn apart. —SC

The way the survey was pitched to participants was as an absolute question: *Do you think you have ever experienced this mental state yourself?* In theory, assuming memories do not fade too much, the percentage of limerents should progressively increase with age. That isn't what happened. There was an obvious high point.

For eighteen to twenty-four year olds, 55 percent reported having experienced limerence. At early midlife (thirty-five to forty-four years) the number rose to 76 percent, but declined in later midlife and by ages above fifty-four it had apparently settled down again, to an average of 61 percent.

The early midlife peak for limerence seems real. Unless there is a generational change in propensity, the simplest explanation for the peak is that for that age group the experience of limerence is more current, more present in their lives.[16]

Attachment style

The last question asked of our survey participants was whether they thought they had an anxious attachment style. We covered the intersection of limerence and attachment in the previous chapter, and how there is an overlap between the features of anxious attachment and some of the negative aspects of limerence. To test the idea that limerence is more common in the anxiously attached, the final question in the survey was this:

> *Some people feel anxious about their romantic relationships. They seek frequent reassurance that their partner still loves them. They spend a lot of time worrying about the security of their relationship. Small disagreements with their partner can feel like a big threat. They seek a lot of intimacy and want to spend as much time as they can with their partner. Do you think you have this attachment style?*

For the people that answered "yes" to this question, 79 percent also answered "yes" to having experienced limerence. Quite a correlation! For those who answered "no," they do not have an anxious attachment style, 55 percent had experienced limerence.

That's a significant result when it comes to the discourse around limerence and attachment theory. The idea that limerence is a manifestation of an anxious attachment style, or even that limerence is an attachment disorder in itself, is a popular view. In fact, more than half of the population who do not have an anxious attachment style are limerents. But—and it is a big but!—eight out of ten people who have anxious attachments are limerents.

A final cautionary note at this point is that of all the people surveyed, nearly 41 percent reported having an anxious attachment style, based on the description in this question. Again, that number suggests an overrepresentation of people with this trait in our data, as estimates of the prevalence of anxious attachment in the general population is around 15 to 20 percent.[17]

So, how common is limerence then?

After that barrage of numbers and statistics it's natural to wonder: *Yeah, but what does this all add up to?* Perhaps the broadest conclusion that can be drawn is that in every category and every demographic group, at least half of the people sampled had experienced limerence. Limerents are everywhere. All ages, personality types, genders, sexualities, and ethnicities are susceptible.

The other takeaway from the survey is that despite this general prevalence, some demographic groups are more likely to experience limerence than others. The most striking examples are bisexuals, early midlifers, and the anxiously attached. As it happened, both bisexuals and anxiously attached groups were overrepresented in our limerence survey sample compared to census data for the general population. If I had to guess why, I'd say that people who have enjoyed stable romantic lives would have a lower tolerance for answering questions about irrational love, and were more likely to abandon the survey unfinished, due to boredom, irritation, or because they found it intrusive. In contrast, people who have sometimes struggled with their romantic temperament would be more motivated to stick with it to the end. It's hard to know how dramatic this bias is, but the overall effect would be a significant overestimation of how common limerence really is. Our survey average of 64 percent is likely to be higher than the "true" percentage of limerents in the general population.

Given all these critiques, and trying to carefully balance out the sources of bias, my best estimate is that around 50 percent of US and UK adults have experienced limerence, and 25 percent found it so disruptive it affected their enjoyment of life.

It turns out that, when thinking about the ways that people experience romantic love, there really are two tribes out there in the world.

CHAPTER 7
WHY DOES LIMERENCE EXIST?

Nature's little joke

It's obviously important to understand how limerence begins in the brain, why it feels so powerful, and which kinds of people experience the phenomenon, but all this analysis and sense-making leaves a rather big question unanswered: Why does it exist in the first place? Why do some of us have a mechanism for runaway romantic addiction built into our brains?

Scientific studies of love and romance tend, with irresistible gravity, to be drawn toward evolution. Love, in all its forms, is inescapably tied to reproduction. It's not a coincidence that the typical period of limerence (eighteen months to three years) corresponds neatly with the time taken to conceive a child, carry it to term, and protect it through the most vulnerable early stages of life. Limerence is an extraordinary force for romantic and sexual attachment that would clearly increase the chances of successfully mating and providing a stable environment in which an infant would thrive.

While this reproductive benefit is undeniable, it must be incomplete as an explanation since limerence is also a feature of nonreproductive bonding. Same-sex couples, asexuals, and people well past their reproductive prime are all able to succumb to limerence. Equally, non-limerents are just as capable of forming happy, stable, loving pair bonds that provide all the same benefits to their children—indeed you could reasonably argue that it's an advantage to not have to deal with the excesses of limerent bonding.

How can this be reconciled? If limerence is not needed for reproduction, happens even when reproduction isn't possible, and isn't even necessarily the "best" strategy for success, why does it exist? How did a feature evolve if it is only tangentially related to reproductive success?

As ever, the satisfying answers take a bit of digging to unearth.

Reproductive drives only have to work

Most of the deeply rooted subconscious drives that we have built into us focus on two forces for the propagation of our genes: survival and reproduction. It's reductive, but also true, that our most stable and widespread instinctive behaviors increase the odds of succeeding in one or both of these aims.

However, as has often been noted, evolution is blind.[1] It is driven by chance (principally due to random gene mutation) that is directed by natural selection (the fight for survival and reproduction). For a gene, structure, trait, or behavior to persist into future generations, it must promote—or at the very least not compromise—reproductive fitness. That reality means that the instincts, drives, impulses, and biases that we have all inherited are a patchwork of chance outcomes that worked. They were not designed or engineered purposefully, they appeared by chance and were then refined by the ruthless competition for survival and reproduction. The blind forces of evolution only require behavioral drives to succeed; they can easily be riddled with imperfections, instabilities, and inefficiencies.

Our brains are a system of systems, sometimes working together, sometimes not. If we see a stimulus that suggests a desirable mating opportunity (a muscular physique, a flash of cleavage, a seductive wink) it will provoke lust. If we see our partner flirting with an attractive competitor, it will provoke jealousy. If we feel stressed, and our partner gathers us into a loving hug, we feel affection and comfort. All of these drives promote reproductive success, but they are loosely coupled to each other. They can work independently as systems in the brain: we can lust for people we don't want to bond with, we can feel deep affection for someone we don't want to have sex with, we can feel jealousy over people with whom we've not formed a relationship.

This functional independence is best illustrated by the difference between erotic and romantic desire. From a behavioral perspective, lust is the direct drive to copulate—an impulsive, urgent desire for sexual gratification. There are multiple layers to this impulse, but the most immediate and rudimentary is when a sexually charged stimulus provokes a reflex response.[2] In the brain, nitric oxide signaling increases sexual appetite, and the same signal also increases blood flow to the genitals (in both men and women, although the consequences for men are obviously more . . . prominent). In contrast, romantic desire is focused on bonding, and emotional as well as physical consummation. It's driven by the oxytocin and vasopressin feedback to the reward centers discussed in Chapter 3. This distinction again illustrates the principle of parallel neural systems that intersect (orgasm releases oxytocin, intimacy raises libido) but are also able to operate semi-independently. Lust and love are not completely separate, but they are only loosely coupled from a neuroscience perspective.

The point is that these drives exist because they are expedient. They are useful mechanisms for making us more successful at reproduction, but they are not rational, elegant, or harmonious, and they don't always work in unison. Many more people can erotically excite us than romantically appeal to us. We can fall in love with people with whom we cannot reproduce. We can want to bond with people who don't want to bond with us. The drives are built in to trigger certain *behaviors* not certain *outcomes*. From a genetic perspective the only thing that matters is that the behaviors statistically increase the likelihood of an evolutionarily advantageous outcome.

Once those loosely coupled drives are set running in a human, all kinds of crazy, wonderful, or destructive things can happen. Because our romantic and erotic impulses are the automatic responses of neural systems, which are sensitive to particular environmental cues, they can be stimulated in a way that evolution couldn't anticipate. Indeed, under the wrong circumstances, they can even be driven into a state of derangement.

Supernormal stimuli

The capacity for primitive brain systems to be destabilized was brought into tragicomic clarity by the discovery of so-called supernormal stimuli. The classic example of the phenomenon was described by the Nobel Prize–winning ethologist Niko Tinbergen, in stickleback fish.[3]

Male sticklebacks will instinctively fight for territory, and Tinbergen was trying to understand what cues triggered this aggressive behavior. During his experimentation, he discovered that the males would attack a crude wooden model of another male, as long as the model was painted with a prominent red belly. By trial and error, he found that he could design some wooden shapes that would be attacked even more aggressively than an actual stickleback—it was possible to fabricate a fake cue that was even more powerful at provoking hostility than the natural threat (and that the neural systems for aggression had evolved to respond to).

Tinbergen showed that if you can identify a sensory cue that animals react to, and then exaggerate an essential aspect of that cue, animals will show a heightened response to that "supernormal" stimulus. In effect, the neural systems could be overactivated by an artificially pure form of the stimulus.

Numerous other examples of this phenomenon exist. Some bird species will neglect their own eggs to obsessively brood a gaudy porcelain super-egg (this is the same phenomenon that the cuckoo exploits when laying its eggs in a reed warbler nest). Male butterflies will spurn females to enthusiastically mate with paper models that have been designed to maximize their mating reflex. Herring gull chicks will relentlessly peck at painted wooden sticks in the hope that they will regurgitate food, and can be triggered to peck even more fervently at sticks painted with specific patterns of red and yellow stripes than realistic models of female Herring gull heads.

The conclusion is clear. Instinctive behaviors can be pushed into a state of overdrive if the stimulus that activates the relevant neural systems can be identified, isolated, and perfected. Evolution haphazardly selected for neural systems that worked; scientists identified and exploited the imperfections and instabilities.

The implications of these discoveries for human behavior have not been missed.[4] Supernormal stimuli abound in our modern environment. Some popular examples are junk food, pornography, advertising, and social media. These take the stimuli of sugar/fat blends, sexual display, and status anxiety, and concentrate them into a pure form designed to elicit a disproportionate craving—the refined manipulation of our core drives for survival and reproduction. It is not hard to see how people with a reward system more sensitive than average to these supernormal stimuli could end up addicted to the highs.

This perspective on how our neural systems can be driven into a state of hyperactivity helps frame our understanding of limerence too. In this context, when it comes to the brain of a limerent, their limerent object could be described as a highly personalized supernormal stimulus for romantic infatuation. Something about them provides the optimal combination of sensory cues to drive the neural systems that cause limerence into a frenzy of overactivation.

The benefits of pair bonding

Let's accept that our neural systems for bonding and reward can be overactivated by the supernormal stimulus of a limerent object—what would be the benefit of this phenomenon from an evolutionary perspective?

Most evolutionary theories of love and romance focus on the costs and benefits of instinctive behaviors from a kind of quasi-economic starting point. From this perspective, there are lots of strategies that can work, lots of ways to increase the odds of reproductive success. This is evident from the magnificent number of mating habits, strategies, and peculiarities that abound in nature. Even among our nearest evolutionary relatives, the great apes, there are numerous different approaches observed—from the fierce harem-guarding of silverback gorillas, to the near-indiscriminate promiscuity of bonobos.[5] The one abiding feature of reproduction in all contexts, and the basis for most evolutionary analyses of love, is the central role of competition in sexual selection. Only a certain number of males will be able to father offspring, and both males and females have inherited drives that increase their odds of conceiving healthy children through overt or covert means.

Pair bonding as a reproductive strategy is rare among primates. Humans are unusual in adopting it as the dominant style of mating, suggesting that there might be some quirks of our physiology or psychology that favor its adoption. When it comes to pair bonding, there are several factors that contribute to calculations of reproductive fitness. First, it increases the direct odds of reproductive success. Second, it promotes sexual fidelity and paternity assurance. Third, it secures parental investment in offspring. Fourth, it increases psychological and emotional security. Fifth, it promotes commitment and mate guarding. Collectively, these ideas can be captured by an umbrella concept known as "fitness interdependence" where the pair help each other to thrive, and together improve the odds of their children carrying their combined genes into future generations.[6]

Some of these benefits are fairly self-evident. It obviously helps the chances of a child reaching maturity if the parents feed, protect, and support it through early childhood. It is also a lot easier to face a difficult and dangerous world together than alone, sharing burdens and resources. But beyond these obvious benefits, there are some nonintuitive advantages to mutual commitment too.

The general, commonsense view of sexual politics is that men prefer to sow their wild oats as widely as possible, whereas women need to be choosy because of the additional physical cost involved in bearing children. So, for men, the optimal reproductive strategy would be to find as many mates as possible in a rather indiscriminate way, whereas women should guard their wombs against attack, except by the most fit males. Like many commonsense notions this is, of course, wrong.

From the perspective of an individual man, indiscriminate mating is a lousy strategy—and not just ethically lousy, but mathematically lousy. Women are only fertile for a limited period of time around ovulation so the chance that an opportunistic sexual encounter will result in pregnancy is low. This is especially true because—unlike other primates—human females do not broadcast their fertility (compared to, say, the visibly swollen genitalia of female chimpanzees). Given this uncertainty around fertility, a much more effective strategy for a man is to remain with a woman for a prolonged period, having regular intercourse, thereby increasing the probability that fertilization and implantation will occur. From this perspective, male and female goals are aligned—commitment to a pair bond maximizes the odds of conception, and defrays some of the risks and costs of child-rearing.

Such dispassionate calculations based on reproductive fitness and gene frequency in populations are not a conscious part of falling in love and forming a pair bond, of course. We feel the bliss of mutual love, the volcanic jealousy of mate-poaching, or the shared joy of parenthood, independently of any transactional utility. The desire for ecstatic union, mutual care, and sexual exclusivity all arise from the natural operation of those expedient drives that evolved because they happened to promote behavior that delivered the reproductive advantages of fitness interdependence. Nor is it a foolproof strategy—covert opportunistic mating outside of the pair bond is common even in nominally monogamous species—but pair bonding is an abiding phenomenon, a widely stated preference, and a culturally endorsed feature of almost all human societies. It has undeniable utility for reproduction.

Given that, the existence of limerence becomes more understandable. Limerence is a distillation of the drives that promote pair bonding into a pure form—a desire for mutual commitment so intense that it crowds out all other considerations.

Limerence as extreme pair bonding

Limerence is a supercharged version of pair bonding. What better way to secure the benefits of this reproductive strategy than to have the desire for a specific mate overwhelm all other priorities? People with the capacity to be pushed into an altered state of mind that causes romantic monomania will maximize the chance of benefitting from the interdependence gained through monogamy.

From the perspective of evolution, though, this extreme approach seems like a risk. There are obvious dangers. The first is that the choice to cleave so adamantly to a single partner excludes the opportunity to find a superior mate (however you might define that in personal or evolutionary terms). It's the "all your eggs in one basket" problem. The glimmer is also quite idiosyncratic and egalitarian. We can easily become limerent for oddballs and eccentrics—people that our friends and family scratch their heads over, wondering how they caused such devoted attachment. We don't all become limerent for people with obvious "high mate value."

The second risk with extreme pair bonding is that the commitment might not be reciprocated. We could bond with someone who is following a different strategy, someone who is not limerent for us, and who is playing the field while we crave exclusivity. How is it beneficial to commit so fully to someone who may not warrant it? Fitness interdependence only really works if both partners are strongly bonded. This comes back to the problem highlighted at the outset of this chapter: Why does limerence exist in a world where non-limerents are equally abundant?

This is a common dilemma in evolutionary theory. Why should some behavioral traits that seem to confer both costs and benefits persist in populations through time? Classic examples of this sort of conundrum are the peacock's tail, the giant antlers of the Irish elk, self-sacrificing altruism, homosexuality, and male spiders that are eaten after mating. How is it that behaviors or encumbrances that seem to put an individual at risk can nevertheless be selected by evolution?

There are many explanations offered. Sometimes, it is about the statistics of gene propagation—if you save near kin by selfless acts, you will increase the odds for survival of genes that you share.[7] This is also where game theory illuminates evolution—cooperation can often give a more reliable payoff than competition, despite the apparent risk to the individual.[8] When it comes to the complex interactions within a population it doesn't really make sense to think of a single "best" strategy for propagating genes. In practice, the most stable situation in nature is often a state of dynamic tension, where drives for selfishness and altruism, competition and cooperation, are balanced.

Sometimes, the risk calculation is a gamble that successfully mating and propagating your genes is more important than surviving afterward (when you no longer matter to evolution as an individual). In other cases, a particular male trait can be especially esteemed by females, and "sexual selection" can result in an arms race where males constantly escalate their efforts to showcase their fitness.[9] This concept is exemplified by the peacock's tail and is known as handicap signaling.[10] The rationale is that females will select healthy, vigorous males who are able to impress them with a display of opulent feathers, as a demonstration of their fitness. The absurd excess of the peacock tail is signaling the ability of the male to commit so much resource and energy into its mating display that it must be extraordinarily fit. As humans, we can of course see the perversity of signaling your strength by squandering it, but sexual selection combined with male competition can lead to these peculiar outcomes.

I suspect that limerence is like a peacock's tail. This is speculation—we can't really answer the question of why limerence persists in human populations, as we don't have enough data and it's very hard to design experiments to test it—but I think the argument makes sense.

Limerence acts as a form of handicap signaling. It's a display of such ostentatious commitment that the limerent is willing to handicap their chances of mating with anyone else. It signals to your limerent object that you are so infatuated, so dedicated, so profoundly and insanely besotted with them, that there is no risk of you straying. If they commit to you, they will not be abandoned or cuckolded. The milkmaid in love with the farmhand would not be swayed by the prince. The billionaire in love with the waitress would not be swayed by the socialite. Each partner can be assured that their investment in the connection is not going to be wasted by the quasi-economic calculations of sexual transactions. Their romantic attachment is so powerful that it transcends rational self-interest.

The limerent is temperamentally incapable of risking the

bond, because it matters more than anything else to them. They willingly forsake other options to commit to the benefits of fitness interdependence. If their mate is also limerent, then they enjoy the ecstatic union of mutual infatuation.

It's an all-in strategy that can sometimes pay off spectacularly.

Limerence, then, can be understood as a drive to bond, which exists because it can work as a way of improving fitness interdependence in a partly competitive, partly cooperative world. The blindness of evolution means it can also be triggered in situations where reproduction is not actually possible, because it's an instinct to bond intensely in response to certain kinds of (supernormal) stimuli, not an intelligently engineered way to make babies. All that is required for limerence to persist in our species is that it provides enough of a boost to the odds of reproduction in a complex, interpersonal world.

From limerence to limerent objects

Limerence arises from a formidable union of factors: the operating rules of fundamental systems within our brains, how instinctive behavior can drive those systems into a state of person addiction, and how evolutionary pressures can select for these traits because they promote pair bonding. It's not just a crush. There's an impressive amount of psychological heft behind it.

Modern neuroscience and psychology can explain the basis of this altered mental state, but to understand limerence fully we need to get out of our heads and consider the influence of the wider world. Obsessive infatuation is a personal battle, but it happens in a social context.

Other people are involved, and that makes everything much more complicated.

PART 2
UNDERSTANDING LIMERENT OBJECTS

CHAPTER 8
SOCIAL AND CULTURAL FORCES
*Romeo and Juliet, Beatrice and Dante,...
and a thousand high school movies*

Sir Terry Pratchett once described human beings as Storytelling Apes.[1] It's true. We think in stories.

Limerence is, by definition, an exceptional experience. It is out of the ordinary. Your perceptions change, the world around you seems to transform. Your mood swings from euphoric highs to sickening lows, your priorities realign, your whole emotional landscape is reconfigured. And, at the center of it all, blazing like a romantic supernova, is that one special person. It's a "lifequake" that demands an explanation.

Although the emotional turbulence of limerence is an internal force, those of us who are members of the limerence tribe instinctively look outward for explanations. We cast about for role models, social precedents, and cultural touchstones that will make sense of the experience and allow us to fit it into our existing worldview. We search for parallels between our own personal romantic upheaval and the great wealth of stories that we have absorbed throughout our lives, and that have shaped our beliefs about love. We seek an explanatory narrative that feels emotionally satisfying. We want the world to make sense, and the way that we usually force it to cooperate is by telling ourselves a compelling story.

When it comes to limerence, there is—it is fair to say—an embarrassment of riches to draw from. A long history of books, movies, TV shows, and pop songs about romance saturates our culture; stories that seem to confirm that other people have wrestled with the same exquisite agonies. Naturally enough, we try to fit our own personal adventure into this dramatic legacy. We make sense of our limerence by finding a narrative that feels true to our experience.

That instinct comes with advantages and disadvantages. The story we tell ourselves will determine how limerence affects our lives.

Why stories are so powerful

Making sense of a complex and confusing world is difficult. If we were to try and reason things out from first principles whenever we encountered the unexpected, we'd be paralyzed by uncertainty. We evolved in an environment where deep deliberation was costly for time and resources. Food, shelter, and safety were hard-won and fragile, and indecision or trial and error experimenting was often ruthlessly, lethally, punished by nature. Our ancient forebears didn't live in communities crowded with chin-stroking philosophers. They needed to learn critical lessons in survival quickly and efficiently. Stories were the perfect vehicle.

Humans are social animals and evolved in tribal communities.[2] To live harmoniously in a community requires the ability to develop empathy, to understand other people's motives, to have shared points of reference, agree to cultural norms, and find common purpose. Stories are an excellent way to develop these interpersonal skills and forge shared bonds.[3] Stories also allow us to learn indirectly from others who have gone through life-threatening trials, made serious errors of judgment, been complacent about risk, or found clever solutions to difficult problems. Stories are a way to communicate real experience, to transfer knowledge in an engaging and persuasive way, to preserve discoveries in the collective memory of a community.

Last but not least, stories go beyond direct experience and allow us to invent new scenarios in our imaginations. Stories are a safe way to rehearse possible strategies for dealing with fictional threats, to test the plausibility of ideas without having to literally take a risk and experiment in person. Even our physiology is tailored to this aim—we *feel* the emotions conjured by imagined dangers or rewards as though we are experiencing them firsthand. Stories are arousing, gratifying, frightening, pleasurable.

The imprint of this deep history has shaped our nature. Every parent knows how hungry for stories children are, how bewitched they are by their favorites, and how agonized their pleading for more is when a chapter ends. The frustration of an unfinished narrative is like a nagging psychic itch, the satisfaction of a happy ending is an emotional balm. Great stories hold within them the archetypal essence of human universals.[4] The stories that survive longest are the most highly condensed and refined summaries of human wisdom. The actions of the heroes and villains, mentors and fools, lovers and haters, rulers and paupers that populate our tales provide the archetypal role models we need to make sense of the world. It's an incredibly powerful mental shortcut for making decisions. Instead of analyzing the situation, scrutinizing the evidence, and making calculated choices about the best course of action, we just play out the story in our mind based on the archetypes we have internalized. We follow the conventions of the plot, the narrative logic of the story we are inhabiting: What would a hero do? How would a mentor act? What is the noble choice? Is it time to embrace the darkness within?

Instead of having to figure out a complex world from scratch, we greedily consume stories about archetypal heroes and heroines facing fictional trials, and subconsciously absorb the refined lessons of all the generations before us. It's very efficient.

Stories bypass conscious thought. They speak directly to the subconscious beliefs that we have accumulated over a lifetime of consuming books, songs, films, and art. Stories *move* us. In other words, they speak directly to that part of the brain where limerence lives.

Limerence in culture

It's not hard to find the imprint of limerence in the vast catalog of stories that have been created over the centuries by lovestruck authors, musicians, and poets. There are lots of narrative frameworks available to make sense of the ecstatic agony of romantic yearning, and limerents can find validation of their feelings in these tales.

An obvious starting point is stories about star-crossed lovers. Here, love is thwarted by external forces—parental, religious, cultural—which are hostile to the lovers' connection. The power of love is so compelling in these tales that the narrative leads inexorably to either tragedy or liberation. The lovers may fight internal battles to resist their desire, or they may battle against the external forces, but ultimately love endures through all this resistance.

Romeo and Juliet is the prime example of a tragic ending, where social forces destroy the young lovers. *Pride and Prejudice* is a happier example, which plays out the liberating ending where love triumphs and society is brought to heel. In both cases, social barriers, familial disapproval, and old prejudices prevent the open acknowledgment of romantic destiny, but fail to stop the irresistible momentum of mutual love.

A second archetypal story that seems tailor-made for limerence is the rescue fantasy. This takes two main forms: the damsel in distress and the tortured soul. In these stories, a lost soul must be saved from their doom—either an external source of malice, or internal darkness—by the noble love of a suitor. Fairy tales are laden with damsels in distress. Cinderella, Rapunzel, and Sleeping Beauty are all trapped in states of despair; victims of dark forces. The heroes (princes, all) are stricken with love for their damsels and do battle to save them from the abusive guardians who imprison them. Usually, the dyad of prince and damsel win out, and the villains are robbed of their power and forced into retreat.

The tortured soul story is a variant on the rescue fantasy, where an innocent lover must save someone whose worldliness has corrupted them. *Beauty and the Beast* is probably the best-known example of this narrative. Sometimes the tragic hero rejects the salvation offered by the innocent lover, dooming himself forever—*Eugene Onegin* being a particularly bleak example.

Another story archetype is the chaste lover. Here, the protagonist of the story loves someone they cannot be with, and so resolves to love them from afar. The object of love is venerated as an almost divine figure. The lover dedicates their lives to them, using them as a muse and source of inspiration, where their love is expressed as sacrifice. Dante's adoration of Beatrice fits this mold, with her being referenced as the embodiment of grace throughout *The Divine Comedy*, and ultimately guiding Dante through Paradise. This chaste admiration was also the intention of Lancelot in his love for Guinevere in Arthurian legend, where finally giving in to their base desires leads to the collapse of Camelot. Conversely, in E. M. Forster's *Maurice* the lead character tries to suppress his romantic desires in a society hostile to homosexuality, determined to live an admirable, if loveless life. Ultimately, his redemption comes through accepting his true nature and embracing love, in defiance of social conventions.

This is just drawing from the classics. The same themes, the same narrative pull, is there in innumerable other romantic stories. The star-crossed lovers of *Brokeback Mountain*. The damsel in distress of *Pretty Woman*. The redemptive power of love in *When Harry Met Sally*. The chaste admiration of *Lost in Translation*. These films have naturally been given a more modern sensibility, wary of stereotyping, but they all still play on the old themes.

While these stories do not all have a happy ending, they all share a central message: Love is a life-defining force. Failure to embrace and enable love leads to pain, disharmony, spiritual sickness. Thwarting love leads not just to potential tragedy for the characters, but the wider community, as the world becomes more troubled and filled with conflict the longer the lovers are prevented from uniting. Love must be accommodated, and often the world has to adjust around it to recover proper harmony. A thousand high school movies culminate in this truth (even if the stakes are a little lower).

Capital-L love is a force greater than simple human concerns. It could even be considered a mystical or supernatural force. It's natural that limerents would fit their own overwhelming, soul-consuming desire into this narrative framework.

Spiritual stories

One of the most affecting aspects of limerence is the profound sense of "rightness" limerents feel when bonding with a limerent object (LO). In terms of neurochemistry, this can be explained as the impact of oxytocin and vasopressin linking reward to bonding with a specific person—the neuroscience that underpins limerence, as discussed in Chapter 3. The combination of bonding hormones and dopamine reward signals acting together explains the joy caused by connecting with the LO, but it doesn't *feel* like that for the limerent going through it. It feels like a life-affirming, euphoric rush, exactly like all the grand love stories—as though the limerent has been spellbound, smitten by a thunderbolt or discovered True Love.

It's easy to see how being overcome by a wondrous and terrifying attraction to another person leads to thoughts of otherworldly powers. It does feel as though an external force more powerful than your own will has overtaken you. For those with a different cultural or spiritual background to (taking a random example) skeptical neuroscientists, very different narratives present themselves. The numinous, fervent sense of connection to a LO is taken as proof of spiritual union. The experience of limerence—especially the first time it is experienced—is likened to what it feels like to meet your soulmate.

> *A tremendous upwelling of affection and adoration poured forth. I felt it physically in my chest. It felt like I had been living in an emotional desert for years and suddenly it was springtime. I associated songs of love and loss with her. I would sob in my car thinking that I could never be with her. —B*

> *What I'm sure of though, is how good LO makes me feel. At home I feel inadequate, useless and guilty, while when I see him, I'm happy, I'm smiling, I'm alive. I'm holding on to those feelings to survive. That's I think the key to this limerence lasting so long. —E*

In time [LO] captured me, and once I am captured, I idolize and idealize my LOs and have an exaggerated sense of loyalty to them that is nearly unbreakable. —J

When I look at LO, I feel I am looking directly into her soul, and she into mine. I feel so comfortable and safe discussing literally anything with her, yet we don't even know each other that well. —B

For many people, the power of limerence is taken as proof of a deeper connection than mere mutual affection. The language used is often an indication of this perspective: "You complete me," "You are The One," "This was meant to be," "No one else has ever made me feel this way." The desire is for total immersion, fusion of two lives, bonding at every level: emotional, spiritual, and sexual. Again, there are abundant stories that capture this intense yearning for blissful union—*Dr. Zhivago; Sense and Sensibility; Jane Eyre; Truly, Madly, Deeply.*

Once limerence is conceptualized in spiritual terms, the narrative can go beyond fiction into belief. A popular interpretation for the symptoms of limerence is the idea of "Twin Flames" or mirror souls. This concept is that a single soul can be incarnated into two bodies, and the sundered halves will seek each other and when they meet feel an astonishing affinity. The term "Twin Flames" appears to have been coined by the spiritual leader and author Elizabeth Clare Prophet, but the idea of wholeness coming from the communion of two complementary spirits or souls dates back to antiquity, and has many echoes through history (not least, in the ideas of Carl Jung).[5]

Spiritual narratives elevate the experience of limerence beyond the everyday, to the sublime.

Cautionary tales

So far, all the stories that we've considered approach the issue of limerence from a rather grandiose and self-serving perspective. That's understandable too, as we generally favor stories that make us feel good about ourselves and flatter our egos. The obvious starting point for understanding limerence is to look to the great love stories of the past, but there is another direction that the narrative-weaving could take. Other stories that lead not to harmony and spiritual communion, but to darker places. To vanity, hubris, and ruin.

There are many passions that are not true love, many stories that warn us of the perils of forsaking responsibilities to pursue sensation, of indulging lusts and other dark temptations for selfish gratification. For every Robin Hood and Maid Marian, there is an Anna Karenina and Count Vronsky. Literature is rich with tragic figures who bring destruction and pain in their pursuit of romantic madness: Madame Bovary, the Phantom of the Opera, Lady MacBeth, Heathcliff.

Cautionary tales of the corruption of debauchery are just as common: *The Picture of Dorian Gray*, where a portrait takes on a libertine's foulness to preserve his innocent façade; Dr. Jekyll succumbing to the addictive power of the potion that turns him into the monstrous and uninhibited Mr. Hyde; Bluebeard and his bloody chamber full of murdered wives.

As a counterpoint to these cautionary tales, there are also many tales of heroic resistance to temptation, and how nobility of spirit can save us from madness. When Odysseus passed by the island of the Sirens, he took care to protect his crew from their irresistible song with wax earplugs, and tied himself to the mast so he could not act on the maddening desire.

One of the most useful insights that comes from recognizing our propensity to think in stories, is that it gifts us the ability to take control of the narrative. We are the authors of our own tale. We draw from the well of stories to make sense of our limerent experience—a well overflowing with romantic epics, romantic comedies, and romantic tragedies. The story we choose to tell ourselves will shape our fate.

To an extent this is play-acting. Casting ourselves into epic narratives might feel a bit ridiculous, given that we are actually living in the modern world, not the age of myth. Part of the reason this may seem odd is that modernity has led to a disdain for classical narrative structures. Contemporary fiction is more often concerned with existential ennui than grand narratives, but archetypal stories deal with powerful themes. They offer ways of conceptualizing ourselves, and our aspirations, allowing us to reorient ourselves emotionally into a new role that is very satisfying at a deep level. We know how heroines should act. We know what good mentors should do. These are inspiring ideals; noble versions of ourselves worth striving toward. The stories give us an integrated framework for behavior, once we decide what role we want to play. Who are we in the pantheon of archetypal characters? Are we the Innocent, seduced by a Villain? Are we the Mentor, tested by unwelcome desires for the Innocent? Are we the Hero, facing trials as we explore the world? Or are we the Victim, trapped by a Monster and battling to free ourselves? Where are we in our own personal hero or heroine's journey? The way we cast ourselves in that story helps guide our decisions.

Our minds will effortlessly play out the story we choose according to its inherent narrative momentum. If we become limerent for someone we could form a healthy bond with, then the grand love stories can lead us into a state of bliss. If we instead become limerent for someone who we cannot form a bond with, then there is danger in telling ourselves a story of "love thwarted by cruel fate." That narrative will appeal to the limerent mind because it casts us as a hero fighting for love; a less flattering but equally credible narrative is the hero tested by temptation. Stories act as cultural validation for our state of mind, but we don't have to accept the narrative that acclaims our limerent feelings—we could just as readily craft a narrative around resisting the siren song of limerence as being victimized by the strictures of a dutiful society.

Stories have amazing emotional potency. It's inevitable that we will make sense of the neurochemical storm of limerence by interpreting our feelings in terms of the grand romantic stories. The cultural and social forces effortlessly fit those feelings into a grand narrative. If we want to take control of our own situation and the consequences that limerence brings into our lives, it pays to choose the story we tell ourselves wisely.

CHAPTER 9
WHY DO THEY SEEM SO SPECIAL?

Where the glimmer comes from, and how adolescence shapes our romantic lives

Limerence happens inside our heads. Once we feel the glimmer for someone, the gathering momentum of reinforcement begins. The arousal, reward, and bonding circuits are stimulated in just the right way to begin the cascade of events that leads, if unchecked, to a state of person addiction. Knowing that such a vulnerability exists is obviously essential to overcoming the downsides of limerence, protecting yourself against unwanted episodes and thriving in future romantic relationships, but there is another big piece of the puzzle that needs to be fitted into place: What makes someone attractive in the first place? Why do some people seem so special that they go beyond the usual laws of attraction and become idealized to the point of becoming a limerent object (LO)? What is it about certain people that causes the glimmer to begin? Why can some individuals activate our limerent circuits with the manic overload of a supernormal stimulus, when other equally attractive and admirable people just can't kindle the same bewitching spark? For all the issues of idealization, rationalization, and objectification of an LO that clearly distort the judgment of infatuated limerents, there is, undeniably, something special about them that triggers the neurochemical cascade. What is it?

Getting to the bottom of these questions requires some emotional excavation of the limerent's past. Why we find certain people attractive is going to depend on a very heady brew of past experiences, beliefs, influences and—most likely—romantic disasters. Our own unique limerence template will lie in our personal history.

Universal appeal

A starting point for trying to understand where attraction comes from is to analyze those factors that are universal—the traits and cues that make people objectively attractive. Good-looking people can be recognized across cultural and social boundaries, and often benefit from their widely recognized beauty when it comes to life success. The basis of this generic attraction is well studied. Most of the research focuses on what might be called predictors of mate appeal. Examples include facial symmetry, a clear complexion, youth, pronounced secondary sexual characteristics (jaw line, height, depth of voice, hip width and bust size, to give a few examples), and—perhaps counterintuitively—averageness. People consistently rate computer-generated composite faces of hundreds of individuals (smoothing out the idiosyncrasies and creating "average" features) as more beautiful than actual, individual people.[1]

Along with these markers for general attractiveness, a number of studies have investigated how hormonal and behavioral cues can affect sexual appeal. Variously, evidence suggests that mate preference can be influenced by fertility (with women showing greater preference for masculine faces during ovulation), body odor, libido, charisma, and simple familiarity.[2]

This scientific approach to the analysis of attractiveness helps highlight an important principle—while there are some universal factors that can mean people are generally ranked highly on sex-appeal, the exact combination of factors that makes someone attractive as a mate to a specific person are surprisingly flexible and idiosyncratic. They also depend to a large extent on our own psychology and physiology. It's another example of nature and nurture working hand in hand to shape our fate.

While there may be a weighting toward certain features or traits increasing an individual's "mate value," many of the most important cues are personalized. As an example, two factors that have significant predictive power for attraction are odor and face-similarity.

It's a favorite experiment in popular science that when men or women wear the same shirt for several days, without any deodorant or perfume, it turns into a potent mate-selection tool. Asking other men and women to smell this accumulated body odor, and rate the attractiveness of the potential mate, reveals strong preferences. Interestingly, the best predictor for whether a given stinky shirt was appealing to the sniffer was how genetically divergent the wearer was from them.[3] Genetically different people found each other's scents more arousing.

A similar result was found by asking individuals to rate the attractiveness of faces for pictures that had been engineered to resemble the test subject, or not. So, a heterosexual woman presented with composite male faces that ranged from very similar to very different to her own facial structure, was asked to rate them for attractiveness. Interestingly, the results suggest that we find faces similar to our own more trustworthy, but less sexually attractive.[4]

From an evolutionary perspective, this makes sense. Offspring vigor will be improved by mating outside of kin groups because it would reduce the risks of inbreeding leading to genetic disease. We are attracted to people who are genetically different, and we are able to subconsciously detect this with both sight and smell.

Romantic templates

These sorts of studies seem to go against the old adage that "men marry their mother and women marry their father," and there is a countervailing theory in psychology that challenges their conclusions. It argues that childhood "sexual imprinting" is an important factor in determining adult romantic preferences—we subconsciously develop a "romantic ideal" template for future mates, based on the role models around us during childhood.[5]

Several studies have reported suggestive correlations, where researchers found that hair color, eye color, and other markers of facial similarity between people's marriage partners and their parents were much more common than expected by chance.

This idea is known as "phenotype matching" where the traits of the opposite sex parent become an archetype for adult role models of successful, and therefore desirable, partners.

As you might expect, given the wide variety of parenting styles and skills that exist in the world, the quality of the relationship between child and parent is an important element of the process too. The apparent effects of sexual imprinting are strongest when the relationship between child and parent is positive. For those people who had neglectful, abusive, or disordered parenting, the correlation is weaker or negative—suggesting that imprinting is not just about elementary visual associations; there are aspects of emotional security and behavioral stability that contribute to positive selection of mates who resemble your parents.

Another important factor is that, while parents are obviously the most visible and prevalent role models for children, there are many other adults around as we develop through puberty and adolescence. We grow up surrounded by adults who shape our emotional development, and our romantic sensibilities. Teachers, aunts and uncles, friends of the family—and of course the celebrities that saturate our cultural environment in the modern age—all can come to embody presexual archetypes of manhood and womanhood. The mental model that we form into an idealized romantic template will be an amalgam of all these influences. Feed in the stories of fairy-tale romances, family sagas, romantic comedies, erotic thrillers, and the rest, and you have a pretty wide-ranging set of factors that contribute to our sense of what an attractive person is like. Quite a medley of ingredients.

The idea that we each have a favored romantic type does have some experimental support. In a study carried out in Germany to test how similar the personality traits of people's romantic partners were, a group of young adults were followed over nine years, and their romantic partners asked to fill out a self-assessment of their own personality profiles.[6] The results showed that there was striking consistency between sequential partners for individuals who had serial relationships—their new partners were like their ex-partners. This might seem a little perverse (why would we want to replicate a relationship that had failed?), but it is a reliable result and illustrates a principle known as "assortative mating." We tend to preferentially form relationships with a particular type of person who is often similar to ourselves.

An exception to this principle was that people who scored high in extraversion—who were open to new experiences and energized by being in social settings—sought more variety in their romantic partners. This leads to another complicating observation: Who we are sexually attracted to is not the same as who we form relationships with. We may form pair bonds with a particular type, but we can be attracted to a wide variety of people. Indeed, one of the persistent challenges of monogamous relationships is the tension between the comfortable, affectionate bonding of long-term love, and the lusty thrills of sexual novelty.[7] Having a romantic type might define the people you form bonds with, or become limerent for, but it does not exclude erotic desire for wildly different people.

Formative experiences

Clearly, many factors can influence the development of our romantic preferences during adolescence, but we don't just absorb these influences passively, like sponges. We interact with the world and the people within it, and the outcome of those dynamic experiences also has a profound effect on our attitudes to love.

Starting, once again, with the most formative relationships for most people, childhood bonding experiences will determine how we associate the desire for intimacy with different behavioral styles. If you grow up in a family that is characterized by banter, teasing, competition, and boisterousness, that sort of dynamic is going to feel familiar and "right" in a future relationship (particularly a serious relationship that may be the nucleus of a new family). Contrast that with those who grow up in a calm, supportive, studious environment and it's easy to grasp why some people who may be powerfully attracted to each other sexually end up being incompatible. The quiet librarian may be drawn to the raucous athlete, but the odds of bonding are against them.

The popular idea of "love languages" exemplifies this principle.[8] We tend to favor some ways of expressing and receiving love—compliments, gifts, quality time, service, or intimate touch—which have their roots in the behavioral frameworks we observed during childhood. Mismatched expectations about what a loving relationship involves dooms many a hopeful couple.

Beyond simple familiarity, there are darker influences too. Childhoods marred by neglect or abuse can give rise to adults who subconsciously repeat the patterns of unhealthy bonding, seeking to heal old wounds by forming a mirror relationship and "making it work this time." This is the area where attachment theory is most likely to intersect with limerence, as the stable, anxious, or avoidant attachment styles determine who is most attractive to the limerent and how they will respond to the cues given off by the LO. Such limerents might be belittled as having "Mommy issues" or "Daddy issues," but while their behavior can seem irrational to others, in reality they are just trying to make their emotional world right at last.

As we age, the influence of our family of origin lingers in the subconscious, but is superseded by the influence of peers. New formative experiences arrive once we become romantically involved with other people. Sometimes, a first love can cast a long shadow, setting a standard that others struggle to match. This can even be an unconsummated crush—an infatuation that leaves such a strong mark that a mortal man or woman cannot compete. Other times, the influence is decidedly negative. Many people still shudder at bitter memories of romantic humiliation that shook their self-confidence during adolescence. The first crushing rejection. The time she mocked his lack of prowess in front of the whole school. The time he openly bragged to his friends about how far she'd gone with him. That horrible feeling of not knowing what to do or how to act—ashamed by simple naivety—when first getting intimate with someone new. These moments have lasting potency that can shape limerent vulnerabilities.

Most of us are insecure about our own attractiveness, which has inevitable consequences for how we react to others, and who we rate as attractive. If individuals consider themselves to be desirable and are confident in their own appeal, they tend to be more critical and discriminating in their rating of others. In one study, women who scored themselves highly for attractiveness had a strong bias for the masculine traits that predict male attractiveness.[9] In simpler terms, we seek matches aligned to our own perceived status.

Another common consequence of personal insecurity is that believing someone else is attracted to you can be a surprisingly powerful aphrodisiac. If we detect some hint that another person has romantic interest in us—say from flirting, holding eye contact, or giving any of the other cues that suggest they are aroused by our company—it can make us reevaluate their romantic appeal. While many of us will recognize this from personal experience, there is also some scientific corroboration of the concept. Unacquainted couples asked to engage in mutual eye contact (or touch) before rating the attractiveness of their partner tended to score them more highly than couples who had not shared that romantically suggestive intimacy beforehand.[10]

> It was only once I thought she was into me that I became interested in her. In many ways, she really isn't my type, but once I thought she liked me it was game over. I was hooked. —VL

Attractiveness, is not a fixed, immutable trait. Many circumstances can influence our judgment. Many factors determine who we can become addicted to.

What causes the glimmer?

By this point, eagle-eyed readers may have noticed a slight problem. The collective evidence shows that we are attracted to people who are different from us genetically, but also remind us of our parents. We often have a romantic type who is similar to us in personality, but we also seek novelty. We internalize a blended version of the people around us into a romantic archetype but can find many different people attractive. And all of these opinions can change, depending on our self-esteem and whether they are attracted to us.

It's fair to say that humans are complicated.

So, have we made much progress? Can any of this conflicting evidence help us to figure out what causes that glimmer of recognition when a limerent meets someone who could become a LO?

For a limerent, some ineffable cue from the other person triggers their reward circuits in a particular way—whether it's the LO's face, smell, personality, or demeanor—and ignites a spark of limerent excitement. The glimmer is a special, highly personalized form of attraction. This means that population studies that consider everyone (limerent and non-limerent; hetero-, bi-, and homosexual; high and low libido; and every personality type) may not help us home in on the specifics of what makes the glimmer unique. All this uncertainty might seem dispiriting, but there is a simple shortcut that sidesteps a lot of these difficulties: Accept that we will probably never understand all the influences that shaped us.

Our own personal glimmer triggers are buried somewhere in the jumble of genetics, early life experiences, half-remembered stories from childhood, celebrities and role models that affected us in adolescence, and the formative experiences we've had through the years. There's value in excavating this historical rubble, but you may never fully get to the bottom of it, or successfully disentangle all the many contributions. Instead, as an adult, it's enough to know that your own personal history imprints a kind of romantic archetype in your subconscious that you recognize quickly if you meet someone who fits your personal template. That insight allows you to identify your own triggers, and make better decisions about how to react when you experience the glimmer in the future.

Learn your triggers

When Tennov first defined limerence, she interviewed many people who were suffering through the experience and asked them about what had first attracted them to their LOs. The answers illuminate the point about personal templates very well—they were quirky, idiosyncratic, and sometimes surprisingly trivial.

Here are a few examples:

> *I liked Betty's hair. It was long and very dark brown with waves, the kind of hair that moved when she turned her head.*

> *The first thing that attracted me ... was his height. Barry was exactly the same height I was, and I loved it.*

And, with a nice touch of self-awareness:

> *I fell in love with Bernard because I thought he might love me in return. I must also admit that his money and success and all the power that seemed to go with them probably also played a role.*[11]

A similar pattern is evident in the thousands of comments on the *Living with Limerence* blog. Here are a few quotes from limerents who have reflected on their own experiences and identified some potent triggers:

> *It was his lightness and effervescence—like champagne—that was so attractive. I can be serious, analytical, lost in thought and a bit melancholy—but not with him! I felt like a child on an adventure. —J*

> *What makes him special? Kindness, humility, conscience, sense of humor, pragmatism, calmness and a lively intelligent mind. And not forgetting he is my boss and I have come to realize that this really, really does it for me. —A*

> *I was fascinated by how ordinary she was, and how a lot of her interests were boring to people. It just made her all the more adorable, and I couldn't figure out how to express this to other people. They just couldn't understand her appeal. —LW*

> *This comes from a need to feel validated. I measure my worth as a man to what I can do for a woman. LO sparked that somehow.*

> *If I can help her with problems she has then she will see me as a worthy man. By extension, I will then prove to her that there are men better than her ex. Even if I am not available, I can at least show her how a man should treat her. —A*

> *LO is always telling me "I appreciate you so much," "thank you for always being there for me," and "you're so sweet." Those expressions of gratitude become addictive and make me want to do more and more for LO just to experience her gratitude. —LS*

Eye contact

One of the most common triggers for the glimmer was eye contact. It's a very powerful way of communicating romantic interest, and many limerents recognized it as the critical moment of realization that they were becoming infatuated.

> *I noticed he was looking at me intensely and thought to myself "I think he likes me." Later, he was with the group of guys, as I walked over to join them, I noticed that he had turned toward me and looked me straight in the eyes. Our eyes locked, he did not look away. That instant, he became my LO. —R*

> *Eye contact is what captured me and keeps me chained to LO still. —SW*

> *For me the glimmer came from the eyes. I told her it seemed like she was looking into my soul. —JR*

> *Today I was having a conversation alone with my LO and she was keeping very direct eye contact (which seems to happen a lot when we are alone). There was a moment when I felt something passed between us and it gave me the fuzzy-brained, lightheaded feeling I've known well in the past when dating someone. Almost magnetic. —R*

Eye contact can rapidly escalate affection, as it's a powerful mode of nonverbal communication (although one very prone to misinterpretation). It's a way of sharing intimacy when in a crowd, and it can make you feel hopeful, but not certain, about reciprocation. A potent combination of factors for fueling limerence.

In summary, the crazy witches' brew of influences from our personal history makes us vulnerable to particular cues that certain people broadcast. We can't undo the past and alter our formative experiences, but we can identify our own proclivities and triggers to build up a picture of the kind of people who reliably push our buttons—our personal limerence "avatar." This knowledge helps us to anticipate our vulnerabilities, and so respond more cautiously when we meet a potential LO in the future. It's worth spending the time to develop this self-knowledge as it equips us with the skill to respond to the glimmer in a much more thoughtful and deliberate way. We'll make better decisions once we understand ourselves.

CHAPTER 10
WHY ARE SOME PEOPLE SO ADDICTIVE?

A rogues' gallery of limerence enablers

It's valuable work to understand your own limerence triggers and your own particular vulnerabilities, but it should also be acknowledged that some people do seem to be especially good at triggering limerence in others. They are potent limerent objects (LOs).

If limerence is viewed as a state of person addiction, these folks are the most powerful intoxicants. Although they appear like regular individuals outwardly, there's something magnetic about them that draws people in. They intrigue.

It's important to remember that limerents—by definition—objectify their LOs. Anyone caught in the limerence trap has to recognize that they are not necessarily responding to their LO's behavior in a neutral, genuine way. Even under the best of conditions, anyone can misunderstand another's motives and interpret their behavior incorrectly. During limerence, that tendency is distorted even further by wishful thinking so that completely unwitting behavior on the part of the LO is overinterpreted as evidence of reciprocation.

Mastery of your limerent drives cannot depend on an LO behaving exactly the way you want. It's obvious when stated so bluntly, but in the reality-distortion field of limerence it's easy to misread their intentions, feel hard done by, and that they've "led you on" or encouraged an attachment that means much more to you than them.

Despite that clarity of purpose, it is also undeniable that the behavior of an LO can make a dramatic difference to how bad a limerence episode becomes. Some people really do make it worse, whether they mean to or not. There are some behaviors that can reliably induce limerence in a receptive person.

The addictive qualities of limerent objects

If you've felt a glimmer for someone and begun to feel the hungry stirrings of limerent desire, anything they do that increases hope and uncertainty within you will fan the flames. Again, these behaviors may be conscious or unconscious on their part—their motives may be a mystery, even to them—but looked at from the perspective of a dispassionate observer, some habits or mannerisms will predictably increase the strength of limerent feeling.

Let's work through some of the biggest triggers.

Flirting

Nothing stokes hope like a bit of flirting.

> *My LO is a big flirt, he loves playing with words and dropping light-hearted innuendos throughout his conversation with anyone in our friendship group. With me he always amped up the innuendo because he would generally get a response from me, if he overstepped my boundaries I would just blush and he'd smirk and push harder. —LA*

> *My limerence started because the flirting felt different, more sincere rather than fun. First time I had that vibe with another woman in 25 years. —R*

> *My LO flirted outrageously with every female in sight. So he was a "player" I guess. He knew that he was very, very attractive physically, almost irresistible to the opposite sex. He was the kind of male that other straight males dislike and/or avoid on principle. —S*

It's fair to say that opinions vary on how troublesome flirting is, and the social contexts in which it is appropriate. At one end of the scale, the most laid-back people see flirting as harmless fun—a way to flatter, to communicate admiration, to make people feel better about themselves, and to generally add some sparkle and playfulness to social interactions.

> *Most people figure out by a certain age that 90 to 95 percent of flirting is sport. Means nothing or very little, is indicative of not much and no one intends to move on it. It's just something fun to do. —M*

This type of comment presupposes that everyone involved in the interaction has the same understanding of how the flirting was intended. In reality, it's highly subjective. We vary dramatically in our emotional sensitivities, social preferences, and cultural expectations. The motives of the flirt aren't the only relevant factor.

At the other end of the scale are people who consider flirting to be intrusive, to cross personal boundaries, and to be inappropriate in most social contexts. In professional settings flirty behavior can be seen as sexual harassment. Again, this is perfectly defensible as a position to take, but it is a strict standard. If coworkers know and trust each other, and there are no overt power imbalances (such as boss to subordinate), most people are tolerant of some light-hearted flirtation as a natural element of social life.

As well as disagreements about the appropriateness of flirting, there's also a big gray area of uncertainty about what constitutes flirting. For some people, being smiley, open, and vivacious is just friendliness, but it can be misinterpreted by others as romantic interest.[1] Similarly, complimenting another person on their clothes or appearance can be intended to be courteous and flattering, but might be experienced as unwelcome commentary on their physical attractiveness. Likewise, physical touch can be meant as a sign of familiarity and affection, but felt as an invasion of personal space. For some people, bawdy jokes build rapport and trust, others find them distasteful.

Flirting is complicated enough as one of those areas of social life that people have strong disagreements about, but for limerents it's a minefield. First, there is obviously the fact that having your LO flirt with you is tantalizing evidence that they are attracted to you. Oh, glorious hope! If they are sparkling at you, and apparently relishing your interest in them, it's natural that you can become quite optimistic. Unfortunately, the nature of flirting is that it tends to be more of a tease than a declaration. Part of the fun—part of the game—is that the hints of admiration and attraction should dance along the borders of propriety. That introduces an element of uncertainty, further heightening the limerent reinforcement. You can tell they like you, but you can't tell how serious they are. Are they flirting *with meaning*?

A second risk is that the instinctive response for most people when someone they like flirts with them is to flirt back. Unfortunately, we are not all blessed with the elegance of a virtuoso when it comes to joining the dance. Even if we do generally have good social skills, the mind-altering influence of limerence robs us of our poise. Addled by dopamine and overconfidence, limerents blurt out clumsy innuendoes, hold a hug too long or too tightly or embarrass themselves by oversharing intimacies.

They overdo it.

> *It was like a bad movie. Literally the conversation stopped and silence fell just as I declared to LO, "You should be careful what you promise, you know how dirty my mind is!" Everyone at the table just stared at me, then laughed. —K*

> *I still cringe when I think about it. The look on her face when I said, "Careful or I might fall in love with you!" because she offered me candy. I am 38. —HP*

Flirting is a delicate business, full of pitfalls for the unwary. Unfortunately, limerents try to navigate those hazards while love-drunk.

Love bombing

An extreme form of flirting—and really a crossing of the boundary into more direct disclosure of romantic desire—is a phenomenon known as "love bombing." This is when someone is highly effusive in their praise and admiration and seems to be struggling to rein in the strength of feeling they have for you. Unsurprisingly, this confirms to the limerent that there are strong grounds for hope. It feels pretty great to find out that someone is head over heels about you.

Love bombing can take different forms. It isn't always obvious protestations of love, it can also be expressions of how close they feel to you, or how easy it is to talk with you, or how no one else has made them feel this safe, or this special, or this happy. It might be very public praise of your abilities or accomplishments, it might be gift-giving, or confidence-sharing, or acts of generosity. Love bombing is characterized by extraordinary gestures of admiration that border on adoration.

One of the consequences of love bombing from an LO is that the limerent experiences the thing they desire more than anything else: reciprocation of equally strong feelings. It makes sense that a limerent progressing along the delirious path to person addiction would interpret love bombing as evidence of mutual limerence—after all, they are experiencing a similar extraordinary upwelling of feeling.

Unfortunately, love bombing is rarely a sign of healthy, genuine feelings of love.[2] Most limerents learn fairly early on in their romantic adventures that it is wise to hold the strength of their feelings in for a while, so as not to derail a promising relationship with excessive enthusiasm. They instinctively know that showing such immoderate infatuation is unsettling for the other person. At best, love bombers haven't learned how to moderate their overflowing emotions, at worst they are being manipulative.

Another reason why love bombing reinforces limerence is that it can often be surprisingly short-lived. An early period of delicious affirmation is followed by a sudden, distressing cooling off. Once the explosive release of the love bombing is spent, these LOs lose their enthusiasm—and in the worst cases move on to a new target. The befuddled limerent is plunged into doubt and uncertainty. What went wrong? Why have they stopped adoring me? Is it worth fighting to get the old devotion back?

> *He's got me tied up in knots, and my heart has been breaking since he started to withdraw several months ago after an initial period of love bombing. And yet, occasionally I will receive some poetic text wishing me eternal peace and serenity, usually right as I'm in the midst of stewing over the fact that he hasn't responded to my text from 3 days ago. —LL*

> *I see him turning on the attention that hooked me in on some other hapless gal, and then she falls for him and then he moves onto the next... and all of us still adore him. —AF*

Love bombing makes the limerent believe they have secured reciprocation, but the excessive and unstable nature of the glorification leads quickly to confusion and uncertainty. Perfect conditions for limerence reinforcement.

Mixed messages

Another major cause of limerence amplification is the sending of mixed messages by an LO. This scenario can take many forms. Sometimes it's ambiguous statements, sometimes it's inconsistent behavior, sometimes it's genuinely due to the LO experiencing their own shifting emotions about the limerent, and so blowing hot and cold about the relationship.

Mixed messages have hope and uncertainty built in—some warm, positive interactions that are occasionally punctuated by moments of panic when the hope is cast into doubt. The limerent is kept guessing about the LO's true feelings. They get caught up in cycles of rumination, running through past interactions for positive signs, wondering where they might have misjudged the situation, planning for future interactions, and trying to dream up the perfect combination of words that will unlock their LO's secrets. The LO is front and center in their mind, a singular focus for psychological fixation. Examples of some classic mixed messages are:

- Sometimes responding enthusiastically to texts or messages, but other times being unresponsive
- Making ambiguous declarations like "You're so wonderful, but my life is really complicated at the moment" or "You should keep away from me, I'm trouble," or "If only we'd met in another life"
- Being affectionate when alone, but cold and distant in company
- Using pet names or other personal intimacies that suggest you have a special bond, but not seeking genuine closeness
- Insisting they want to spend time with you, but never actually being available
- Canceling dates at short notice or making other empty promises

There are, of course, many potential explanations for these sorts of events, both innocent and deceptive. It's easy enough to explain away individual examples—who hasn't had to sometimes cancel an appointment at short notice? The point, though, is that the fact that there are reasonable and unreasonable explanations is why mixed messages can be so maddening. The limerent will chronically overanalyze the situation: Are they trying to warn me off? Or let me down gently? Or encourage me to try harder? Should I send another text to find out what's going on, or will that seem too needy? I know they've read the last DM, why aren't they responding?

One of the worst-case scenarios for mixed messages is a LO who is emotionally conflicted themselves. These are LOs who give some definite reciprocation but then pull away, perhaps because they're unavailable for an honest, open relationship. Sometimes that's because they are married, or the limerent's boss, or in the closet about their sexuality. These indecisive LOs may be wrestling with mutual desire, but unable or unwilling to act honorably, and so end up "leaking" signs of their attraction while trying to maintain a façade of professionalism. Understandably, the limerent can be confused by the contradictory messages of intellectual discouragement but emotional encouragement when an LO who has verbally distanced themselves from the limerent lets their guard slip and reveals their desire.

Ultimately, the cause of mixed messages is immaterial to the consequences it has on the psyche of the limerent. They are trapped in limbo, mood swinging back and forth, wondering what their future holds, thinking that maybe if they just hold on and keep trying, they will finally break through the uncertainty. Mixed messages from a LO makes them an enigma to be solved, and reinforces the mental habits that deepen the addiction.

> *I wasn't quite sure about the guy to begin with, but he'd alternate between running away from me and having these long, deep conversations. It sent my limerence through the roof.* —GM

> *It's such a high when he messages me nice things and tells me how close we are, then sometimes he'll disappear for days. I find myself planning what to say to bring him back to me. Or persuade myself to play it cool when he comes back to scare him into seeing what he could lose.* —C

> *I've been stung again by the LO who told me that I've misinterpreted a bunch of his comments. He's sorry if he's muddied the waters but he's started seeing someone bla bla bla. Oh please.* —H

LOs who give mixed messages are like human slot machines. Sometimes they pay out with sparkly lights and lively music, but other times they deliver a disappointing thud. Limerents keep pulling the handle in the hope that they'll get the prize, training themselves into person addiction with that most potent conditioning force—intermittent reinforcement.

As a final observation, it is also possible that limerents could seek out this "zone of uncertainty" as their romantic niche. Consciously or unconsciously, they learn to associate unreliable behavior from an LO with limerent excitement. They come to need the uncertainty to trigger the thrills of limerence euphoria, unwittingly trapping themselves in a pattern of unstable attachments. They end up dwelling in the gray zone of limbo.

Manipulation

Another possibility that needs to be confronted is that there are some people out there in the world who harbor darker motives. They delight in receiving limerent attention and use it to their own advantage. Some people deliberately set out to beguile others, using the combination of hope and uncertainty to intentionally reinforce attachment through intermittent reward, mixed messages, love bombing, and other forms of psychological manipulation.

The best-case scenario here is that they just like the attention. After all, discovering that someone is besotted with you is top-notch ego validation. Maybe they're feeling lonely, or perhaps it's rare that people show desire for them. Whatever the reason, they are grateful for your romantic interest, and want you to keep coming back. Not malicious; just a bit selfish, really.

The worst-case scenario is that the manipulative LO is a narcissist, sociopath, or some other flavor of personality disorder, and they feed on limerent supply. They sense and cultivate your interest, perfectly happy to fabricate reciprocation—enough to keep you hooked—but never commit themselves openly. Manipulators live in the gray zone of plausible deniability, enjoying the hinting and game playing and cheeky frisson of pushing boundaries, but not wanting anything to be publicly transparent.

Manipulative people will also often seek out your personal vulnerabilities as a way to get closer. They may try to implicate you in unethical behavior, social transgressions, or the sharing of inflammatory secrets as a way to bind you to them; to entangle you in their dramas.[3] Having compromising information about you gives them power. Unfortunately, limerents can often be all too eager to share their secrets as a way of bonding and showing trust. Once person addiction has set in it is very difficult to undo, and the limerent often finds themselves trapped in a toxic connection.

> Sometimes I wonder if I was actually manipulated into limerence... because being neurodiverse is very lonely most of the time and I am very much susceptible to becoming very attached to people that I feel "get" me. And this LO seemed

> to understand me more than anyone else (but he knew I was neurodiverse.... I do wonder if he was saying the right things on purpose to get me limerent for him?). I remember that he was oversharing a lot of personal things with me before I began oversharing things with him as typically I have my guard up with everyone... perhaps that is what triggered all of this. —NL

> He has said on multiple times that he is going to leave his wife and that he loves only me, but then he says he cannot do that to his daughters and begs me to be patient. He has done this [...] three times now and I am feeling desperate. —JD

Other red flags that you are dealing with a manipulative LO are unpredictable shifts from praise to ridicule, excessive or insincere flattery, asserting that past events didn't happen as you remember them, a focus on your loyalty, and extreme concern for their own privacy (but disregard for yours). While it's fun to condemn anyone who's wronged us in love as a narcissist, these are, of course, only indicators that the conduct of a LO will make the limerence worse.[4]

Archetypes

Finally, a last eclectic group of people who can also be uncannily addictive are those LOs who fit a romantic archetype. Our tendency to think in stories, as we saw in Chapter 8, means we relate to these people not as individuals but as representatives of a certain type of person. They seem to somehow be larger than life, like a character who has stepped out of a book. Let's work through the rogues' gallery and allow ourselves a bit of cheeky cynicism about what sort of psychological buttons they might be pressing.

The damsel in distress: The embodiment of the rescue fantasy. Someone who seems lost, scared, vulnerable, maybe struggling with hidden psychic wounds. Perhaps their partner is wicked or neglectful. Only you can save them!

The tortured soul: They've wandered from the path of the light, embroiled themselves in dark deeds or dark thoughts, and suffered for it. Perhaps the burdens of the world are too much for their sensitive nature? Perhaps you are the beacon that can light their way back? There's nothing so alluring as a damaged soul you're sure you can fix.

The agent of chaos: Their life is a shambles, but you understand them better than anyone else. Thank God you came into their lives! They feel so much healthier now. You, on the other hand, can look forward to a descent into chaos. Every day brings a new catastrophe that they need your help with.

The bad boy/girl: The loveable rogue. The seductress. You know they're trouble, but they are also powerful and desirable. They embody the thrill of playing with fire. Their reckless and erratic behavior keeps you guessing, keeps the uncertainty up, and keeps you in a state of insecurity. They can also trigger the rescue fantasy—they are clearly a damaged soul who only acts out because they need a noble limerent to teach them how to love.

The rock: The opposite of the rescue fantasy—the rescuer fantasy. They are utterly dependable, sure-footed, calm. A port in the storm. A refuge from the trials of life. Someone to cling to.

The leader: A variant on the rock. Someone who has both solidity and power. The noble monarch. Someone who has achieved impressive feats; someone who has authority. Wouldn't it be something if someone like that saw the value in you? Or maybe even fell hopelessly in love with you?

The guru: Wise, insightful, actualized. They have found a path to the enlightened life. They are able to see your inner self and understand your true needs. Both guide and master, they are bound to uncover the secrets that you seek.

The free spirit: Nothing can constrain their artistic soul. Free of possessiveness and free with love. Liberated, nonjudgmental and daring. But don't make demands. They are a delicate nightingale, who mustn't be caged by responsibilities or personal sacrifice of any kind.

The man/woman of mystery: The irresistible draw of the unavailable, the unknowable, the enigmatic. The lone wolf who has cut themselves off from love. What fascinating secrets lie in their past? What hidden deeds have shaped their life? Could you break through their shell? Could you become the one person they trust to enter their world? What a challenge!

Archetypes are enthralling. They can be especially seductive as we project our own romantic aspirations onto them to meet our own emotional needs. Although this catalog is tongue-in-cheek, it has more serious intent: It's useful for limerents to know the kind of person that presses their buttons and activates their limerent circuits. Recognizing your own emotional vulnerabilities is a valuable step in managing limerence because it allows you to predict the sorts of people who are likely to cause the glimmer for you. Archetypes can be especially powerful because they connect to deep emotions forged from formative experiences and hazy memories.

On reflection, many limerents realize that they have become addicted over the years to several limerent objects who may look different but have the same archetypal personality. Their romantic type is defined by their urge to rescue, or play, or compete, or seek comfort.

> *It's uncomfortable to realize how deeply I convinced myself that I alone could heal my damaged, distant LO through the power of my love, and how deeply I was able to fool myself about it.* —T

> *I am always limerent for unavailable women.... The less they care about me the more into them I am. I could text my LO 5 times. She could ignore it 4 times. Then she'll respond and it's the greatest excitement. The limerence just gets worse.* —T

> *My damsels have only sent ME the distress signal (in my mind at least), and so I'm special in some way. To everyone else they're this outgoing, effervescent type who is the center of a room. But they've chosen me to divulge a hidden vulnerability that I then believe only I can fix. That's the intoxicating blend of ingredients.* —V

People who tap into those deep drives are especially addictive. The reason they resonate strongly is not only down to our own personal history, but because they fit a trope—we see them as representatives for a personality type that we have encountered many times before in stories and art. At a subconscious level they are recognizable, and we have prebuilt expectations of how they will act and what a relationship with them would be like.

Through them we hear echoes from the past.

CHAPTER 11
DATING WHILE LIMERENT

Finding the right match

Most people don't put a lot of thought into dating. It may be an important part of their lives, and meeting someone special might be a priority, but they generally approach the actual process of dating in a rather improvised way. They wing it on intuition and instinct.

A typical dating mindset is something along the lines of: seek out potential matches, arrange a date, hope for a spark, and follow up if things seem promising. As a strategy, this clearly works—people continue to meet, date, and fall in love, after all—but the downside is that there can also be a lot of pain and misunderstandings along the way. Some of that is unavoidable (life being what it is), but many of the problems of dating can be sidestepped once you realize that people can have wildly different expectations of what falling in love should be like. In particular, once you understand the nature and causes of limerence, many of the common mistakes and missteps of dating start to make a lot more sense.

> *If there's one thing I hate about conventional dating it's walking that fine line where if you show too much interest you look needy, and if you play it too safe it looks like you're just looking for friendship. Then again, I'm a dork, so that's probably on me (and being a serial limerent doesn't help, either).* —B

Fundamentally, people who experience limerence will have a profoundly different set of hopes and expectations to people who don't. Sadly, when embarking on a date it won't be clear at the outset whether your date is a limerent or non-limerent. The two tribes will have such different instincts about romance that following their intuitions about what feels right will almost inevitably lead to heartache. A lot of human folly can be explained by the mismatched beliefs and desires when the two tribes encounter each other in the wild.

Another major factor complicating life for single people seeking love is how rapidly the conventions and mechanics of dating are changing. An ongoing study at the University of Stanford titled "How Couples Meet and Stay Together" has been tracking dating habits among heterosexual couples in the United States since the 1950s and has reported some remarkable results.[1] Up until the 1990s there was a broad mix of ways and venues in which couples first connected, with friends, work, family, and bars being the major contributors (each varying in the 20% to 40% range), with other sources like school, college, and neighbors making up the remainder. In 2022, when the latest data was gathered, around 60 percent of couples had met online. All other sources had dropped below 10 percent apiece.

This is a dramatic social change. What impact it will have in the long run is unclear, and as with any innovation, there are likely to be positives and negatives. The overall shift is from haphazard encounters in a local community of friends and acquaintances to active selection from a far greater pool of potential candidates. Finding a potential match has shifted from being a relatively open process within a shared social circle to a more private affair—often kept separate from existing friendship and peer groups. More independence, choice, and variety may have wonderful benefits, but it will also come with unintended consequences.[2] For example, choice overload may lead to indecision, short-term thinking, and fear of missing out, rather than an increased chance of meeting the perfect match.

The combination of changing norms and different starting expectations means that the presence or absence of limerence will have an impact on the dating experience at every stage of the process. Indeed, the consequences of the mismatched intuitions of the two tribes start at the very beginning.

First contact

In the past, dates would usually be set up after you had spent a bit of time with a new person in a social setting—some set of circumstances had thrown you together, you'd sensed some personal chemistry and decided to meet more privately to see how things might go. Even blind dates began when you met face to face and so exposed yourself to the full suite of the other person's attributes—their appearance, personality, mannerisms, scent, voice, sense of humor, and all the other little cues that can contribute to attraction. First contact with a date was in-person, and identifying an ineffable spark of connection was straightforward, even if the meaning of that "spark" would differ. For limerents, a spark really means the glimmer of limerent recognition—that special sort of romantic potency that excites at a subconscious level. For non-limerents, the experience is unlikely to be so viscerally stimulating—the spark of attraction is closer to admiration than intoxicating desire.

With online dating, first contact is profoundly different. Instead of meeting in person, you decide on a possible match based on a picture and a brief biography. You try to judge attraction from a few carefully selected images, plus some sales patter. With so few cues, it's natural to fill in the blanks with your imagination. For limerents given to daydreaming and projection, it can be surprisingly easy to begin the process of limerent idealization at this early stage, even with such limited material with which to work. If you also exchange some bantering messages with your potential date before meeting, the idealization process can intensify further, as you start to mentally embellish their personality based on their online "voice."

Given these risks, some jaded users of dating apps recommend limiting any electronic preamble to the minimum necessary, having learned through experience that the imaginary person that they had conjured up during hope-filled texting did not match reality once they met (leaving both parties disappointed). It's also a useful way of filtering those people who are not really serious—those who are only seeking validation from collecting matches, looking for an ego-boost, or the outright fakes who are catfishing.[3]

> *I keep to some pretty simple rules when online dating: If there's chemistry and mutual interest, we meet within a week. Otherwise, I delete him. —B*

Meeting online is best treated as a quick, preliminary process. Actual dating then moves into the old realms of coffee shops, bars, and restaurants where you can properly assess the prospects of a meaningful connection.

> *I can't imagine getting the glimmer from someone I haven't met face to face. I have to see the person in the flesh, watch them move, eye contact, smile, laugh, natural scent [...] to have an emotional response to them. I guess I'm both lucky and unlucky in the sense I can't fall for someone I haven't met in person. —S*

Getting to know each other

Assuming the first few dates go well, the next stage of dating is a process of getting to know each other better, and seeing whether the initial good vibes might lead to something more serious. This phase is also going to be experienced differently by limerents and non-limerents. The two tribes have fundamentally different perceptions of what falling in love feels like and how quickly it should happen.

For limerents, once the altered state of mind of limerence sets in, romantic desire will escalate until it becomes obsessive and difficult to moderate. They are likely to want ever more frequent and intimate contact with their new paramour, and to deepen the connection as quickly as possible. Delay and caution will take conscious effort, and time apart is likely to be dominated by daydreaming and rumination. They will prioritize opportunities to be together over everything else, and be hyperaware of any signs of doubt or dissatisfaction from their limerent object (LO). That's the natural trajectory that limerence will follow, as reward-seeking leads to person addiction.

For non-limerents, the progression of love would be more measured. They will likely get an enlivening boost of "new relationship energy" and enjoy the excitement of getting to know someone stimulating and desirable, but it is unlikely to become the one, dominant obsession in their lives. Rather than ever-deepening immersion, non-limerents would want to find a happy balance, integrating the new romance into their other friendships, relationships, and goals. A good romantic relationship would be seen as an essential element of a happy life, but not its single-minded focus.

Unsurprisingly, these different expectations can lead to discord. An excited limerent will be desperately looking for signs of mutual limerence as they get to know their LO better. Their instinct will make them seek a blissful immersion into a deep union that seems, to a non-limerent, like an unhealthy fixation. Faced with the more level-headed bonding process of a non-limerent, limerents often overreact by seeking ever more intimacy to regain hope and reassure themselves of the intensity of the connection. Meanwhile, the non-limerent will be feeling increasing disquiet about the erratic, needy behavior of the limerent. Each person is expecting their own feelings to be mirrored. The mismatch in behavior will be alarming and only worsen as their individual intuitive responses (to get closer or pull back, respectively) heighten the discrepancy.

As a final irony, the mix of hope and uncertainty generated by these mismatched expectations is the perfect recipe for driving the limerence engine into overdrive.

Keeping things casual

Another potential source of discordance between the tribes is the recent shift in attitudes toward the role of sex in dating. In past eras, dating was a more chaste affair, aimed at establishing mutual attraction, personal compatibility, and how genial you found one another's company. In those days, sex was often a secondary consideration, sometimes even waiting until after marriage, but certainly until after a public commitment of some sort had been made. Emotional intimacy tended to precede physical intimacy, and the goal of dating was to assess the feasibility and desirability of forming a pair bond.

The etiquette of modern dating is different. The more transactional nature of swiping on photos to select a date has coincided with a more casual attitude toward sex. Sex is now commonly viewed as an expected part of the early, recreational period of getting to know each other, rather than something that signals an intention of commitment. Pair bonding is only a hypothetical outcome if things go well. Accordingly, newspaper columns are now filled with advice on how to avoid "catching feelings" for a date, how to navigate a "situationship" (a limbo state where casual sex is ongoing without any clarity about how serious or exclusive the connection is), and how to generally manage the emotional ups and downs of "hook-up" culture.[4]

It makes sense for people to discover early on whether they have a good erotic connection, but many limerents who intend to date casually as a gateway into exploring this compatibility instead discover that casual sex with someone that you have felt the glimmer for turbocharges limerence.

Putting it bluntly, sex is not just masturbation with another person. Skin-to-skin contact, scent, taste, and eye contact all have profound effects on our brains.[5] Bonding is not an exclusively psychological process—we are physical beings. The release of bonding hormones during sex, in unison with dopamine reward signaling, intensifies limerence dramatically. In a situation already charged with hope and uncertainty, that bonding intensification can quickly escalate into full-blown person addiction.

Some people are able to emotionally separate sex and love, but it's also easy for a limerent to talk themselves into pretending they can while struggling to suppress their limerent feelings. They may try to force a "friends with benefits" relationship to work because they'll accept whatever terms they can get if it means they can be with their LO. In reality, few limerents are able to keep their emotions so neatly compartmentalized.

We've been together for nearly six months and it started as hook-ups that got more serious, and the whole time I feel like I've been trying to hide my obsession so I don't scare him off but now I'm going crazy with the fact that I want him to feel the same as me. He's not doing anything wrong, he's just so chill that I feel like he doesn't care enough, you know? It's eating me up that he isn't having limerence for me. I know it's unhealthy how obsessed I am, but I want him to be the same. —G

I started a friendship with a coworker as soon as he finished a long-term relationship (I felt very, very attracted to him). Of course, very soon sparkles started and we ended up in a sexual relationship "just for fun" (due to his recent break up). I lied to myself pretending that I could handle [it], but I started obsessing for this guy (as I did with other guys in the past). I started being weird and he started to pull back. —J

Many limerents end up "catching feelings" to a spectacular extent, all while trying to kid themselves that they are happy with an easygoing, casual relationship. Sadly, they discover that faking the persona of a "chill" lover when they in fact want to be a "withdraw from the world and luxuriate in mutual infatuation" lover, ends up trapping them in an awful situation. The casualness of the relationship was agreed in advance in a mature and open way, but their limerent mind is going mad with uncertainty and insecurity.

How to pick well as a limerent

This last point illustrates a key principle for navigating these pitfalls of dating—you have to be honest with yourself about what you really want. You have to be clear on what you are seeking, and engage with other people on a sincere and authentic basis. If you are a limerent, starting casual and seeing what happens might seem entirely rational at an intellectual level, but it can quickly plunge you into unintended limerence. Once that altered state of mind sets in, you will be carried along by the emotional rollercoaster, with all your careful plans to take it slow and steady left in disarray. Your heart leads you to what it really wants—deep, intense bonding—however much you might feign a more casual attitude.

The way to avoid this hazard is to be more conscious and deliberate about the process of dating from the outset. Perhaps the obvious starting point is to reflect on whether it is better to seek limerent or non-limerent partners for yourself. This is not necessarily a straightforward choice.

Limerent–Limerent At first blush it seems that mutual limerence would obviously be the most desirable outcome. It would certainly smooth the path ahead if you are aligned in your emotional and psychological expectations and desires. Mutual infatuation, mutual obsession, and deep immersion is most likely with limerent-limerent couples.[6]

The downside to mutual limerence is that it doesn't last. Once reciprocation is secured, and the limerent passions are sated, then the mania will inevitably fade. Limerent euphoria is only ever going to be an early phase of any relationship—it is more like a sugar rush than long-term nourishment. If you seek only mutual limerence through dating, then you need to anticipate the fact that a limerent partner (who isn't all wise and enlightened like you) may well interpret the deterioration of limerent feelings as evidence that they are falling out of love. Once the giddy limerence tingles pass, many people conclude that they are no longer "in love" with their partner, and they move on to seek the next limerent glimmer. This leads to serial limerence, with sequential short-term relationships that are glorious at first, but inevitably disappoint. There is a risk of being caught in that cycle if you aim to exclusively date limerents.

Limerent–Non-Limerent A second scenario is that you have already felt the glimmer for someone but discover during the "getting to know you" phase that they are a non-limerent. They just can't provide reciprocation of your limerent feelings. That just isn't what falling in love feels like for them. Accepting that reality is actually freeing. It means you can avoid the cycles of self-doubt and false hope that come from believing that if you could just twist yourself into an ideal shape, or accommodate their needs perfectly, you could make yourself into their LO. Instead, you can direct that energy into finding strategies to align your limerent tendencies with their non-limerent tendencies.

The principal challenges will be moderating your limerent instinct to seek ever more entanglement and intimacy, and managing your emotional volatility when they behave in a way that is natural for a non-limerent. Your chance of success is a lot higher if you are open about what you are experiencing, but also open about your willingness to compromise. For example, if they are being noncommittal and taking things slowly, and it is driving you mad with limerent panic, it would be better to express that openly (in a diplomatic way) than to try and choke it down and stifle your limerence.

As a general principle, communicating your own emotions clearly, in a way that focuses on your internal state rather than their conduct, is the best way to make decisions that benefit both parties. "You know, I feel really bad when you date other people. I have to admit I get jealous and anxious. What do you think about becoming exclusive?" is a clear and honest way to express your feelings without implied judgment about their behavior. It can be transformative to invite direct honesty like this. It might not work out as you hoped: They may say they are not that into you, thought this was only for fun, or that they want the freedom to see other people. That will obviously hurt, but it will also tell you your limerence is likely to become increasingly toxic if you continue to try and bond to someone who can't return your commitment. It's also an excellent way of distinguishing between someone who is just dating for fun and someone who is a non-limerent but nevertheless taking the relationship more seriously. Ironically, as an extra bonus, developing these advanced communication skills during dating will also help you succeed in any longer-term relationship that might develop.

Limerent–Non-Limerent Object The third big challenge in picking well when you are a limerent is the question of whether a relationship with someone who is not an LO will feel unsatisfying. Many limerents are a bit unsettled by the idea of forming an attachment to someone who they do not feel the glimmer for, and who does not cause the giddy, emotional thrills that they associate with love intoxication.

> *I care very deeply about my current "significant other," and I feel that our relationship is one that could potentially offer a lifetime of mutual care and support. However, it unnerves me that I never felt limerent for this person.* —SK

Most limerents associate the feelings of early limerence with the definition of romantic love. A natural fear is that falling in love more slowly with someone who is compatible but does not cause the euphoria of limerence means they are "settling"—that the lack of fireworks means the relationship is somehow diminished. The reality is that there's no reason to think that the factors that determine who you become limerent for are the same factors that determine who you can form a deep, loving bond with. A stable, long-term relationship does not require mutual limerent fireworks at the outset. As Dorothy Tennov put it:

> *A relationship that includes no limerence may be a far more important one in your life when all is said and done, than any relationship in which you experienced the strivings of limerent passion. Limerence is not in any way pre-eminent among types of human attractions or interactions; but when limerence is in full force it eclipses other relationships.*[7]

Limerence is inevitably going to fade. Any long-term relationship has to be built on foundations of love that endure beyond the initial pyrotechnics of limerence, and in some cases, limerence can be a direct liability.

Some poor souls become limerent for people who are incapable of forming a healthy long-term bond. If you become serially limerent for unavailable people, narcissists, manipulators, ditherers, drama-seekers, or philanderers, you're unlikely to find any of your LOs are good prospects for a life partnership. If you identify your "limerence avatar," and discover that they are the sort of person that is likely to avoid any attempts at commitment, then choosing to "follow the glimmer" will result in a series of tempestuous but short-term relationships. That's fine if it's what you want, but if you are looking for a serious, monogamous partner it makes sense to avoid people who cause you the glimmer.

Clarifying what your goals are is important because you can make better judgments about whether the person you are drawn to is a good prospect at an early stage of dating, and manage your expectations going in. Understanding how limerents and non-limerents differ in their attitudes and behavior is invaluable for making sense of how someone you are dating is likely to act at each stage of the process. If you can figure out whether they are a limerent, it allows you to predict how they will express their romantic feelings and hopes, and how you should respond to their behavior. That insight can help you make informed choices about how to proceed, rather than letting your instinctive emotions pull you back and forth.

The two tribes have always had to find ways to compromise and accommodate each other's temperaments and needs, often without the benefit of knowing that such different ways of experiencing love exist. The modern world is adding ever more complexity to that already challenging situation, as the conventions and consequences of dating evolve at a rapid pace.

Limerents and non-limerents are pioneering this new frontier of social and romantic communion together. It's a brave new world. As well as the dating apps themselves, the wider online world of social media and social networking has had profound effects on how we manage our interactions and process our feelings. It provides all new ways to kindle hope and uncertainty, new channels for contacting a limerent object, and endless opportunities for rumination and reinforcement.

For limerents, it can be a perilous realm.

CHAPTER 12
SOCIAL MEDIA
A limitless database of rumination fodder

A lot has been written about the seismic changes in social behavior that have been caused by the invention of the internet.[1] For those who grew up before the arrival of social media and dating apps, it's difficult to appreciate how profoundly different it is to become limerent in this new, socially transparent age. Like all cultural shifts, it will take time for the good and bad to settle out, but for all the rapid disruption that the tech giants have ushered in, the neural pathways through which we make sense of the world—and each other—are not so changeable. With an understanding of the forces that drive limerence, it's possible to predict how social media will affect the progression of person addiction: it makes it worse.

Above all, limerents seek contact with their limerent object (LO) because it is so rewarding. Daydreaming and rumination reinforce the mental connection between the LO and reward, and so even this apparently innocuous behavior ends up promoting the transition from exciting crush to person addiction. Limerence is also an insatiable desire, and so any opportunities for direct or indirect contact with the LO will be seized, and exercising restraint will be difficult.

Even with such a cursory review of the main forces driving limerence, it's obvious that social media supplies them in abundance, and all available 24/7.

A whole world of limerent object exposure

The most obvious and striking impact of social media for limerents is that it provides almost limitless opportunities for exposure to their LO. Assuming their LO has an ordinary degree of engagement with the main platforms, posting updates every few days, it's easy for an excited limerent to find photos, posts, opinions, tweets, even videos of their LO going about their lives—furnishing the online world with their personality and presence. As a motivated limerent, getting access to your LO's social sites is like immersing yourself in an infinity pool of limerent rumination, and luxuriating until your fingers go wrinkly.

That database of easy LO hits is also on standby in case of disappointments. If you have a negative interaction with an LO in real life, or are not able to see them for some time, the indirect contact of checking their socials can give some fleeting relief. The pain of craving can be partially soothed by revisiting that favorite photo of them looking dazzling on the beach, or at the charity gala, or trekking in the Peruvian rainforest. It becomes a secondhand bliss hit.

Access to the online social world of an LO also offers a wonderful source of hope and anticipation if you can connect on one of the platforms that have restricted access and direct messaging. When an LO accepts (or, even better, sends) that first friend request or invite, you receive blissful affirmation, followed by the excitement of gaining access to a new, private channel of communication. This takes you beyond the public-facing pleasures of haunting an LO's Instagram or X accounts, and into an inner circle of sorts.

In the past, it took time to get to know someone's life history, tastes, opinions, and preferences. You would have to spend time with them, or phone them, or cross-examine their friends—all of which telegraphed to everyone else in the community that you had a particular interest in them. Nowadays, it takes much less effort to get access to an LO's private life, and it can be studied quietly and confidentially. Over time you can build up a mental image of the LO that blends their online and real-world identities. This hybrid will include plenty of misconceptions, given the limerent tendency to idealize LOs, but that is part of the objectification process—social media makes it easier than ever to engineer someone into the LO you want them to be.

In principle, the easy access to all that social media evidence about the LO could potentially work against the forces of hope and uncertainty that drive limerence. You could discover some distasteful opinion or secret of theirs that is so off-putting it short-circuits your reward centers. Exposure to their "content" could break the limerence spell early. Equally, though, it could turn out to be a treasure trove of positive reinforcement, as your glimmery brain diligently unearths exactly the evidence it's most motivated to discover (skipping over the bad photos and concentrating on the ones of them looking lovely). The likelihood of this outcome is even greater if the LO behaves in the way most people do when it comes to their social media posts—carefully curating them to make the best possible impression.

> It's astonishing the power of social media on a limerent. Something as innocuous as a new profile pic, and I am ruined. I know I should hide her from my feed, but that's about as effective as locking the liquor cabinet when the alcoholic still has the key. —B

As if our brains weren't already masters at glorifying the LO, the input from social media comes prepolished to present them at their very best. Browsing their feed is the psychological equivalent of bingeing on highly refined LO sugar.

The temptation to impress

Most people craft their social media presence to represent a favorable version of themselves. For a limerent with access to the online repository of the LO's life, the temptation to tweak their own online persona to align themselves with the LO's tastes is hard to resist. Once you get a sense of the LO's opinions and beliefs it's an obvious strategy to adjust your own persona to match their preferences.

In the initial phase of limerence, when the infatuation is building and hope is blossoming, it's natural to take more interest in their worldview and explore how well you can fit into it. All of us have a natural tendency to mirror the people we esteem.[2] This unconscious impulse to mimic arises from a desire to show affinity—to empathize and build rapport. As limerence deepens, an LO can affect us not just in terms of haunting our minds (and cropping up suspiciously frequently in conversation), but also in transforming our own mindset and personality. A good clue to the fact that an LO has captured your imagination is that you start adopting their mannerisms, idiosyncratic turns of phrase, and quirky opinions. Every new aspect of their lives is a delightful discovery that makes you feel closer, and it is quickly integrated into your present sense of self.

> *I found myself adjusting my route when walking around, hoping to run into him. I found myself coming up with questions for him, just so I could go talk to him. One of the most stupid things I did was start smoking for a short time, because he did and it enabled me to run into him more in the smoking area. —DL*

That impulse to align yourself with your LO leads naturally into immersion in common online communities, networks, and sources of news. Online life can be very tribal.[3] Once inside the LO's bubble, it's inevitable that your opinions and interests will begin to harmonize—especially if it's a shift that you welcome because it means you're getting closer. As the limerent eagerly joins the LO's virtual world and adjusts themselves to be as compatible as possible, the influence on the limerent's own identity can be profound.

As well as the impulse to align personae, online connection is also a chance to impress at a more straightforward level. To show off, basically. Most limerents have an urge to peacock a bit in the hope of catching the LO's attention. They finally find the motivation they need to improve their health, appearance, and desirability in wanting to present their best self to the LO. No harm in dressing to impress. Maybe post a few more photos on Facebook. Perhaps a bit more risqué than usual. Take a few dozen more selfies till you get the angle, lighting, and smile just right. While these habits have benefits beyond the desire to impress, they are usually undertaken in a fairly calculated way. You want them to notice.

As well as physical appearance, the desire to impress carries over into demonstrating your virtues—especially the ones the LO admires. Maybe it's your wit, wisdom, compassion, stoicism, or snarkiness. If the LO responds positively to a post or meme, you'll want more of that lovely reward and refine your online behavior accordingly to emphasize the traits that seem to please them. You "lean in" to the things about you that they seem to like.

Much of this personality refinement, preening, and posing is not conscious. It's a natural habit that limerents drift into, a current that carries them along as part of the excitement of strengthening a limerent bond by getting closer to the LO. We present our best, try to mirror what we think they want, and track their responses with single-minded dedication.

The power of intermittent contact

The online database of photos and personal information about the LO is a constant temptation. It's on a semi-public site for anyone to casually sift through, with no incriminating traces if you've been careful with your browsing history.[4] Not all social media is so passive, though. Some platforms can give you live feedback about when an LO is online and what they are doing.

> *I can't stay away from the computer and Facebook for more than an hour or so.... I have to keep checking, is he on there, has he posted, did he "like" anything that I posted ... and of course the inevitable sadness when there's no response to my post, and then the euphoria, if he happens to respond in any way ... then the cycle begins all over again ... trying to figure what to post that might elicit a response. —M*

Messaging apps are a particular torture.

> WhatsApp was the big problem for me. Those two ticks and the last seen ... limerent's nightmare! LO would do this infuriating thing where she'd send me a message, I'd reply, she'd then leave it "unread" for about 24hrs and then reply. Drove me crazy waiting for the response, checking to see if she'd been online (she had). —V

> We transitioned to WhatsApp and ... it's torture to see those double checks appear but never turn blue. Like, why is she not reading my message? And then they turn blue and she doesn't respond, but she's changing her profile pic and posting new things on Instagram so I mean, what, less than nothing to her? Why yes, yes I do. —F

The ability to like and reply to posts is a form of intermittent reward, exactly the type most likely to promote obsessive behavior and limerent reinforcement.

> I used to go on Facebook obsessively to see if he had liked my last post. I'd get such a rush of excitement when he did. It ended up getting to the stage where almost everything I posted was chosen to try and get a like out of him. —BL

> One of the things about Instagram that drove me crazy was why my LO always showed up as the FIRST liker on any Instagram post he liked—he might not be the first person to like it, but the minute he did, he bumped right up to the first position so the notification says "LO and 7 others liked this." What is the algorithm picking up??? —E

These indirect ways to get contact are especially psychologically potent because they allow the limerent to send a message at any time, hoping to provoke a response, but they cannot control when they might get a hit. Even worse, the limerent is left waiting and guessing and ruminating about all the possible reasons why the LO may have seen the message but chosen not to respond yet. It becomes impossible to predict if (or when) a "bite" will come, but there is no barrier to casting out additional hopeful lures, like a relentlessly optimistic fisherman.

It's like a terrible psychological experiment—trying to discover what will attract the LO's attention, gathering data on engagement, trying to improve response time, and all the while being completely blind to what is actually going on with the LO and why they are behaving as they are. It's no wonder limerents can end up frantic with hope and uncertainty as they try to read meaning into every little interaction. Like the gambling addicts trying to find a "system" for payouts from a slot machine, the limerent keeps trying to secure an unpredictable reward but just ends up trapped in a state of uncertainty—until they are queasy with overanalysis and social media poisoning.

Perhaps the purest example of this problem is when a limerent logs on to a social media platform to see what the LO is up to, and then spends so long browsing the updates that they suddenly realize "I've been on so long now that LO could have posted something new while I've been distracted!" Then they loop all the way back to the beginning and start the cycle anew.

That sort of behavior reveals another pernicious aspect of social media.

Compounding addictions

The tech giants know their business. Social media is addictive.[5]

In much the same way as limerence transitions from active pleasure-seeking into person addiction, the use of social media can shift from a stimulating diversion to a compulsive habit. The sites are optimized to hold your attention and maximize engagement by providing you with carefully delivered doses of reward and arousal (in the forms of gossip, scandal, or competition) that are finely tailored to stimulate your curiosity. It is hard to self-regulate use because social media companies have devised ways to hook you even if you aren't intentionally seeking contact. Notifications and alerts—big red circles, bells and popups—are designed to catch the eye. Something is happening! What could it be? Don't miss out!

Seeking an LO on social media mutually reinforces two reward-seeking habits under one impulsive behavior. The cravings compound, as each behavioral addiction keeps exposing you to cues for the other. This multiplying effect of social media is one of the most disruptive influences on the life of a limerent—countless hours of life can be spent languishing, staring at a screen, distracted, neglecting work, perhaps neglecting family and friends; ill-tempered and absent. The opportunities missed during all those listless hours of futile scrolling are depressing to contemplate.

At its darkest, this mutual reinforcement can lead limerents into a pattern of use that borders on cyberstalking—following the LO's feed relentlessly, searching for old material in the dusty corners of forgotten sites, tracking where they are and what they are doing in real life—all in the hope that it will somehow give emotional relief to the endless hunger for contact. Instead, it intensifies the craving.

For limerents who have contact with their LO in real life, the forces of social media can easily drive the progression of limerence from pleasant intoxication to unpleasant toxicity, but the power of social media for cultivating limerence can even go beyond simply reinforcing existing infatuation. A new phenomenon has recently arrived in the world of romance—limerence in an online-only relationship.

Although it's easy to focus on the negative aspects of social media on our behavior, the sites have been such a spectacular success because of the *social* aspect of their function. They are addictive because they are rewarding. It's an invaluable way to keep in touch with friends, find online communities built around personal interests, hobbies, and shared passions, and it allows us to connect with kindred spirits around the world. Understandably, this offers tremendous opportunities to get to know other people.

It's surprisingly easy to feel connected to someone even if your interactions are exclusively online. You might have a few pictures to work with and can build on them to conjure a sense of their personality from their writing style. This begins the idealization process. It also feels safe to share some personal details about your life because of the security of emotional and physical distance. In fact, many people report that it's easier to open up emotionally to a pseudonymous stranger on an online forum or social media site than a real-world friend.[6] These are ideal circumstances for creating a limerent *object*—perfect conditions for projecting your own hopes and needs onto someone who is not immediately present to spoil the illusion.

Imagine the temptation. You are perhaps a bit frustrated with mundane life—tired, stressed, demoralized. In your pocket is a device that allows you to instantly, from wherever you are, open a dialogue box with a secret friend. A friend who excites you with limerent energy, whose only demand of you is to carry on the shared conversation, who is partly real and partly imagined; the blanks of uncertainty filled in with your own idealization.

> *My [online] limerence experience was never really illicit but it was deeply personal. I was responding on a level that should have been reserved for my wife. The more the LO revealed, the more I wanted to know about her. The more I learned, the more attracted I became. Over time, I got in too deep.* —LE

As the intimacy deepens, all the phases of limerence from euphoria to addiction will play out. Being an exclusively online connection, there are other factors that contribute too. First, it is easy to compartmentalize the relationship from the rest of your life as it can only be accessed through a technological portal. Second, it is easy to self-justify that this isn't a "real" relationship and disregard the usual boundaries that would be expected for in-person connections. Third, if the limerent is already in a long-term relationship, there is plausible deniability that there is no real transgression happening because you have never met the LO, and only chat online (though, in reality, it is the emotional transgression that can cause harm).

> *I'd never met the LO, never actually spoken to her, and we were on opposite coasts. I told my therapist that we weren't in a relationship. She looked at the email and said, "Oh, yes, you are."* —LE

Online-only limerence dwells in a strange hinterland, where the LO exists half in the limerent's internal fantasy world and half in reality. They are a real person, of course, but the limerent's contact with them is filtered exclusively through social media communication channels. The impossibility of physical contact also seems to constrain the LO into the category of "friend" because all interactions are entirely virtual. It's a blurring of boundaries that confuses both the limerent and any outside observer who wonders about the strength of the connection.

The inbuilt ambiguity of online-only limerence also serves as a useful case study for one of the most difficult challenges in managing any kind of relationship with an LO. Although the limerent will be cycling through the agony and ecstasy of addictive reward, in principle they can keep that emotional carnival to themselves. They don't have to share their feelings with their LO, or anyone else. They could swear off any hope of romance and instead keep the relationship platonic.

This train of thought leads to a question that is inevitably asked by anyone who is struggling with limerence for someone with whom they cannot openly bond.

Is it possible to be friends with an LO?

CHAPTER 13

CAN'T WE JUST BE FRIENDS?

Unrequited limerence, forbidden love, and last-ditch bargaining

Life is complicated. There are a multitude of reasons why it might not be possible to openly seek a romantic relationship with someone you've become limerent for. That frustration is distressing enough, but it also creates a new emotional predicament: Can you just be friends with a limerent object (LO), given how powerfully you are attracted to them?

The most obvious cause of this dilemma is that your LO does not reciprocate your romantic feelings. It is an unfortunate fact of life that, statistically, the odds are low that someone we find attractive will be attracted to us too. That makes unrequited love an almost inevitable part of the human experience. A natural impulse in the face of this disappointment is to try and remain friends in the hope that you can reconcile yourself to a platonic relationship—to salvage some good from a sad situation.

Alternatively, the problem might lie in our own insecurities. Many limerents find themselves so overwhelmed by the power of their feelings that they become paralyzed by indecision. The romantic stakes are so high that they fear taking any action because making a mistake could destroy their hopes forever. Declaring themselves is intolerably risky and so they conceal their true feelings, perhaps persuading themselves that they are buying time until the perfect moment arrives to disclose their secret passion.

A third impediment to open bonding with an LO is the presence of social, cultural, or geographical barriers to romantic attachment. If either the limerent or the LO are in a committed relationship, have a professional connection, a duty of care, a religious incompatibility, live on different continents, or are thwarted by any of the myriad other reasons why a relationship cannot be ethically or practically pursued, they must resist their limerent urges. Again, a natural response is to try and tough it out and maintain a cordial relationship without ever giving in to the limerent desire. Just ignore the forbidden fruit. It probably isn't deliciously sweet.

All these scenarios share a common problem: The limerent finds themselves unable to satisfy their limerent desires but determined to maintain contact with their LO. When faced with this dilemma, it is an obvious and reasonable conclusion that being friends is better than nothing, and so the route forward involves keeping in touch with the LO while swallowing the limerent feelings until they go away. It seems logical enough—you do, after all, enjoy their company, and they really seem to understand you, and you care about their happiness. Surely those are all important aspects of being a friend?

Unfortunately, regardless of the motives for wanting to "just be friends" with an LO, the nature of limerence makes the plan perilous. Limerence blooms in uncertainty and ambiguity. Friendship with a LO is a category error. You're attempting to do two contradictory things: deepen an emotional connection while simultaneously reducing your limerence. You are consciously exposing yourself to their intoxicating company, but also hoping that your desire for it will decrease. It's like an alcoholic who tries to drink socially—a constant game of brinkmanship with temptation.

Given all these causes for caution, it's essential to be honest with yourself about your true motives, self-aware enough to understand why you make the choices that you do, and clear-sighted about the consequences of those choices. There will be a lot of obstacles in the way of friendship with an LO. It's one of those scenarios in life that tests our ability to confront emotional pain with composure, and put wisdom before feelings.

The psychology of wanting to stay friends

One of the most important lessons to internalize about limerence is that once you are in that altered state of mind, your judgment is compromised. It doesn't mean that you are not able to make decisions or take responsibility for your actions—you are not a hopeless victim of your affliction, buffeted by fate—but it does mean that you are highly likely to indulge in motivated reasoning. Our brains are excellent at rationalization. The executive regions of the cortex are supposed to be feeding back information to the reward centers to contextualize desires and help us make better decisions, but they can just as readily invent creative rationalizations for why LO-seeking behavior can be justified. Rationalization stems from a desire to avoid feelings of discomfort by telling ourselves ego-protecting stories.

What makes the job of rationalization easier is that there *are* lots of reasonable arguments that can be made about why you should remain friends with an LO. Some are founded in a sense of duty or loyalty, others in practical constraints. Limerents often react very defensively to the suggestion that friendship with an LO is misguided. For some people, friendship is a serious, heartfelt commitment, and so taking any action to detach would be a calculated betrayal. Instead, the inability to control their limerent feelings becomes a personal failing that they should strive to overcome. The rationalizing inner voice starts its arguments: *It is thoughtless and selfish to discard a friend just because I'm struggling to manage my emotions. They are a good person, and I'm just being pathetic. I'm not going to let limerence decide who I can be friends with! We help and support each other, and that's worth preserving. A real friend wouldn't give up on someone just because they've got a crush on them.*

Other rationalizations involve external limitations: *I have professional responsibilities or social commitments that mean I cannot avoid them. They are enmeshed in my friendship network. It would look odd if I suddenly started avoiding them. I shouldn't have to lose out on opportunities because I'm trying to avoid them.* Again, legitimate reasons all, but ultimately irrelevant to the intractable problem of trying to simultaneously strengthen the bonds of friendship while weakening the bonds of limerence.

Another form of motivated reasoning is bargaining. Here, the limerent builds a case as to why a friendship is possible with optimism that borders on wishful thinking. *I can handle it. I'll take it slow and get used to it. I only see them a few times a week, so it's not so bad. In fact, it's probably a good idea to expose myself to their company to desensitize myself, like building up a tolerance. Once I get to know them well—flaws and all—it will demystify them and break the spell.*

To reiterate, none of these arguments are without merit. They are all convincing to varying degrees, and so it's easy for a limerent to persuade themselves (especially while addled by limerent bliss) that it's fine to continue to spend time with them as friends.

Deep down, when they are honest with themselves, most limerents know that this is an evasion. A self-serving excuse. The true motivation for wanting to stay friends with an LO is that it means you can maintain access to the limerent highs. You're okay with keeping up a façade of friendship if it means you can still enjoy some of that sneaky fizz. Furthermore, it also feels unbearable to think about breaking contact with them. The complete death of hope is too grim to face, and so through friendship, a limerent can keep the pilot flame of their limerence furnace burning.

> [If I'm] 100% truthful to myself, I don't really (really) want friendship with my LO. I fancy LO, I like how it feels when it's nice and LO reciprocates and it feels like we're "getting somewhere" (though I don't think we truthfully were, whatever was said). That's what kept me coming back to their company. Of course I liked them, more than liked them . . . but really? As a friend? —T

While we're being honest, another uncomfortable truth is that many limerents settle on friendship in the hope that they can maybe win over their LO at some point in the future through dedication and perseverance. The distorted reasoning is that maybe reciprocation of romantic feelings can be gently cultivated over a prolonged period by cleverly demonstrating your virtue as a worthwhile friend. In fact, this urge can be quite deeply buried by rationalizations and self-delusion. We're just friends! I have no ulterior motive.

Meanwhile, the limerent wallows in the shallow end of the relationship pool—the friendzone, if you will—and bathes in their LO's loveliness while yearning for more depth.

Why friendship is impractical

Battling your own hidden motives is not the only barrier to sustaining a friendship. Friendship is a mutual relationship, and you cannot single-handedly control or predict the way it will develop because you can only control your own conduct (and sometimes not even that). The behavior of the LO will also have a dramatic impact on how difficult it is for the limerent to manage their emotions.

If the limerent has concealed their feelings, the LO will be unaware of what's going on, so it's not surprising if they unwittingly act in a way that worsens the emotional turmoil in the limerent. The LO is acting in the way that feels natural to them, but the typical friendship dynamic of mutual affection, sharing of secrets, laughter, and easy-going intimacy feeds the limerent's subconscious mind direct evidence that the LO likes them. To sustain a friendship under these conditions, the limerent would have to overrule that emotional input with the intellectual argument that the LO's affection has limits. In most cases, that mental conflict causes anguish.

Ironically (and it's a bitter irony), even disclosure of limerent feelings doesn't solve this problem. Indeed, one of the hardest emotional traps to escape from when it comes to friendship with an LO is the gentle rejection. Most well-adjusted LOs who discover that one of their friends has developed romantic feelings for them will react with a complex mixture of feelings. Everyone likes to be admired, but for compassionate people, the flattering ego boost usually gives way to sympathy and concern pretty quickly if they don't have romantic feelings for you. They don't want to lose you as a friend, they don't want to string you along, but they don't want to hurt you either. Unfortunately, this caring response can prolong the limerence as it frequently leads to mixed messages—or at least messages that can be distorted through the limerence lens into false hope. They might use humor to avoid embarrassment, they might assert how much your friendship means to them, they might even show you extra attentiveness and concern to make it clear that your declaration hasn't scared them away. They aim to "let you down gently" by praising your virtues in the hope that it will quietly close the door to anything deeper. Unfortunately, in the grip of limerence, anything less than an unequivocal slam that shakes the walls can make it seem like the door of opportunity might still be ajar.

Finally, another scenario that needs to be confronted is that some LOs might not be the compassionate and thoughtful friends that we would hope for. Some LOs like the attention. They may turn down an offer of romantic connection in a purposefully confusing way because they are titillated by the idea of your devotion. These LOs can even become more flirtatious and suggestive to deliberately stoke the fires of your infatuation.

> *I got caught because he flirted with me and I was blind to his behavior toward other women. I am not used to [being] flirted with, so I developed a crush quickly. When he started to talk to me and cuddled with me, I was elated. Only to be brought crashing down when his girlfriend showed up a few hours later and I realized I was nothing to him. Nonetheless, he continued to flirt with me, even with her there. —N*

Some LOs are bad news. Trying to stay friends with them is an invitation to suffering.

I'm taking a hard line on this issue because the attempt to maintain a friendship with an LO is a major source of pain for many limerents and comes with a serious cost to their psychological health. I hear from many limerents who have fallen into the trap of *limerence limbo*: an endless cycle of intermittent contact, rumination, caution, anxiety, and inaction. The only decision they have made is to wait and see if things might somehow change for the better. In the meantime, they settle into the familiar passivity of daydreams, regret, and a free-floating promise of a delayed future.

> *I waited around far longer than I care to admit for something to happen with my LO, even though, deep down, I knew after about the first six months that nothing ever would.* —M

> *Two years of limbo and although my LO knew I was struggling to move on, he'd do and say enough to keep me hooked. It's been a terrible waste of time.* —B

Friendship is not a consolation prize, or a way to numb the pain of thwarted limerence. Trying to force yourself into the mold of friend when you want to be their lover is literally and figuratively deranging. You are too invested. There is an asymmetry in desire that is dishonest to conceal. You won't react to them the way you react to your other friends, and inevitably, in those moments when you relax your vigilance, the limerence will begin to reassert itself—perhaps in neutral ways, like realizing after a wonderful day together that you are more deeply infatuated than ever, or perhaps in darker ways, like the stab of jealousy and resentment when you find out they are dating someone new.

> *We've all had that one platonic friend who's a little too possessive, haven't we? And I think this sort of behavior often makes people cringe when they're on the receiving end.* —S

Trapping yourself into a limbo of second-rate bonding can mutate limerence into the most toxic form of person addiction. The psychological toll of frustrated desire can turn you bitter and spiteful, blaming the LO for the pain caused by your own choices. A comprehensive failure of friendship.

What is friendship?

To clarify why limerence and friendship are incompatible, it's worth spending some time analyzing what friendship is really about and why limerence prohibits the authentic connection that's needed.

In the fourth century BCE, Aristotle devoted some of his philosophical energies to examining the nature of friendships.[1] He distinguished three main categories of friend on the basis of the benefits that they provide: friendships of Utility, Pleasure and Goodness.

Utility-based friendships can be seen as the simplest form, where you both get benefit from the friendship at a somewhat transactional level. Examples would be the friend who shares your interests in sport, music, or some other hobby that involves community spirit. Or the friend who goes for lunch with you because your schedules match, or a colleague who you know you can always chat with at business events. Basically, someone whose company is congenial, but who you only really see in a particular context. This kind of social friendship is a blessing, of course, but not very stable. If your interests change, the friendship would naturally fizzle out.

Pleasure-based friendships are considered a level up from utility friendships. A Pleasure friend is someone that you can chat with freely and openly, and who you implicitly trust, someone who you actively seek the company of because you really enjoy being with them. These are friends that know about your life history, commiserate with your bad luck, and share your triumphs. The majority of friendships probably fall into this camp. These are people you care about, who often have some shared interests and opinions, who you can rely on to make you laugh, and who are basically on your side.

A Good friend is the Aristotelian ideal (and alternatively can be called a "perfect" or "virtue" friendship). Here, friendship is a proper connection of souls. In Aristotle's view, true friendship comes from seeking goodness in others and cultivating it in yourself. Exactly what is meant by "goodness" is a bit elusive, but essentially it signifies moral integrity, personal authenticity, and a will to live well. Good friends seek each other's company from a desire to help each other improve as people through mutual respect for one another's merits. There is generally complete trust and honesty, with the recognition that a betrayal of that trust would be an irrevocable harm to the friendship as it would destroy its foundation. These are the friends that last a lifetime, through relocations, long absences, or big changes in life. The great benefit of such a Good friendship is that the other, lesser forms also come automatically: we tend to gain Pleasure and Utility from the company of a Good friend, as well as the virtuous uplift of socializing with someone we admire as an individual. To gain the friendship of such a person requires us to live well too.

Looked at in this framework, it's clear that limerence creates conflict at all three levels. For Utility friends, you will be constantly seeking increased closeness as you try to move them into a more intimate relationship. They want to go and watch the match; you want to find out all about them. Friendships based on Pleasure are even more fraught. This is the most well-trodden road into limerence limbo, as you spend time together chatting and bonding and reinforcing the limerent habit. There's a lack of sincerity about this because your LO wants a coffee and chat, and you want *them*. This is not an authentic basis for friendship. You are keeping a major secret from them that would fundamentally alter the dynamic of the relationship.

Finally, limerence for a Good friend would be agony. This kind of friendship requires emotional intimacy and vulnerability. For an unavailable LO, this depth of friendship would be near impossible to sustain without falling into the worst kind of limerent obsession. If the limerent has a partner themself, that relationship will destabilize. If the Good friend has a partner, the closeness of your friendship is likely to cause tension and conflict within their relationship. A Good friend is someone whose time and company you esteem and enjoy, but with whom you do not want to form a romantic bond. If you try to be Good friends with an LO, how could you not fall in love with them?

The limerent desire to always drift into deeper intimacy will conflict with the terms of reference for lesser friendships and lead to personal agony and inauthenticity within a more intimate friendship. There are many splendid people in the world. We should seek Good friends from those that are not also potential LOs.

A ray of hope

I've taken a very dreary perspective on the prospects of remaining friends with an LO, principally because of the danger of pain all around. Losing a good friend is one of the most demoralizing costs that limerence can inflict. It's a legitimate loss.

One way to come to terms with the unfairness is to accept that you can't realistically be a beneficial friend to them. You could try, but you'd probably fail because of the way that they trigger limerent craving in you. It's nobody's fault. You just have to live with it as a sad outcome. In the end, it is likely to be more compassionate to yourself to detach and recognize the sacrifice as necessary for your well-being.

To leaven that cold comfort a little, it's worth trying to look at the problem from a more positive perspective and to mentally reframe the situation. First, a pertinent question to ask yourself is what would a good friend do once they have realized that their limerent feelings are interfering with the friendship? The obvious answer is to be honest. Concealing major aspects of your own internal life is an insurmountable barrier to genuine connection. If you cannot (or must not) express your feelings because of larger responsibilities, continuing in a compromised friendship is not in anyone's best interests. If you care about them, don't carry on under false pretenses. It's better to detach with grace.

A second, more optimistic, perspective is that accepting you cannot be friends with an LO is freeing. You disentangle yourself from the emotional barbed wire that has captured you and escape from limerence limbo. Distance is a good way to recover clarity. Until you can escape the gravitational pull of limerent desire, your motives and actions will be distorted. Getting away from that influence is an essential step for recovery.

That brings us to the last, most hopeful perspective. Despite all the pitfalls outlined above, and all the sobering difficulties, it is possible to be friends with an LO. The catch is that it's only possible with an ex-LO, which means you have to get over the limerence *before* you can attempt to establish a genuine friendship.

> I am [now] good friends with the person who used to be my LO. I couldn't be friends with the LIMERENT OBJECT, but when he ceased to be an LO, he became a real person, and over time, I became friends with that person. We like and trust each other, support each other through difficulties, rejoice in each other's happiness. I can cry and share my feelings with him and not feel any desire for him in a romantic way. —OT

When someone is an LO they are an ideal construct, a vehicle for romantic hopes, a screen to project a fantasy movie onto. It's hard to get to know anyone on those terms. Being with them just bombards you with emotional reward and arousal, drowning out any real chance of hearing them clearly, or interacting with them authentically.

Friendship is only feasible on the far side of limerence. You have to get out of that altered state of mind first, truly accept that you want no romantic connection, and prove it by getting to the point where you feel no romantic excitement at the prospect of being with them. The embers of limerent desire have to be completely extinguished. Realistically, the only way to get to that point is to intentionally and decisively separate yourself from the LO until your recovery is complete.

And if the very idea of deliberately going "no contact" causes a stab of intense emotional discomfort, that's a strong sign that you are not yet ready to be their friend.

CHAPTER 14

LIMERENCE AND LONG-TERM LOVE

Life as a limerent

For most limerents, the first time they experience the altered state of mind of profound infatuation with another person their life changes forever. Before limerence, romantic love was a concept that they understood in an abstract way—an idea from stories and songs, understood as a force that brings lovers together, perhaps a more powerful version of the unromantic love that children have for family and friends. After the first bout of limerence, everything changes.

The transcendent nature of limerent euphoria seems to make sense of the fairy tales, makes the concept of true love believable and credible. The rational knowledge that a perfect soulmate can't *really* exist is shaken, along with any belief that you are able to choose who you fall in love with. Limerence trumps everything you thought you knew. Once limerence has been experienced, the concept of love is reset, and mutual limerence becomes the standard to aspire to. The goal of attaining ecstatic union with the limerent object (LO) is the new measure of romantic triumph. Willingly, blissfully, you surrender.

There are many consequences to this personal transformation. Sometimes it is a cause of new agonies because the manic passion is not requited. Sometimes, though, the limerent desire is secured and the limerent begins a romantic relationship with their LO. Surely then, all their dreams will be fulfilled, their hopes made real, and they can look forward to enjoying their happily ever after just as the fairy tales, high school movies, and romantic comedies promised? After all, love conquers all!

Yeah, right. Some hope. Even if a limerent gets to form a pair bond with their lover, it turns out that the Shakespearean adage is true: The path of true love never did run smooth.

Limerence fades. Regardless of how spectacular the thrills are at the beginning of a relationship, expecting that euphoric connection to last more than a few months is unrealistic. Quite apart from how exhausting it would become, it doesn't make sense from an evolutionary perspective. Limerence is the drive to form a pair bond tight enough to result in conception; it has no real role in making it last. Once a child is born and has survived through the most vulnerable period of early life, familial bonding between parent and child takes over as the dominant force for reproductive security. After that, evolution is done with our romantic needs. Sustaining limerence would be wasteful.

That leaves our love-dazed limerent in a quandary, and with a lot of questions. What does the fading of limerence mean for the future of a relationship? When the fireworks have fizzled out, does that mean they are no longer "in love" with their partner? How important is chemistry compared to compatibility, and is it possible to keep both?

Making sense of love

Throughout this book I've built a case for limerence being a consequence of the reward, arousal, and bonding circuits of the brain being driven into a state of supernormal activation that resembles an addiction. By its nature, limerence seems so immoderate that it isn't surprising that many people view it as an unstable and defective manifestation of love. While I've argued that the capacity for limerence exists because it powerfully promotes a pair bond, a case could be made that it is instead a distortion of the healthy bonding process. Looked at from this perspective, limerence is sometimes described as "false" or "immature" love based as it is on emotional volatility.[1] It's all spectacle and no substance. Limerence can be selfish, jealous, deceptive (in misguided attempts to impress LO), and psychologically unstable.

Reasonably enough, these features of limerence are contrasted unfavorably with "real love," which is selfless, free of jealousy, honest, nurturing, and stable.

This disagreement in perspective arises, once again, from the problem of defining "love." While it is absolutely true that limerence lacks the qualities of stable affectional bonding, it's a misguided critique because limerence begins as a burst of explosive emotions at the very outset of the bonding experience. The selfless, deep bonds of affection that characterize lasting love cannot sincerely develop until a long period of mutual trust and intimacy has been established. In this context, the features of "real" love would in fact be just as false during the early stages of a relationship between two non-limerents. Developing deep feelings of selfless, unconditional love for your partner in the first few months of a relationship would also be a sign of an irregular romantic attachment.

The problem of definitions and mismatched meanings has bedeviled the study of romantic love since antiquity. We all have a personal experience of love that often conflicts with the attempts of others to draw universal lessons. Poets, philosophers, and scientists have tried to capture the essence of love but are thwarted by the many flavors in which it can be tasted.

For the Greeks, there were seven forms of love: *ludus* (playful love), *eros* (erotic love), *philia* (friendship love), *storge* (familial love), *pragma* (companionate love), *agape* (spiritual love), and *philautia* (self love). Sometimes an eighth form is included: *mania* (obsessive love). More modern researchers have built from these foundations to find other classifications, from color wheels to triangles and languages, but even sticking with the Greeks, it's easy to see how limerence could be interpreted within this framework in many different ways.[2]

Those who see limerence as unhealthy, jealous, and destructive would likely classify it as *mania*. Hysterical, unbalanced love. False love. Those who have experienced limerence personally know that the reality is more complex. Limerence involves many of the other types of love blended into a wholly distinct state of mind. While they would no doubt concede that *mania* captures some of the more distressing symptoms of limerence, there are also the enlivening aspects of the experience: erotic desire, a deep yearning for intimacy, and a sense of the numinous or transcendent power of connection.

Limerence doesn't really map neatly onto a specific "type" of love. It integrates many of the different forms, and which ones predominate depends on the individual limerent experience. Unrequited limerence that cannot be escaped can lead, distressingly, into *mania*, but mutual limerence is more likely to be a bonanza of *eros* (erotic), *philia* (friendship) and, maybe, eventually, *storge* (familial) love.

To make sense of this philosophical tangle, it is better to look at love not as separate types or forms, but to think instead about how love changes over time. Our experience of love develops as a relationship progresses. The phases of limerence (laid out in Chapter 2) illustrate this principle—the positive, exhilarating, life-enhancing thrills of limerence come first, and whether they deteriorate into the much more negative experiences of person addiction depends on the circumstances for both limerent and LO. Neither love nor limerence are static.

This switch in perspective is well illustrated by the idea of organizing the process of falling in love into sequential stages. The biological anthropologist Helen Fisher proposed a model of love that follows three stages: lust, attraction, and then attachment.[3] For a particular person falling in love, the blend of the different forms of love will shift over time. Early on, *eros* will dominate (lust), transitioning into a mix of *eros* and *philia* (lust combined with desire for emotional intimacy), and ultimately—ideally—a blend of *eros*, *philia*, and *storge* (adding affectional bonding to romantic attraction).

A metaphor is useful. The love life of plants is very different to ours, but there are some funny parallels. Flowers are the first, exuberant, showy attempt of plants to reproduce. They can be beautiful, but also a bit over the top. Flowers use insects or wind to try and secure cross-pollination, to become fertilized and to bear fruit, but it doesn't always work. Sometimes they just wither and die. In this metaphor, limerence is the flower and long-term love is the fruit. It makes no sense to dismiss a flower as a "false fruit" because it is not juicy or laden with seeds, just as it makes no sense to dismiss limerence as "false love" because it doesn't have the features of long-term affectional bonding. Limerence is the drive to form a bond. It's the urgent compulsion to gain intimacy with someone, and that may only be loosely related to the factors that determine whether the bond will last beyond the initial phase of euphoria. The flamboyance of a flower does not determine the chances of fertilization or the richness of the fruit.

To understand the relationship between limerence and long-term love, the better question to ask is not whether one form of love is superior or more "real" than another, but what determines whether the early, delirious phase of limerence can successfully transform into a long-lasting and healthy attachment.

Should you seek or avoid limerent objects?

Perhaps the most important factor in a successful transformation is the kind of person for whom you become limerent. Some limerent objects will be auspicious for stable bonding. If you consistently become limerent for people who are kind, generous, reciprocal, supportive, and make you feel good about yourself, then following the call of limerence increases your odds of forming a lasting, loving relationship.

Other LOs will be more neutral when it comes to predicting future success. If your glimmer is kindled by factors like long hair, a weird sense of humor, quiet dignity, or some charmingly quirky mannerism, then limerence won't correlate in any meaningful way with the factors that determine romantic compatibility. If you're drawn to tall, dark, and handsome, it's just as likely that they could be a good partner as a bad partner in the long run.

A third scenario is that the limerent and LO are incompatible—sometimes people just aren't right for each other—but the most challenging scenario is a troubled or troubling LO. If you are drawn to unavailable people, manipulative people, emotionally distant people, wounded souls that need to be rescued, or any of the other characters who promise an unpredictable and uncertain relationship ahead, then limerence is more of a warning signal to avoid than a beacon to head toward.

One of the most common mistakes that limerents make about romantic love is believing that the strength of their limerence determines how promising the relationship is. In reality, the intensity of limerence has almost no connection to whether a long-term relationship with an LO is practical or desirable.

Successful transformation of limerence into affectionate love depends critically on the character of both the limerent and LO, and their mutual compatibility after the most volatile period of chemistry has burned itself out. Limerence is a weak predictor for the viability in a relationship, and occasionally, it runs actively counter to the goal of forming an enduring pair bond. You have to know yourself well to understand which scenario is true for you.

> As someone who's only known dating in the context of the glimmer and the inevitable limerence that follows, I have no idea how to tell when it's right to try and take a relationship "to the next level" with someone in situations when there isn't that intense burst of feeling. —B

Navigating the transition from limerence to stable love

The loss of limerence—the transition back into an ordinary state of mind—can often be a crisis point for limerents. The passing of the infatuation phase of the relationship means facing a future based on affection and compatibility rather than thrills and chemistry. Most people tackle this critical decision by . . . hoping for the best. They assume that there will be enough romantic momentum left over from the explosive launch of limerence to carry them through the difficulties of navigating real life with another person. They just hope it will all come naturally.

Sometimes this assumption proves correct, and the pair bond remains strong beyond the fading of limerence. In other cases, it becomes clear that the emotional firework display had been blinding the couple to problems lurking in the shadows—romantic chemistry had been masking incompatibilities that become too big to ignore. The real art of relationship mastery is passing through this crux point wisely—being honest about how important ongoing chemistry is for you, but also being conscious of making intelligent choices. It's easy to go astray. Are you mistaking the end of limerence for the end of love? Should you abandon a good relationship to chase new limerent thrills? Are you settling for comfort because that's what you want, or are you avoiding decisions because of embarrassment or fear? Can you find a way to expertly blend the many forms that love can take?

Making decisions solely on the basis of chemistry or compatibility is risky. Uncritically pursuing the thrills of limerent chemistry risks bonding to someone fundamentally incompatible, or chasing one short-term bond after another, naively hoping that one day the limerence will last. Conversely, swearing off emotional excitement to choose pragmatic compatibility can lead to a slow, complacent slide into a sexless union—until the lack of fulfillment and stimulation make you vulnerable to regret and resentment (or new limerence).

The ideal scenario is to find a balance: someone who has lasting erotic appeal while also being compatible enough to mean everyday life is happy and harmonious. The feasibility of this Goldilocks scenario depends very strongly on understanding the basis of your own limerence. A clearer understanding of your personal "limerence avatar" will help you predict the consequences of being led by chemistry or compatibility—heart or head. The chance of finding lasting happiness depends on being honest with yourself about how your romantic temperament matches the universal predictors for relationship success.

Signs of a good relationship

Love comes in many forms and many phases: it transforms, it ebbs and flows, and it gets tangled up in contradictions. Is it possible to feel both excited and safe? Can we feel erotic desire for someone and nurse them when they are vulnerable? Can we enjoy both novelty and familiarity? It sometimes seems that we ask too much of love—we want to eat our cake and have it too.[4]

A solution to these apparent contradictions can be found in a state of creative tension—a dynamic but balanced conflict of forces. For love to be sustainable, there needs to be both chemistry and compatibility, a balance between emotional needs and intellectual good sense. Although I've been a bit snarky about our tendency to wing it on hope and instinct when it comes to love, intuition is enormously important when it comes to romantic relationships. Perhaps more than any other aspect of life, romantic attachment depends on emotional congruence. If it *feels* wrong, it almost certainly is wrong.

This is an important protection mechanism. It helps us to identify incompatibility—or even danger—and sense at a deep level that something isn't right. Anyone who has found themselves in a situation that escalates out of their control knows how forceful the stomach-lurch of emotional fear is. The problem for limerents is that the glimmer can be so intoxicatingly attractive, it can feel so right, that the instinct to seek ever closer connection is not questioned. The giddy thrills of limerence can even overpower those other instincts and emotional fears. Unfortunately, it's only after you've become addicted that you discover any incompatibilities, by which point, ironically, you are also committed to rationalizing them away. The desperate desire for the LO could even drive you to try to change yourself to resolve the problems, rather than face the possibility that the LO is a bad match.

> I've had some very lucky escapes (which didn't feel lucky at the time) from what would have been awful relationships. And I threw away good relationships with kind and good partners. —CC

Once you learn that limerence can distort your intuition, you begin to doubt your feelings as a guide to finding long-term love—especially if you are serially attracted to incompatible LOs. This is when the counterbalancing force of wisdom can be used to improve decision-making. The overall goal is to hold off on full surrender to limerent ecstasy until you have done some due diligence about what exactly it is you are responding to. You need an unbiased way to be sure that you aren't becoming too lovestruck, and the answer is to use your rational brain—your executive center that learns from past mistakes and spots patterns and dangers—to set guardrails along the edges of your romantic adventures.

Trying to sustain a relationship with an incompatible LO is futile. Fundamental clashes of moral values, life goals, and personality are not going to be overcome without self-negation or constant emotional friction. If they love to socialize and you hate it, trying to fake a "soul of the party" persona won't work out well for either of you. If they are competitive, outspoken, and independent, but you are compassionate, shy, and generous, you will more likely cause each other continual stress than balance each other out. If you are orthodox and devout, and they are an atheist, there will be trouble ahead. It's unlikely to end well.

Fortunately, applying wisdom is more straightforward than unravelling the psychological tangle of emotional decision-making. There are some core features that all good relationships need for any hope of success:

- **Mutual respect:** If you lose respect for your partner, it's very hard to recover the relationship. Why would you want to bond to someone you disdain? Similarly, if they treat you with disrespect, it is corrosive to your psychological and physical health. It's better to walk away than to slowly diminish as they grind away your self-confidence.
- **Mutual affection:** A close second. You need to care for each other, want the best for each other, and love each other. This is usually expressed through physical contact. The importance of sex is debatable, but hugs, kisses, and affectionate touch are essential for most people.[5]
- **Trust:** For a partnership to work you both have to feel safe. Equally, you need to have freedom to do your own thing, have independent interests, and not feel that the relationship is precarious if you don't get things exactly right all the time.

- **Intimacy:** You should feel able to share your thoughts, feelings, and emotional vulnerabilities, and receive loving support in return. Equally, you should give that support when needed and protect your partner's privacy. The bond between you should feel special and unique.
- **Honest communication:** You have to feel able to say what you really think and feel and not fear judgment or scorn. Equally, you should avoid keeping secrets or concealing your true desires through a misplaced belief that always giving your partner what they want will make you both happier.
- **Common purpose:** Relationships work best when you have shared ideals, shared beliefs, and common purpose. If you disagree on important issues (e.g., sex, money, children), it takes more work to reach a consensus. All relationships involve compromise, but constantly battling over the fundamentals makes for a wearisome life.[6]

These principles are the bedrock of successful relationships, the factors that determine compatibility. Fortunately, they are also skills that can be learned and used to improve a relationship that has started to stagnate—you can cultivate trust and intimacy and improve the quality of your communication. Making this effort and developing these skills is the practical wisdom part of making love work.

Creative tension can add some buzz to the relationship. Although your fundamental values should align, superficial incompatibilities in tastes, vocation, and habits can be very useful. Indeed, one of the most gratifying and life-enhancing aspects of a good relationship is how your partner helps you grow. The ideal scenario is to find someone who is different enough to be interesting, but similar enough to be compatible (with a bit of compromising). The absolute sweet spot is when the compromising actually ends up enhancing both of your lives.

Relationships work best when two people are working side by side to build a life they both desire, while still having enough differences to be interesting. That's the state of dynamic, creative tension that seems to magically foil the contradictions: independent but partners, committed but autonomous, together but self-determining.

Everyone's Goldilocks scenario will be different. Once you understand your triggers and vulnerabilities it becomes possible to find the right balance between intuitive attraction and protective wisdom. Some limerents should avoid LOs because they promise incompatibility and heartache. Some limerents should actively seek LOs because they are drawn toward people who are good matches for lasting love. Most limerents should aim somewhere in the middle: open to the hunger for limerent excitement, but cautious about overindulging it.

Mastering that ability to balance forces, to walk the emotional ridge, is the best hope for finding lasting happiness. Limerence will pass. Love will remain. By taking care on the way into limerence, you stand a better chance of passing through it and moving onward into a love that endures.

CHAPTER 15
LIMERENCE AND INFIDELITY

"I love you but I'm not in love with you"

Limerence can be the prelude to successful, affectional bonding that transforms into long-term love. Unfortunately, in defiance of the love stories that promise a happily ever after, limerence isn't always done with us yet.

Even those lucky souls who succeed in navigating their way from limerence into a happy long-term relationship can sometimes face a rude awakening. They become aware of their limerent nature when it takes them by surprise. Secure bonding in a healthy relationship is not always sufficient protection against the intrusion of new limerence into a calm and well-managed life. It can sometimes gatecrash a stable relationship, uninvited and unlooked for.

For people who had only previously known limerence as the giddy elation that marks the beginning of love, its reemergence when already in a committed, loving relationship can be quite a shock. It shakes the established pair bond, upends old certainties, and challenges long-held convictions. It is a test of moral fiber.

At best, new limerence causes deep, personal reflection into the nature of love and the status of the existing relationship; at worst, it is a wrecking ball that can destroy families. Limerence can lead to adultery.

Why limerents are vulnerable to affairs

There are lots of reasons why affairs happen. Some people are selfish and want to indulge in opportunistic and promiscuous behavior while also having the security of an unaware partner. Some get a sexual kick from deceit. Some hunger for novelty. Some regret their marriage. Some seek constant validation from the romantic interest of others. Some have found themselves in relationships where they feel sexually or emotionally neglected to the point where romantic interest from someone else is impossible to resist. There are lots of reasons, but the limerents I hear from most frequently have simply fallen into a pattern of settled complacency, enjoying the security of being able to take life for granted.

Most relationships of long standing can get a bit dull. Once companionship overtakes erotic excitement as the dominant expression of love in a relationship, a hidden vulnerability can grow.[1] Life is full of stresses and demands, compromises, sacrifices, everyday toil.

> *Classic midlife episode here with an LO 14 years younger than me. I think some of the attraction is that LO reminds me of my wife in our early days together. Before parenthood and the pressure of midlife began to prise us apart. LO offers fresh, fun conversations and it's nice to talk to someone who seems interested in you rather than whether you've put the rubbish out. It's escapism really and I'm probably selfish for wanting and enjoying the attention. —R*

Unfortunately, once limerence begins, unthinking, instinctive behavior can carry the complacent limerent along a predictable path, past a series of tipping points, each of which reinforces the addiction to the new limerent object (LO). This is not usually intentional or devious. At every stage, the moral transgression seems small and easily rationalized, but like compound interest the consequences multiply quickly. Several decisive thresholds are crossed in turn:

1. **The glimmer.** The start of it all. The moment of recognition that you've met an LO.
2. **The first flirt.** Usually a subconscious reaction to the glimmer. The point at which your attraction to LO reveals itself.

3. **The establishing flirt.** The point at which you flirt with more intent to try and find out whether they are attracted to you too.
4. **The fantasy affair.** The rumination begins. Enough positive feedback has given you the hope of reciprocation and you immerse yourself in reverie. You fantasize about being with them, and entertain the idea (not seriously—just a little self-indulgent fantasy) of what an affair with them might be like.
5. **The first moment of "oversharing."** A step beyond normal friendship. You share an emotionally intimate experience or thought, and hope that they will hear you, empathize with you, and respond with further intimacy of their own.
6. **The first moment of deceit.** This is the most morally consequential tipping point. The first time you lie to someone else about your feelings for the LO, or lie about your plans or commitments to get more time with the LO. The first time you prioritize limerent reward over personal integrity.
7. **An emotional affair.** An established pattern of sharing thoughts and feelings that you know deep down should really be reserved for your partner. The affair can deepen further as you start to discuss love, sex, and the problems and disappointments of your existing relationship.
8. **Disclosure to LO.** A declaration of love. At this point, there is no deniability, no rowing back, no easy deescalation. You have declared yourself to the LO and pushed your partner into the role of cuckold.
9. **Sexual contact.** Physical contact or lewd photos intended for sexual gratification—kissing, caressing, sexting, or actual sex. Outright adultery.
10. **A physical affair.** An established sexual affair with the LO that carries on in secret.

The order of these tipping points may vary, and the time taken to move from one to the next will vary too. Some limerents may rush all the way to physical affair, some may teeter on the edge of a tipping point they know they cannot ethically cross, hoping the limerence subsides before their resolve crumbles. Unfortunately, most limerents don't realize the danger they are in until they have already crossed too many lines and are deeply compromised and trapped. It's only once they are fully ensnared that the limerent starts to ask some pertinent questions: How did I end up here? What the hell am I doing? How do I get out of this mess?

Coping with cognitive dissonance

Once it's established, the emotional storm of limerence crashes against the social barriers of duty, obligation, integrity, possibly even religious vows. There is a simple, direct problem—there is no honorable way to satisfy the relentless limerent craving. The limerent feelings cannot be openly expressed and so interactions with the LO are characterized by hints, ambiguity, plausible deniability, and deceit. This results in a chaotic mix of hope, uncertainty, guilt, excitement, and confusion—all very potent limerence reinforcers.

The fact that such an emotionally demanding experience as limerence has to be kept hidden means it can only be processed internally. There is no outlet for all that pent-up energy, no one to share the consuming obsession with, no way to figure out what's going on except through the internal mental cycles of rumination, reverie, and overanalysis that inevitably transform into intrusive thoughts. Secret limerence cannot be safely discharged or neutralized. Choking it down creates an emotional blockage.

The failure to manage limerent feelings, and the conflict between desire and duty, causes cognitive dissonance.[2] Your brain is trying to reconcile contradictory ideas, to process a mismatch between the urgent, desperate cravings of limerence and your stated values: *I love my partner, but I'm "in love" with someone else. I am a good person, but am being disloyal. I want to start a love affair with LO while also keeping my family.*

If forced to confess their conflicting desires openly, most limerents recognize that they are ludicrous.

> *I wanted something that was a complete fantasy. What I wanted was to have a secret affair with LO, have the time of my life,*

then both of us mutually fall out of love, and then go back to our significant others as if nothing had happened and our primary loves fully intact if not stronger! Talk about delusions! —J

Cognitive dissonance is psychologically distressing—a mental toll that needs to be relieved. There are really only two options available for relief: (1) accept that you have made poor choices, resist the siren song of limerence, and recommit to the relationship, or (2) find ways to justify your desire to be unfaithful. Unfortunately, there are plenty of handy rationalizations that a subconscious turncoat, addled by limerence, can conjure up:

This is True Love so different rules apply.
This is bigger than both of us.
Monogamy is unnatural.
Lots of people have affairs.
My LO seduced me, I am their helpless pawn.
I always do the right thing, it's time to live a little.

Trying to resolve conflicting desires while sustaining a self-image as a good person usually results in casting around for such justifications. We think in stories, which means the narrative that best explains the situation while protecting the ego of the limerent will be the most attractive option. After all, it can always be rationalized later, especially if it's coupled to the addict's defiant boast:

I can handle it. I can stop anytime I like.

Hiding in the fog

Limerence is so mentally disruptive that clear thinking becomes impossible. Everything seems open to question. Conflicted limerents often try to reimagine life from another perspective that could somehow allow them to have that impossible, selfish dream of a consequence-free affair with their LO. From this crooked vantage point, it's also likely that their assessment of the old relationship will be warped. This tendency will be heightened by the fact that the pair-bonding instinct is inherently exclusionary—if you are enjoying exhilarating reward as the bond with LO strengthens, it's inevitable that previous bonds will weaken. When you are limerent for a specific person, any competing romantic attachments create conflict and will be subconsciously felt as a threat to the irresistible new prize.

For limerents, the primary drive for infidelity is rarely sexual novelty; it's pair bonding. The hackneyed claim of the cheater that it was just a moment of madness ("I don't know what came over me") is even less convincing when it comes to the flowering of limerence over time—by the time the limerent has passed enough of the tipping points to become captured, a lot of moments of madness have come and gone. This can cause a defensiveness and deliberate attempts to blur the boundaries of propriety. The limerent retreats into a fog of ambiguity. One area of uncertainty, which is a legitimate area of debate, is what constitutes infidelity.

For some people, disloyal thoughts are betrayal enough. For others, words have to be spoken—flirty texts or oversharing of personal feelings or secrets—to move the disloyalty from a private battle of conscience within the mind of the limerent to an open act of unfaithfulness. The moment limerent feelings are vocalized, they are out in the world causing repercussions. More often, though, infidelity is judged as having to go beyond words to deeds—taking specific actions that reveal divided loyalties. Overt acts of affection, overfamiliarity, private dinners together, any behavior that breaks the social conventions expected for a monogamous union can be considered a sign of betrayal.

One of the most sensitive areas for disagreement is the relative importance of physical versus emotional intimacy. For some, sexual infidelity is as painful a betrayal as they can imagine—a red line that has no ambiguity. For others, "meaningless" opportunistic sex is something that can be forgiven, or at least overcome, as long as their partner has not fallen in love with the other party. Instead, the emotional bond is what matters most when it comes to feelings of betrayal.[3] This perspective leads to the concept of an "emotional affair" where a chaste romantic attachment is formed with someone outside the existing pair bond. It's as though you have a second partner—a deep emotional connection based on affection and companionate love—even if it doesn't involve any actual hanky-panky.

To many people, this behavior is self-evidently unfaithful, but others dismiss the whole notion of an emotional affair as absurd.[4] Sharing secrets or intimacy is not seen as a violation of a monogamous relationship, because friends can be emotionally intimate—indeed, it can be reasonably argued that this is a healthy and normal aspect of friendship, and the gender or sexual orientation of the friend is entirely immaterial to the situation. Stigmatizing such bonds with close friends is taken as unreasonable jealousy and possessiveness. To expect one partner to be a lifelong lover, confidante, carer, and domestic companion is too much to ask of anyone.[5]

Limerents often seek to exploit this lack of clarity, but it is usually a deliberate evasion. The spectacular quality of the limerent craving for an LO is so emotionally charged that claiming they are merely a close friend is a brazenly self-serving lie. While there is certainly some haziness about the nature and severity of different forms of infidelity, if you find yourself looking for legalistic definitions, or seeking specific exemptions or loopholes that give you more access to an LO, you are creating rationalizations to excuse your person addiction. Such willful self-delusion is a powerful force in driving unwise limerence into infidelity.

Escaping the fog

There's a simple way to dispel the fog of uncertainty that clouds the details around relationship ethics. Once you have passed the first moment of deceit, you are deliberately concealing your motives and actively moving toward an affair. No amount of fog can hide you from that truth.

Starting an affair is a dangerous response to limerence. It will not solve any of the problems that may have existed in the long-term relationship, but it will create many new ones.

Infidelity also devalues your character. When you resolve the cognitive dissonance of disloyalty by compromising your morality, it has profound consequences for your self-image and self-esteem. Infidelity emphasizes the lowest aspects of your personality—most obviously lying and cheating. Deceit is needed to sustain an affair, and that makes dishonesty the foundation of your new identity. You multiply your problems and destroy your integrity. Not an ideal outcome.

So, how can a limerent who has crossed so many tipping points begin to repair the damage and escape this downward spiral? The only way out of this trap is to tell yourself the truth about the situation. Your choices led you to this predicament. Whatever past circumstances in your relationship made you vulnerable to new limerence, you now need to balance all emotional, personal, family, and social or professional demands, and decide upon the proper response. That requires self-awareness and honesty. Like *Frankenstein*, unthinking obsession led you to create a monster that you can no longer control and that threatens your old life. You cannot ignore it, or run away from it forever. You have to face it and take responsibility for your actions.

So far, we have focused on the issue of infidelity entirely from the limerent's point of view. This is another big part of the problem. At some point, if the limerent has overstepped too many of the tipping points, a crisis will come. The previously oblivious partner will find out—ideally because the limerent confesses, but often because the partner discovers the secret themselves. At that point, the monster is loose.

It's important to appreciate just how destructive infidelity is to the betrayed partner's psychological health. For the unfaithful limerent, there is an illusory compartmentalization. While they have been behaving as though everything is fine, their old life had carried on exactly as before. Their "side activity" is often totally separate in their mind—something that they do in addition to their primary relationship. So, surely, if they just stop doing it, then everything goes back to normal? What's the problem if no one finds out? In fact, isn't it more considerate to keep the affair secret to spare their partner pain?

For the partner, it's utterly different. They thought they were living one life, but in fact the person they trusted most has been making a fool of them. If the limerent affair has passed beyond the tipping point of disclosure, a central truth about the relationship has been shared with the LO, but not the partner. This humiliation is something that can never be erased entirely. No statute of limitation applies. No matter when the partner finds out, the discovery will undermine their whole mental model of the world. In a moment, they are confronted with a new reality: they can't trust you, all their past memories are suspect, all your promises are potential lies, all their future plans are in jeopardy.

What other massive things have you kept from them? Who else is involved in their life that they didn't choose to have in their world and don't know about? What is going to happen to their family? Who do they go to for support now?

> *It was the singularly most distressing and disturbing episode of my entire life. The initial shock, on finding out, lasted a few days. I couldn't eat, sleep or think, I suppose numbness covers it. I remember wanting to be curled up on the ground, in a room, on my own. The pain seemed almost physical. —K*

It's not surprising that people have nervous breakdowns over this.[6] You should not try to sanitize the consequences of infidelity.

What does limerence mean for a relationship?

Whatever the state of your existing relationship, limerence can potentially reemerge at any time. All that's required is you meeting someone who causes the glimmer for you, and unheedingly following your instincts past that series of tipping points. Just as the inevitable fading of limerence after a bond has been secured does not mean that love is over, the fact that you can feel limerence for someone new does not mean there is necessarily anything seriously wrong with the existing relationship.

One thing that limerence does mean for a relationship is that you cannot keep complacently carrying on with business as usual. If you have betrayed your partner, it will force some harrowing conversations out into the open. This is when the real reckoning begins, when the strengths and weaknesses of your relationship are laid bare. There are only two practical options available: end the relationship or find a path to reconciliation. In the cases where either the limerent or the betrayed partner were unhappy before the limerence set in, because of genuine incompatibilities, a dignified breakup is probably the best option. In the more common case where the relationship was good but imperfect, you will have to negotiate a way forward together.

The only real hope for reconciliation is for the cheating limerent to take responsibility for the situation they created and radically change their approach to communication and dispute resolution within the relationship. Instead of thinking of the limerence as a personal battle, a choice to be made between two possible futures, it should now be treated as a problem that needs to be jointly solved. If you find yourself in this situation, "you and your partner against the problem" is the better mindset, not "how do I choose?"

One of the few positive outcomes that can be rebuilt from the rubble of betrayal is a more durable foundation to the relationship, based on more open and honest communication. What do you really want out of the relationship? Have you been ignoring some serious problems for too long? Can you work together as a team to envision a better future?

It is difficult work, with pitfalls aplenty. The betrayed partner may defer their own needs and accept blame onto themselves to gain some measure of control over the situation. The limerent may be tempted to seize this opportunity to save face and assuage their guilt. Both have to work hard to be honest and avoid such superficial solutions that only put off the difficult decisions.

It's uncomfortable to discover that you created a monster, and natural to want to excuse yourself or downplay the seriousness of your misdeeds, but the anger, doubt, and fear expressed by your partner is understandable, and you need to listen with patience and emotional forbearance. Instead of damage limitation, your primary goal should be to rebuild trust by earning it.

Trust comes from honest communication. That means no more minimizing the seriousness of the situation, no more "white lies," no more evasions, no more hiding in the fog. It is important to be sensitive about how and when you disclose the details of any betrayals, but it is also important to be transparent so that your partner can begin to believe that you are being truly open, rather than drip-feeding them the bad news bit by bit to try and dilute the outrage. It's a delicate business developing the habit of open communication while both of you are dealing with churning emotions within, but you have to try if you are going to emerge from the hole you've been digging, and start climbing back toward the light.

You may find at the end of this process of painful review that the relationship cannot be salvaged. Perhaps you've crossed lines that cannot be forgiven, perhaps there are incompatibilities too big to resolve, or maybe you have just grown apart and the limerence was a byproduct of that alienation. Or maybe it is possible to repair a relationship that was fundamentally good before limerence intruded to disrupt everything. Regardless, you will never get to that truth without honestly communicating with your partner as an equal; the other half of a team of two.

It is important to gain clarity about what limerence means for a relationship, and to work together to make good decisions about the future, but there is still a fundamental issue that needs to be addressed. You can decide that you want your limerence to end, and to recommit to your existing relationship, but that decision—in itself—won't turn off your limerence. To really take control of your life, you'll need to learn how to get rid of unwanted limerence after it's set in, and how to protect yourself against future episodes.

That's the challenge that we cover in the last section of the book.

PART 3
RECOVERING FROM LIMERENCE

CHAPTER 16
FINDING BALANCE

Can the ecstatic union last?

I hate how limerence makes me feel but the prospect of not having it terrifies me a little bit. —R

Limerence, it is fair to say, is both a blessing and a curse. Most limerents have mixed feelings about their capacity to undergo the mental transformation of limerence and the benefits and costs that it brings. At the most basic level, the euphoria is amazing—that's why it is so intoxicating, so powerful a temptation, and so difficult to resist once the habit is established. The reward offered by limerence dwarfs most other sources of pleasure in life. Successful pair bonding is exhilarating; joyous. Limerence undoubtedly adds richness to life when it is free to be safely indulged—perhaps most obviously when you are young and single and looking for love.

Countering this, there is a clear risk that limerence can tip over into misery. The pain of rejection, the psychic assault of intrusive thoughts, the anxiety, the emotional instability can all be so debilitating that any early thrills seem hollow in retrospect. Beyond the emotional costs, languishing in "limerence limbo" also brings the opportunity cost of all those wasted hours that could have been spent enjoying a healthy, productive life focused on meaningful goals.

The costs to other people can also be steep. As we discussed in the last chapter, when limerence is ungoverned it can destroy existing relationships and destabilize families. Clearly there are times when being able to resist limerence is essential to well-being.

That's what this final section of the book is all about: developing the skills needed to manage limerence, to balance the good and the bad, and to make informed and purposeful choices. How to make limerence work for us, rather than letting it lead us by the nose into trouble. Learning how to thrive as a limerent.

Life as a limerent

Out of curiosity, I once posed a question to the community on the Living with Limerence website that addressed the tension between the good and bad aspects of limerence, the joy and the pain.

Would you turn off your limerence if you could?

The answers illustrate the core emotional conflict:

> *I wouldn't turn it off. It's a part of my personality, or has been. It gave me such poignant and wonderful moments and memories and let me experience life in beautiful colors. I just wish I could have handled it better.* —M

> *I would rather turn it off! It has not contributed much to my life, on the contrary, it brought much unnecessary pain and suffering I didn't need. It was a distraction from my quiet sweet life, which confused and worried me much, a waste of my precious energy and time.* —M

> *I know I SHOULD turn it off but I don't think I would.... It makes me feel alive, even though LO probably thinks I'm a bit odd!* —O

> *[Limerence] has been a bittersweet experience, that's how I can sum it up. The highs are awesome, one is literally on cloud nine. The lows, on the other hand, suck big time.* —AD

> *Would I turn it off if I could? Yes, yes I would. BUTTTTTT It certainly was a colorful time in my life. And it drove me to therapy. I lived most of my life in beige, not happy, not sad, just going through the motions. AI-like. Limerence kicked the crap out of that! lol* —A

It's an academic question, of course. There is no "off switch" for limerence that can be flipped. Limerence is a built-in drive, part of the makeup of those of us who experience it, not a disease to be cured, a sign of emotional immaturity or a defect of character.

Rather than attempting to eliminate it, a far more constructive approach is to accept it as part of who you are and find ways to integrate it into life in an effective and healthy way. Limerence can bring energy, creativity, joy, and self-knowledge, and those positive forces can be directed toward productive ends. The fact that limerence can turn pathological in the wrong set of circumstances shouldn't be a cause to reject the phenomenon wholesale as a negative life experience. Limerence is thrilling and energizing. Turning it off would be like willingly sedating yourself—maybe necessary in an emergency, but not a long-term solution. Limerence is like fire— both useful and dangerous; a volatile force to be governed.

Like so much in life, moderation is key. The skill lies in learning enough about how limerence works generally, and understanding your own personal triggers specifically, that you can recognize the difference between exciting romantic opportunities and emotionally destabilizing threats. To push the metaphor—we need to learn the emotional bushcraft needed to keep you warm and cozy without starting a forest fire.

A good starting point for developing those skills is to weigh up the benefits and costs of limerence objectively, and figure out a balance that works well for you.

Energy boost

The euphoria stage of limerence is electrifying. The neurochemical high is unmatched. In the early stages of infatuation, limerents feel buoyant, supercharged with energy, and have the mindset that anything seems possible. The world seems vibrant and full of promise. Many limerents report feeling better disposed toward people and society in general when they are limerent, as they find it easier to be optimistic and are motivated to be active and engaged with the world.

As explained in Chapter 3, this is a real, neurophysiological phenomenon. The reward-seeking drive combined with physiological arousal supercharges motivation, drive, and cognitive performance. Our thoughts are literally quickened. Everything becomes more stimulating, and riding this wave of enthusiasm can help us get things done if we channel the energy into practical ends. At the simplest level, doing things that impress a limerent object (LO) can become a major spur to activity. If you believe that your LO will notice and admire a personal achievement of some sort—intellectual, professional, sporting, or artistic—putting in the hours needed to excel will seem less laborious and more rewarding. It feels good to be in this state. It makes sense to enjoy it, capitalize on it, and get some worthwhile projects done while you're buzzing with vitality.

One of the best outlets for the restless energy that limerence brings is creativity. How many artists have turned their LOs into a muse? We already covered the many examples of limerence in literature in Chapter 8, and that was just the most obvious and unambiguous examples. Even when limerence is not an overt theme of art or story, it's often there, lurking in the background. How many songs, poems, and paintings have in their original motives the urge to capture rapture? To communicate through unique creation the joy, the exquisite agony, of being spellbound by a beloved? The drive to try and transmute the extraordinary bliss of limerence into a concrete form as art is an attempt to embody passionate love. Think how impoverished the world would be without that outpouring of romantic expression.

Of course, our personal creative endeavors may not be quite so elevated as the great symphonies, sculptures, or literary masterworks of history, but limerence gives even the everyday soul a taste of majesty. We may feel moved to pick up a pencil or brush for the first time in years, to compose a love song, to write a love letter (even if it will never be sent). We might even commit poetry.

The desire to give substance to the upwelling of limerent emotions is a positive force—uncynical, genuine, aesthetic, fulfilling and worth embracing.

I was able to write a 242-page novel using one of my LOs as a muse (although I'll admit the revision process is difficult while currently in the midst of a whole new obsession). —N

I'd have to argue that limerence has contributed substantially to my art (not necessarily my happiness, but I suppose if success in art is cause for happiness then it has indirectly contributed to my happiness). As painful and annoying as limerence is, I wouldn't be where I am creatively without it. —C

Self-improvement

Another way to make use of the jubilant energy of early limerence is to focus the creative impulse onto self-improvement. Impressing an LO is a great motivator for getting fit, sharpening up your style, and improving your social skills. Most limerents make the reasonable calculation that their LO will be more attracted to a fit, smart, charismatic, and engaging suitor than a tired, disheveled bore. It can be the impetus needed to finally break the bad habits of poor sleep, exercise, and diet with which most of us struggle. Although the motive might be a somewhat shallow attempt to make yourself more desirable, the outcome for health and well-being is good regardless. The ideal scenario, even though you've launched this lifestyle makeover with the goal to impress, is that you manage to turn it into a lasting benefit by sustaining the good habits in the long term

As well as the benefits of improved physical health, limerence can also stimulate personal renewal. Limerence transforms your inner world and upends the status quo. It's the ultimate wake-up call. It makes you question old assumptions, limiting beliefs and life priorities, and so forces you into a period of self-examination. This experience is obviously psychologically destabilizing and can be treacherous if mishandled. Personal growth through honest reexamination of your nature, your choices, and your purpose is positive, but rewriting the history of your life to rationalize why you should abandon everything for your LO is not. Often, the motivating force for personal transformation is strongest when limerence progresses from giddy excitement to the negative grind of fixation and addiction. The emotional deterioration that follows the passing of euphoria and the ascendancy of distress can cause a crisis of confidence that cannot be ignored.

> Yes, physically it's been a great positive for me, I've lost weight and look the best I've ever done, my energy levels are through the roof and I've never been so productive in my entire life. I am like the energizer bunny on steroids! But limerence has also caused me copious anxiety, sleepless nights, stress, mind bending crazy [...] thoughts, immense sadness of what will never be, internal conflict of my values and integrity, yearning for an LO [who's] unavailable, loneliness, neglecting my wonderful Significant Other and family, two stolen years of my life in ruminations I'll never get back, anger, despair, embarrassment, shame, guilt, thoughts (although fleeting) of what's the point of even continuing to live if this is how I am going to feel indefinitely, and endless rivers of gut wrenching tears. —LA

If we are sufficiently reflective, the harrowing nature of person addiction can help us to drop self-serving rationalizations and confront an uncomfortable reality. We all have ego-protecting pretensions that we use to maintain our self-image, to excuse our bad choices, and to justify indulging in risky limerent behavior. *We're just friends. I can stop anytime. It's just a bit of fun.* Facing that sort of willful self-delusion and scrutinizing yourself honestly can bring sobering insights—it's like taking a cold shower. Unravelling why you were vulnerable to limerence at a particular time and why you were attracted to a particular LO, can teach you a lot about your nature, your psychological triggers, and how your past has shaped your present. That can lead to breakthroughs in self-awareness that transform your life.

Professional therapy can be a valuable part of this process, although there are risks as well as benefits as we'll discuss in Chapter 20. Regardless of how you approach it, honest analysis of yourself and your behavior is invaluable.

> *Attempting to get over my limerence changed my entire life and way of thinking. I realized why I attached to people and became needy and clingy. And ended up learning all about self-love, and that I'm enough, and that being alone isn't a bad thing at all. My attachment style changed and went from anxious/preoccupied to secure. —R*

Spending the time needed to understand the kinds of people that cause the glimmer for you and why can allow you to better manage your emotional response to potential LOs and make better decisions at an earlier stage about whether to embrace or resist the limerent pull of attraction. Without the self-development triggered by a bad bout of limerence, many limerents continue to make impulsive, emotional decisions that worsen the problem.

> *I had this kind of background sense that I was not in control anymore, but would always find an excuse to ignore it. Every time I decided I needed to pull myself together I knew I didn't really mean it. The next time she smiled at me, I would do whatever she asked. —T*

The personal insight that comes from understanding how your own history and choices led you into limerence is a way of salvaging some good from a bad episode of limerence. It can protect you against manipulative or unhealthy LOs and help you identify people who may be a good long-term match. Knowing and accepting your own temperament helps you make wiser choices about romance.

Meeting your match

The final benefit of limerence is in fact the most obvious: it promotes pair bonding. Forming a long-term, committed, loving relationship is an abiding source of happiness and fulfillment for most people.[1] Limerence is a force for creating children and building families. When focused on someone who is a good partner, it can be the joyous prelude to long-term affectional bonding. The problems come when limerence is misdirected onto someone with whom you cannot form a healthy bond.

If you develop the self-awareness and discernment to know when it is safe to embrace the glimmer, it's possible to sort of *hold your limerent energy in reserve* until it is ready to be unleashed. That wisdom allows you to choose when to go all-in on a romantic adventure, or when to hold back and protect yourself. Limerence can greatly enrich life, as long as it is deployed with care and used mindfully. That's why so many limerents would not want to turn off their limerent circuits even if they could—the extraordinary natural high is so invigorating and life-affirming that closing yourself off to it entirely would be a bitter abstinence. Such stringency is only necessary if every LO you encounter is harmful for you, or if you are already in a committed loving relationship. Limerence is not always a sign that a relationship is unhealthy by definition. The promise of a more successful future bond that begins in limerence and transforms into lasting love is worth holding onto if you are looking for love.

Living with limerence means finding the right balance between the benefits and the costs, and that calculation is going to change depending on where you are in your life. For those times when the costs are too high—when the limerence is unrequited, the LO is toxic, or you are already committed—it is vital that you have a clear idea of how to prevent limerence from escalating and derailing your life. It pays to be prepared for the next time you feel the glimmer for someone inappropriate or unavailable, to take control of your capacity for limerence, and act intelligently.

To achieve that goal, it's necessary to understand limerence, the neuroscience that drives it, the habits that reinforce it, and the mysterious alchemy between limerent and LO that cultivates it, but it's also essential to know how to put all that theory into practice.

There are times when it's invaluable to know how to get rid of limerence.

CHAPTER 17
HOW TO GET RID OF LIMERENCE

First solve the crisis, then figure out why it happened

There are many times in life when limerence can be a problem. Perhaps you have fallen for someone who is unavailable or disreputable, and so getting tangled up with them is an emotional train wreck. Perhaps you've already committed to someone else and are building a life together, and a new episode of limerence threatens that future. Sometimes the timing just isn't right, and limerence becomes a drag on your productivity, a waste of mental energy and a distraction from more important goals. Whatever the circumstances, it's obvious that there will be lots of situations in which wild, dizzying, uncontrollable infatuation is inconvenient. Learning how to get rid of unwanted limerence is therefore a life-changing skill.

Developing that skill depends on solving two big problems. The first is universal to all limerents: Limerence emerges from fundamental systems of the brain that can't be switched off. The second problem is personal: We all have our own, unique limerence triggers. These two problems require different solutions, but they are also interconnected. The neural circuits of the brain give rise to limerence, but our individual histories have programmed them to be sensitive to particular people.

If you find yourself in the middle of a destructive episode of limerence, you must confront each of these two problems in turn. To escape the altered mental state of limerence, you need to *deprogram* yourself, to break the habits that reinforce addiction and use the knowledge of how the neuroscience of limerence works to train yourself out of limerence for a particular person. This first stage is the immediate priority—getting out of the mental state of romantic obsession and reestablishing emotional equilibrium. After that, you also need to do the slower work of understanding how your past has shaped your own personal propensity for limerence. Both stages are needed for lasting recovery: first, deal with the crisis, then learn from it. Fortunately, there are several strategies and tactics that can help.

Over the remaining chapters of the book, we'll go deep into the methods that can reverse the habits of mind and behavior that reinforce limerence—reprogramming the neural systems that sustain the altered mental state—and the ways to identify and master your own triggers and psychological vulnerabilities. In this first of the "recovery" chapters, we lay out the scale of the challenge and the key principles that form the foundations of recovery. Managing limerence and integrating it into life is the ultimate goal. By combining behavioral change with personal analysis, you can learn to control limerence, rather than letting limerence control you.

The recovery mindset

An important first step, before delving into the specifics of strategies, tactics, and psychological hacks, is to consider a foundational principle: adopting a "recovery mindset." Developing the right frame of mind at the outset will make it more likely that the techniques for recovery will bear fruit. The goal is to look at the problem from a perspective that helps you frame the limerence experience in the correct context.

This principle is ancient, cross-cultural, and universal: How you think about a problem affects how you feel about the problem. Shakespeare captured it in *Hamlet*:

> There is nothing either good or bad, but thinking makes it so.

It is also a founding principle of cognitive behavioral therapy (CBT), as articulated by one of the pioneers of that therapeutic approach, Aaron Beck:

> *People's emotions and behaviors are influenced by their perceptions of events. It is not a situation in and of itself that determines what people feel but rather the way in which they construe a situation.*[1]

A recovery mindset, therefore, is an attempt to construe the situation in a useful way, to approach it as a problem to be solved, to recognize that limerence is a self-reinforcing mental state that can be escaped from, and to behave in accordance with that perception. This contrasts with a mindset that sees limerence as a divine blessing, evidence of True Love, a prize that must be forgone for reasons of duty, or an irresistible force to which you are a slave. For the recovery mindset, ending the limerence is the path to freedom, to renewal, to restoring yourself to a healthy and purposeful life. For the alternative mindsets, ending the limerence is a burden, a loss that will diminish and impoverish your life. It's obvious which of these two points of view will help you escape.

Adopting a recovery mindset promotes what is known by psychologists as an internal locus of control.[2] This means believing that you have the power to improve your life by the actions that you take, and that it is possible to make progress even in the face of outside pressures that might work against you. In contrast, an external locus of control means believing you are at the mercy of those external forces, and that they will determine your fate. Your efforts could be swept away at any moment by the intrusion of more powerful people, institutions, or forces that you cannot control. Why try if it is likely to be futile?

Unfortunately, limerence can lead to just such a sense of powerlessness. The emotional turmoil is so far outside the range of normal life experience that it's almost defined by a sense of overwhelm.

> *I think the powerlessness of a situation like this is the worst feeling. You feel that your emotions are in someone else's hands and that made me incredibly edgy and fragile.* —A

Our limerent objects (LOs) seem to have sovereignty over us. Our moods depend on their behavior—when they are friendly, we are euphoric; when they are cold, we become anxious and insecure. We feel defenseless—abashed by the desire the LO inflames in us, and unable to resist their magnetism. The temptation to give in, to surrender to them, to abandon ourselves to devotion, is seductive.

Like so many of the distorted perceptions of limerence, that feeling is an illusion. You might well feel powerless, but in reality, you are the one person who actually can take control of the situation and solve the problem. The reason why an internal locus of control is so powerful is that it recognizes this reality—even if there are enormous odds stacked against you, forces working against you, and reasons for despair, the best hope you have is to act as though you can succeed, that it is possible to beat the odds, that there is a path to victory. Because of this truth—that it is better to believe in even a fool's hope than to give in to despair—people with an internal locus of control have lower rates of depression and better life outcomes.[3]

Even better, recovery from limerence isn't a fool's hope. It's entirely possible. Many limerents have done it, many have pulled back from the brink of disaster with their dignity and integrity intact. By adopting a recovery mindset and telling themselves a compelling story about their lives, they escaped the trap of limerence limbo, deprogrammed their addicted brains, learned more about themselves and their needs, and improved their lives in ways that they would never have thought possible when in the depths of limerent despair.

> *Self-awareness is my main discovery over the last 16 months of my limerence episode and has helped me manage my emotions through all this.... I'm not out of it yet, but each time a wave of emotion comes along, I am able to stop, rationally evaluate it and move forward accordingly. That is huge progress. —SW*

> *[The recovery plan] did exactly what it was supposed to do for me: free me from my debilitating and destructive limerence, it has basically disappeared. There might be a hint of feelings left,*

but we're talking about 5–10 percent max. Life has become liveable again. —H

The starting point for recovery is clarifying your perspective on what is really going on, and how best to construe the situation of runaway limerence. Over the years, I've boiled down some of the most powerful lessons into a list of key principles for limerence recovery. Adopting these principles lays the foundations for a recovery mindset.

1. Limerence is happening in your head

The neural systems that can get pushed into overdrive during limerence are a fundamental part of how our brains work. There's no way to stop our brains from using these systems, and it would be a terrible idea to try, as we need the experiences of reward, arousal, and bonding to survive and thrive.[4] Pair bonding is built into us. At a fundamental level, limerence is about neurochemistry.

The extravagant passions of limerence lie within you, are generated by you, and that's where they need to be fixed. We can't expunge limerence from the brain, but we can find ways to turn down the volume and neutralize its effects by reversing the programming that led us into the altered mental state in the first place. It's possible to disrupt the patterns of behavior that reinforce person addiction. Habits of mind can either reinforce or weaken limerence, depending on how effectively you are able to train your executive brain (that highly developed cortical region that should be keeping the reward system in check) to intervene and disrupt old patterns of thinking.

Limerence is happening in your head, and that means it's within your power to reverse it.

2. You make them special

Limerent objects are special. Trying to deny that fact is going to meet emotional resistance and cause cognitive dissonance. Every fiber of your being is urging you to bond with them, and trying to kid yourself that it isn't happening is pointless. I mean, they make you feel fantastic just by being with them—surely, that's evidence of extraordinary charisma?

Your LO is special, but it's *you* that makes them special. The effect they have on you has its roots in your complex personal history. Long forgotten experiences have lodged desires in your subconscious that make you susceptible to idiosyncratic limerence triggers. What limerence practically means is that this person—the LO—has triggered something deep within you, some pattern of traits that is recognized by your subconscious and provokes an all-guns-blazing motivational program to try and get you to bond with them. This is not evidence of divinity. It's not extra-love or super-love. It's a match between the romantic template you have unwittingly crafted through your life and the cues they are broadcasting. Objectively, they are just another flawed human being.

That means that, once again, limerence is all about you. Their specialness is a consequence of your unique life experience. The euphoria, elation, exhilaration—the whole firework display—is happening in your head. They might be the trigger that lit the fuse, but the fuel is your own personality, preferences, and personal vulnerabilities. That means they are not in charge of your fate, you are. Facing the past, and understanding yourself, is the way to understand where their power over you comes from.

3. Check your instincts

When faced with an experience that feels amazing, most people want more. We don't go through life questioning every decision we make, we run on autopilot—doing things that feel good and avoiding things that feel bad. We build up a set of routines and mental shortcuts that help us live more comfortably and effectively, without having to exert too much effort. Generally speaking, our executive brains tend to add a layer of "fine-tuning" on top of our behavior, rather than being the main engine. We mostly run on instinct.[5] This is a problem when it comes to limerence.

During the early euphoria phase, limerence feels amazing, and unless you are already aware that the road ahead is going to lead you to some dark places, the incentive to spend more time with the LO, to daydream about them and feed off the exhilarating energy of early limerence, is very powerful. Unthinkingly, we reinforce the association between our LO and reward. Because of the way our brains are wired, our instincts train us to seek the LO until person addiction sets in. They push us in only one direction, with relentless fervor.

To stop this unconscious drive into addiction, your executive brain needs to provide a countervailing force. Reason needs to step in and moderate instinct, and stop giving the limerent subconscious desires so much latitude. Your mental CEO needs to pay attention and take charge.

4. Don't self-medicate with limerence

Life is full of hardships, and limerence can be a spectacular way to flee from emotional pain by escaping into a fantasy world of romantic gratification. One of the reasons that limerence is so seductive is that it provides an internal source of pleasure and comfort. It's no small thing to have a way of responding to the stresses of life by giving yourself a rewarding hit of bliss. After a limerent learns how exhilarating and motivating limerent fantasy can be, they develop the habit of using limerence for mood repair. It's a short-term high, a learned source of stress relief, a quick fix for downheartedness. Unfortunately, it causes longer-term problems. Repeating the learned pattern of behavior—*I feel bad, I daydream about LO, I feel better*—trains you to become more dependent on them. Once the urge to seek the LO becomes a compulsion, limerence causes more psychological distress than pleasant reward. That leads to that perversely counterproductive outcome of addictions—we still *want* the LO even though we no longer *like* the experience of limerence.

Using limerence for mood regulation is another instinctive behavior that works against the goal of attaining freedom. It's important to learn alternative strategies.

5. Accept that you can't just be friends

Limerence is addictive, and it's monumentally difficult to overcome addictions while still using your drug of choice. Trying to free yourself of limerence for a specific LO while still remaining friends with them is a form of bargaining. Most limerents feel an enormous upwelling of emotional resistance at the prospect of cutting ties of friendship with an LO—a good indication that their subconscious grip is fiercely tight. This resistance is a big barrier to progress (and why Chapter 13 was devoted to the challenges of friendship), so we have to be a bit sneaky about how to manage the situation and not shut down the possibility completely from the outset.

It isn't credible to try and remain friends with an LO during recovery, but there is some benefit to mollifying your limerent brain with a sliver of strategic hope: It is possible to be friends with an LO, but only after you have freed yourself from the limerence. Until that time, be very suspicious of your motives for maintaining an attachment.

6. You're in charge

A limerence recovery plan cannot depend on other people solving the problem for you. It's wishful thinking to believe you can persuade your LO to change their behavior, or reorganize their lives, to take away temptation and make your limerence struggles easier. Any plan that requires an LO to act in a specific way for you to be able to cope is doomed to fail. You may have an LO who makes life difficult by flirting, encouraging your attention, or acting in other ways that make it hard for you to detach. Alternatively, you might feel the problem is with your partner. They might be withholding affection or disrespecting you and making you want to seek solace outside the relationship. If only they could be persuaded to reconnect, you could escape the allure of an LO ...

Unfortunately, these plans depend on factors that are outside of your control. If you try to shift the responsibility of your limerence onto someone else, you are setting yourself up for frustration and failure. It just invites conflict when they inevitably don't do as you ask. No one else can solve the problem of limerence for you. Look to yourself for the solution.

7. Anticipate hardships

It's not going to be easy. Like any process of recovery from addiction there are going to be withdrawal pains, relapses, and missteps. There will be times when life hammers you with stress, and a retreat to the false promise of limerent fantasy will be formidably tempting. There will be days when you don't want to be strong, days when the craving is so bad you *want* to relapse, days when you wonder if the pain of limerence is maybe preferable to the pain of withdrawal. At least it comes with a few thrills.

You're human. Accept your limits. Don't tyrannize yourself with unreasonable demands for perfect discipline, because you will naturally rebel against such unrealistic standards. All free people resist tyrants, if they have any spirit. The secret to setbacks is to reduce their impact by knowing they are coming and anticipating their arrival. Approach recovery with the mindset that you are aiming for gradual improvement over the long term, but it won't always be a straight path without obstacles or failures. If you spend weeks or months (years, maybe) training yourself into limerence, it is going to take time to train yourself out of it again.

Face the inevitable setbacks with humility, but recover your resolve as quickly as you can. Then, get back on track with the recovery plan and try to make the interval till the next relapse longer than the previous one. Eventually, it'll be so long that you'll realize you are free.

8. Believe that a better life awaits

So far, these principles for limerence recovery have focused on the problems: how our brains have led us to addiction, how our history shapes our vulnerabilities, how our behavior keeps us trapped, and how an LO can make everything harder. The last, and perhaps most important, principle is that you have to believe that the obsession will end and that you can look forward to a better life beyond it. There must be some prospect of a happier future to direct your efforts toward.

Recognizing that self-medicating with limerence doesn't work is one thing, but it still leaves us with the problem of how to cope with stress in a healthy way. We, all of us, need ways of making ourselves feel better. The stresses of life will not just disappear, and if we are going to succeed in the plan of stopping LO-seeking, we need to replace the bad old strategy with a new source of comfort. True freedom means not being vulnerable to falling back into old habits when life gets tough, not having to continually exert effort to resist limerent temptation. That requires a vision for a more purposeful life.

> *After being limerent for years during my last limerent episode I finally decided to recover. I went No Contact, I unfollowed LO on social media, I joined a band, I started learning a foreign language, I threw myself into my immensely satisfying and rewarding job, I became more invested in my volunteer work, I made some new friends and strengthened my bonds with my old ones, and I stopped talking about LO. —J*

> *My limerence has decreased massively over the last couple of months and I think a lot of this is because I've really focused and put effort into my work. I've taken on every project that I can and generated work for myself. I'm definitely getting a buzz when things go right and it feels similar to the highs of limerence, but it's a much healthier reward. —R*

The happiness that freedom brings may not be as flashy and exciting as the thrills of limerence, but it is a deeper, more profound contentment. Finding a purpose, a goal you care about, a vision of what your life could be like if you took control of your destiny, shifts you from a state of passive dependency to one of active motivation. Living with purpose means you stop depending on the LO for comfort, stop following their lead, stop letting their behavior dictate your mood. When your energy is focused on achieving something worthwhile that you care about, the need for mood regulation decreases, along with the appeal of shallow gratification. When life has a solid foundation, you no longer lean on unhealthy crutches.

Unshackle yourself from the false comfort of your LO. Seek out new passions, new rewards, new directions to take your life in. Find a new North Star, and follow it to freedom.

CHAPTER 18
BREAKING THE LIMERENCE HABIT
The psychology of behavioral change

Recovery from limerence requires behavioral change. It's not possible to escape by doing the same things that led you into a state of person addiction in the first place. You have to stop digging the hole and set your mind to how you are going to climb back out.

Escaping this predicament is much easier with an understanding of the neuroscience that powers limerence. The neural systems that we explored in Chapters 3 and 4, and the mechanisms that regulate reward processing and the onset of addiction, hold the answers for how to break the limerent habit. The reward centers of the brain lie in the lower portion of the striatum, and that's where the action is for cultivating desire, but they are intimately interconnected with the rest of the striatum, which regulates associative learning (learning the connection between cues and rewards) and "motor" output (control of movement). This integration of functions means that the striatum can coordinate behavior with only minimal feedback from the cortical executive centers.[1] In other words, the striatum can run the whole habit independently and unconsciously. Once that training has become ingrained you can act without thinking. Once limerence is established, your behavior runs on autopilot.

You'll be able to notice if this training has taken place by becoming alert for moments when you find yourself acting impulsively—just like those times when you've picked up a cell phone without having any clear memory of what you intended to do. Your mind is seeking reward. You act first and think later.

During limerence, these habit circuits are really motoring. Cues in the environment that make us think of our limerent object (LO) (just about everything) trigger intense craving, and often cause us to act before we have a chance to think—literally by seeking out the LO to talk, or by texting them. Alternatively, the impulse could be a mental thought loop—both pleasant daydreams and unpleasant fears can become intrusive thoughts, distracting us from the task at hand by pushing us to refocus on the much more important issue (from the perspective of the subconscious) of pursuing the LO. In the thrall of this deeply reinforced habit, the executive brain often finds itself playing catch-up, sometimes even inventing rationalizations and justifications after the fact to construct a narrative to explain the behavior. Sometimes the deliberate transgression of good sense even adds spice to the desire.

> *Part of the reason I became limerent was the transgressive nature of the experience. He was married, and I'll admit that the thought of chucking all of society's rules was kind of thrilling. —M*

Other times, the executive is just disengaged, and provides minimal rationalization or justification to soothe any cognitive dissonance. It's as though reason has taken a vacation, and the executive is lounging in a recliner, chuckling at the mess that the subconscious is making of running things.

> *I feel like my executive brain was a sort of ineffectual parent figure, feebly protesting and then just giving in and ignoring the limerent child stuffing her face with sweets and then throwing up and crying. —CC*

Perhaps the most common experience is that the executive can be clear-sighted, but only when the limerent is away from their LO. In those moments of clarity, the limerent recognizes the dangers of indulging their desire, and resolves to try harder to resist temptation next time. Sadly, once they are in the LO's company, they find those mental barriers offer about as much protection as a sandcastle holding back the tide. This collapse of discipline is another sign of behavioral addiction causing changes at the neuroscientific level: as the subcortical behavioral pathways get strengthened, the cortical feedback pathways are weakened.[2] As the accelerator is floored, the brake is released.

Wanting to recover and hoping your willpower will be up to the job is not a practical plan for overcoming limerence. You need to understand how the brain works and design a strategy that addresses the origins of temptation and emotional resistance to loss.

Stop reinforcing the limerence habit

For any addict, having access to their supply is a constant temptation. We know this rationally. If you are trying to manage diabetes, having sweets or cakes in the house is not a good idea. If you are trying to manage alcoholism, social drinking is reckless. You are testing yourself continually, and every failure of will doesn't just jeopardize your progress, it also conditions you into believing you are weak. It is the same principle for limerence—if you know that there are ways you can reliably feed the limerence hunger for contact, you will likely indulge when feeling distressed.

Access to an LO is more complicated than access to foods or addictive drugs, but there are four main channels by which limerents can receive some LO supply. The first is direct contact: meeting them in person or in other "real time" settings, like phone calls or Zoom meetings. The second is indirect contact: texting, WhatsApp, DMs, and any other channel through which the limerent can send and receive personal messages. Third is passive contact: that giant database of rumination fodder that's accessible through social media. Finally, there is imagined contact: limerent reverie, daydreaming, fantasizing, and mentally rehearsing or replaying real-life interactions.

Which of these supply lines is most significant for any individual limerent will depend on their personal circumstances, but all of them are a cause for habit reinforcement. Every time you seek LO contact and receive some pleasurable feedback, you reinforce the reward memory and cement the idea "LO gives good vibes" in your subcortical systems. Bluntly, if you are going to break the limerent habit you will need to stop doing that, and instead limit your supply.

The next major cause for reinforcement of the limerent habit is the false belief that your erratic emotions will settle if only you had a deeper understanding of the situation. This can become a source of reinforcement because it sets up a cycle of constantly ruminating about the details of your interactions with the LO. Wondering how they feel about you, overanalyzing their every word and deed, reading too much into everything they do—it all sends you into a mental spiral that ultimately results in involuntary, intrusive thoughts.

This spiral manifests in habits like overinterpreting even trivial interactions: Why did they wait a day to respond to your text? How long should you wait before you send one back? How should you phrase it—friendly or flirty? Should you sign off with a kiss?

Surely, if you could just break the code, you'd feel better ...

> *Here's one thing I've learned from my therapist who specializes in treating obsession: a feature of obsessive thinking generally is the sensation that if you just think about it a little bit longer you'll finally get to understanding or resolution, hovering just out of reach. Then minutes, hours, days, months, years could go by and that elusive resolution would remain just out of reach. That's why the remedy is to just cut off the thinking despite its being unresolved, by shifting focus to something, anything, healthier. —ML*

Relentless analysis keeps your LO central in your thoughts, but it doesn't lead to relief. You'll get caught in futile cycles that don't bring insight but do add even more force to the psychological pull of the LO.

This tendency to get stuck in mental loops of overanalysis is another good example of how uncertainty adds fuel to limerence. Uncertainty is a major cause of the restless energy of limerence, and trying to gain relief can lead to some irrational behaviors that ironically make the situation worse.

Common mistakes that limerents make

1. Keeping hope alive

The first mistake that many limerents make is to think that being careful and cautious about revealing their own feelings is a good way to keep hope alive. Even if the limerent is intellectually clear that there is no realistic prospect of a healthy relationship, decisively shutting the door feels like a step too far. The limerent may think they are just being discreet, keeping their cards close to their chest, or perhaps biding their time; in fact, their indecision is generating more uncertainty, and that will reinforce the limerence.

2. Seeking closure

Another common mistake is the belief that "closure" is needed before the limerent can move on—if only they could just resolve the limerence situation neatly, with no nagging ambiguity left, they would finally recover peace of mind. The rationale is that having a calm and sensible conversation with your LO would allow you to part ways amicably, and this would finally relieve the aggravating uncertainty about what was really going on between you. It's another form of false belief—that the discomfort of limerence was being caused by a lack of external clarity rather than the real cause: internal conflict between desire and reason.

> However, although I have no desire for contact again, I have found myself ruminating about what my LO thinks about how the relationship ended. I have been wondering about what his reaction may have been to me not wanting a last phone call, and what he may have thought when I deleted certain social media apps and other means of contact that we had frequently used. I am totally aware that what he feels or thinks is not important to my recovery, but am amazed that my limerent brain STILL searches for ways to think about him. —S

Another motivation for seeking closure is that limerents often worry that their decision to reduce contact will upset their LO; and if there is one thing they cannot bear it is the thought of the LO existing in the world and thinking badly of them. Certainly, once you make the decision to detach, you will have to handle the transition elegantly, but limerents can make their choice, explain to their LO that they need space or time or to break contact for their own health . . . and then worry relentlessly that they didn't do it perfectly.

As evidence of this failure, their subconscious will cite the fact that they still feel emotionally churned up, restless, and unsatisfied, and so reach the faulty conclusion that it must have been the manner in which they parted that has left "unfinished business." In the most extreme cases, the limerent can even openly declare their feelings to the LO, and directly state that they have to detach in order to manage their limerence, but still suffer the relentless, nagging belief that they somehow didn't do it quite neatly enough.

The knowledge of reciprocal feelings, while great for a little while, is never enough. It doesn't last. My LO told me she shared secret feelings for me when I disclosed. Things were fine for a while after that. Then uncertainty crept back in. Ups and downs. I started wondering: Did I imagine all that? Does she STILL hold feelings for me even though she acts normal and even aloof sometimes? It drives me nuts wanting to disclose again, to get an "update," which sounds so stupid. —B

Closure is an illusion. It's another example of believing that relief can be found through external factors. In reality, no ending will ever be perfect. You won't know for sure how your LO feels about you, feel satisfied that there are no loose threads left hanging, or that there wasn't a better way to have handled it. But that's OK. It's not necessary for recovery. To find peace, you only need to come to terms with the situation yourself and accept that the uncertainty is always going to bother you, but that you can learn to live with it. The only reliable way to get closure is to accept that ending your limerence is not a deal between you and the LO; it is a settlement you are making with yourself. You have decided that this period of your romantic life is coming to an end and are going to take the necessary steps to make yourself well again.

3. Pridefulness

A third common mistake is giving in to pride. Limerence is fed by the combination of hope and uncertainty, and many LOs can give off enough hints of mutual attraction to kindle the glimmer in the first place and keep you hopeful once you're hooked. If you feel led on by an LO, it can be wounding to your pride if they react badly to an attempt to remove uncertainty (e.g., by reducing contact, or disclosing your feelings). If the LO suddenly cools off or feigns complete surprise that their behavior could have led to a misunderstanding, the sting of embarrassment can be sharp. Perversely, even if you instigated the situation as part of your recovery plan, any withdrawal by the LO can cause both fear of loss and hurt pride. That can trigger you into reversing course, and trying to goad the LO into some sign of reciprocation. Pride drives you to try and reignite the old fire and prove to yourself that there was a real connection there. You weren't just imagining it.

4. The false dawn

A fourth mistake is the false dawn. This comes when a limerent has resolved to free themselves at last and break contact with their LO—perhaps after an especially bad encounter, or in a moment of clarity when alone and contemplating their actions. After some success in managing limerence symptoms, they start to believe that escape is possible. The LO's pull seems less powerful. This is a perilous moment. Rationalizations can be especially convincing at this point—*I'm feeling better, I can perhaps relax my vigilance a bit. I never wanted to cut them out of my life for good. I think I'm over this, let's go for coffee!*

This false dawn is often when closure is sought, to finally settle matters now that you're feeling more in control. Unfortunately, it ends with predictable consequences—reignition of the limerence furnace and a serious setback in recovery.

> *I feel so much better now, I thought. I can't cut her off when she needs me, I thought. I've just got to tough it out, I thought. One weekend helping her move house and all my progress is gone. —RV*

Most of these mistakes stem from the same source: the pain of uncertainty. In trying to relieve that pain, limerents make the mistake of thinking that the solution lies outside themselves—that if they can manage their interactions with their LO cleverly enough, they can reduce the uncertainty and get relief from their pain. In fact, the only way to remove uncertainty is to be decisive.

Breaking the habit

The combination of trying to maintain contact with an LO and falling prey to easily made mistakes reinforces the limerence habit. You need to stop doing that. To break the habit, you will have to consciously change your behavior. Fortunately, there is a straightforward three-step process:

1. Limit contact
2. Train your executive brain
3. Spoil rewards

Basically, cut off the supply, disrupt the behaviors that reinforce the habit cycle, and break the association between the LO and pleasure.

1. Limit contact

Limiting contact is an obvious first step. Sometimes that's simple, and it's possible to go fully "No Contact" and immediately sever all ties with the LO, but more often life throws in some complications.

There are many scenarios in which going fully No Contact in person is impractical. If your LO is a work colleague, a co-student, a neighbor, or family friend, you cannot fully control the circumstances in which you might meet in real life.

Even if complete No Contact is possible, it is not necessarily the best strategy. For some addicts the cold turkey approach works well and is the quickest way to bulldoze through any withdrawal symptoms. For other people, cold turkey fails. The pain is so severe that they abandon their recovery plan. With limerence withdrawal, you will not get the bodily effects that come from quitting a drug, but the psychological distress can easily be bad enough to make the acute pain of withdrawal feel worse than the complicated pain of limerence.[3]

An alternative approach is to lessen contact progressively over time. This sort of "staged withdrawal" approach is similar in principle to tapering slowly off a drug addiction. It allows you to adapt to the loss of supply by decreasing it slowly but surely, rather than cutting off all exposure in one go. The idea is that you gradually reduce contact in a controlled way, but with the definite end goal of getting to the point where you have minimal contact. Psychologically, this is powerful because it doesn't cause instant alarm and fear of loss. It also means you don't "ghost" an LO that you had previously spent significant time with, you just gradually reduce the amount of time and establish a new normal for your relationship. It may seem a bit coldhearted to methodically plan to cut ties with someone who thinks of you as a friend, but there are two important points to consider: First, the friendship is already insincere if you are limerent for them but pretending you can handle it, and second, if you have reached the point of realizing there is no way to have an open and healthy relationship with them then it is in everyone's best interest to suspend the relationship as gracefully as possible while minimizing hurt, until you are absolutely and unequivocally over the limerence.[4]

The other important principle for limiting contact is that it applies to all four channels of contact—direct, indirect, passive, and imagined. If you cannot fully avoid contact with an LO in real life, you can control all the other channels for contact. Cut back on unnecessary texting, social media browsing, and daydreaming. In extremis, software tools can be used to make it impossible to contact an LO. Sometimes willpower needs a helping hand—implemented in a moment of calm clarity, to save yourself from future temptation.[5] Limiting contact alone will be beneficial to recovery, but it's often not sufficient. It needs to be paired to other forms of mental and emotional support.

2. Train your executive brain

One of the most important skills to develop is the ability to recognize when limerent impulses are pushing you to act in a way that will reinforce the addiction, and intervene. As we've covered before, our executive brains provide an important feedback signal to the reward circuits to moderate inappropriate or harmful "wanting" drives. Unfortunately, the unconscious training caused by relentlessly repeating limerence-reinforcing behaviors strengthens the wanting impulse and weakens the executive oversight. We need to consciously reverse that process by strengthening the executive override and weakening the power of the reward.

A way to strengthen the executive brain is to train it to be more alert and more assertive. A crucial initial step is to become much more aware of limerent impulses as they occur. During limerence the executive can become lazy and complacent, and even worse get recruited into rationalizing the limerent urges and making excuses. It's time to exercise that flabby mental muscle and start spotting destructive urges and intervening. Amazingly, even just becoming more aware of your thoughts is a powerful step toward the cognitive behavioral goal of "construing events in the correct way." Becoming aware of a habit loop beginning helps you see it for what it is, rather than following the impulse on autopilot.

Whenever you feel yourself feeling a limerent urge, *notice it*. That's it—just notice. If you respond to a cue in the environment that reminds you of LO, feel an urge to contact them, experience a pang of loss or regret about losing them, or drift into daydreams because you are feeling sad or lonely, tell yourself explicitly: "That was a limerent urge!" It will jolt your executive into wakefulness, shunt your thinking out of autopilot mode, and into active analysis mode. You can follow up the noticing with additional self-talk to direct your thinking at this stage too, such as "I choose not to act on it," but in the early stages, noticing is enough.

This sort of mental exercise develops the skill of "metacognition"—awareness of your own patterns of thought.[6] It breaks the habit cycle of subconsciously taking limerence-reinforcing actions by erecting an executive barrier that halts the behavior in its tracks. Train yourself to spot the habit cycle as it begins and bring it to the forefront of your mind. You don't have to be flawless about never taking action, but you do need to exercise your executive leadership until you become more vigilant.

> *Even just repeating the word in my head—limerence, limerence, limerence—when my thoughts turn to LO, reminds me that my feelings are abnormal, that limerence is a "thing" that I can control, that it's not even about LO. I feel like such a fool when I look back objectively at the past three years, but I feel hopeful that the next three will be different. —N*

3. Spoil rewards

Finally, the last of the three stages is about breaking the link between the LO and reward. This process may have already begun if you have advanced to late-stage person addiction with debilitating cravings, intrusive thoughts, and using limerence for mood repair, but, as you've no doubt noticed, you still want the LO. To reverse this problem, we need to know how learned behaviors are unlearned.

In Chapter 4, we covered the mechanisms of "habituation" and how desire can be weakened at the level of the neural circuits. One important observation was that learned behavior is never really *forgotten*, it is *overwritten* by new lessons. To suppress a previously learned reward, you need to train yourself into a process known as "extinction."[7] This is a slow rewriting of the old link between a cue and a reward by changing the rules and turning that cue into a neutral or aversive stimulus.

If a slot machine suddenly stopped paying out any money when the lever was pulled, even addicted gamblers would eventually learn not to waste their money and time. Dopamine signals "reward-prediction errors," so failing to get an expected reward decreases dopamine levels and makes you feel bad. Repeat that process enough and extinction of the old association succeeds. You learn the new rule (this machine sucks now).

A good way to accelerate the extinction process is to not just withdraw the reward, but to couple the old stimulus to a new "*punishment.*" Instead of slowly learning that the slot machine lever no longer gives prizes, we could couple the lever pull to an electric shock. That would very rapidly overwrite the old program.[8] We can use that principle to our advantage. Instead of trying to merely neutralize the reward by limiting contact and disrupting habitual behavior, we can be bolder, and make the process of limerent reverie punishing.

The idea is to devise a negative feedback program to hasten extinction and overwrite the original positive association. You flip the script on the old fantasies and happy memories by deliberately spoiling them. That giddy fantasy about somehow being in a consequence-free bubble universe with your LO? It has to be ruined. That happy memory of a time together when you felt blissfully connected? Replace it with a memory from a time when you felt ridiculous and humiliated. Does looking at your favorite photo of them make you feel warm and hopeful? Find the least flattering one you can, and look upon it until it becomes the strongest mental image of the LO that you have.

This approach of deliberate devaluation of an LO and ruining your old memories and dreams might seem disrespectful and manipulative, but it isn't. After all—it's all happening in your head. No LO is actually harmed by your internal mental coaching, you are just reversing the old positive programming by doing the opposite (although it's worth noting that you should take care that this doesn't spill out into hurtful behavior toward them).

Instead of exaggerating their merits and idealizing them as you did during limerence programming, you are now doing the opposite and diminishing their merits by focusing on the negatives. That's just balanced. The positive view was no more realistic than the negative. Your only real hope of seeing them honestly and clearly is to break the spell completely.

So, that's the plan. Three steps—limit contact, exercise executive oversight, and devalue rewards—but before they are put into practice, there is one last note of caution. The process of mental "deprogramming" is powerful and effective, but it can be demoralizing. You don't want to just ladle on the punishment relentlessly, there has to be a source of hope and light to aim toward, a brighter future beyond the labor of escaping life-limiting limerence. That must be a critical final stage of any recovery plan.

We'll cover that goal in Chapter 21, but first you'll need to be well on your way out of the altered state of mind of irrational infatuation. The next stage is to apply this plan to a specific LO.

CHAPTER 19
GETTING OVER LIMERENCE FOR A SPECIFIC PERSON

How to deprogram yourself out of limerence

The previous chapter outlined the three-stage plan for getting rid of limerence: limit contact, train your executive brain, and spoil rewards. Those principles are straightforward to grasp, but being able to put them into practice requires learning a few tactics that can be used in the real world when you are faced with the monumental temptation to seek limerent object-reward. What can you do on a day-to-day basis to help break the old habits, and program in new, better habits?

Every limerent is unique, as is every limerent object (LO), so the specifics of exactly how to implement each tactic will need a bit of adjustment and improvisation. Clearly, a fifty-year-old man suffering his first bout of limerence for another man is going to take a different approach to a nineteen-year-old student who is obsessed with her professor. However, one of the clarifying truths about limerence is that it has universal symptoms and is based in the fundamental systems of the brain. That means the basic tactics will work for everyone; they just need a bit of creative tweaking for your own personal circumstances.

Let's rattle through some of the practical steps you can take.

Ways to reduce uncertainty

Uncertainty is a driving force for limerence. You need to reduce it. Some sources of uncertainty are outside of your control—an

LO who sends mixed messages, or social barriers that prevent the open expression of feelings—but others are firmly within your sphere of influence. Most obviously, your own indecisiveness.

A very common amplifier of limerence is that two people sense mutual attraction but are both apprehensive about expressing themselves clearly. By not being direct and clear in your own communication, you are making that situation worse. If you use hints and winks and subtlety to try and reveal your interest in a slantwise way that preserves pride and deniability, and they respond in a similarly covert way, you can't know if the problem is your failure to clearly telegraph your interest or if they just aren't interested in you. Two people tiptoeing around the direct message that needs to be sent compounds uncertainty and worsens limerence.

Reluctance to make decisions stems from fear. The Latin root of the word "decide" means to "cut off."[1] Deciding on a course of action means cutting off all the other options. We don't typically dither because we haven't got enough information, haven't spent enough time analyzing the situation, or haven't gathered the resources needed for action. We dither because we fear that we'll make the wrong choice, regret our decision and wish we could go back in time and undo it. Indecision means keeping our options open, which feels less risky. Thinking in this (very human and natural) way, is actually an error of reasoning. Indecision is not really open-mindedness; it's delay.

Being decisive means cutting off any uncertainty that you are contributing to the situation. If you are free to act on your feelings, but holding back due to insecurity or uncertainty, then it's time to be bold. Caution is not the same as concealment. If you fake a platonic friendship to cover the churning cauldron of limerent desire within you, it's incredibly unlikely that you will slowly win them over with a long game of a complicated friendship, punctuated by occasional episodes of uncomfortable boundary-crossing. Disclose your attraction to LO and accept the consequences. If they say yes, then you'll kick yourself for not acting sooner, but also get to embark on a romantic adventure that could be life changing. If they say no, then you can commend yourself for your courage, accept the disappointment, and begin the process of recovery now that you know for sure that there is no hope. Your decisive action has cleared away the uncertainty that fuels limerence.

Alternatively, if you are not free to act—because either you or your LO are already committed to someone else—then the decision was actually made some time ago. You are just questioning it because your brain is being bombarded by limerent euphoria and wants to believe that, somehow, the situation could change. This is the classic situation in which disclosure to the LO is a bad idea, and the executive needs to step in and assert itself.

> *I disclosed my feelings for her rather impulsively back in December, and she told me that she felt the same way. It felt amazing for like 30 seconds, and then we both realized we were totally screwed. Because once we'd both disclosed mutual feelings, there was no way to just keep on pretending to be friends, so our only choices were to cut contact or continue in (at least) an emotional affair.* —LS

If you know it would be irresponsible or destructive to disclose your feelings to an LO, you can turn that constraint to your advantage. Use it as the foundation for decision-making. Use it as a way to dispel uncertainty, and short-circuit the mental loops of overanalysis: "*I don't know if LO reciprocates, and it's torture,*" becomes "*I don't know if LO reciprocates, but I'm married, so it doesn't matter.*" Frame the problem from the perspective of a dispassionate judge that is concerned about outcomes and not about feelings—put the executive in charge again. Your "wanting circuits" need to be regulated by your "wisdom circuits" (which probably need some exercise). Having a simple, direct rule like *do not disclose feelings to LO* is a concrete, unambiguous limit that is simple for the executive to enforce.

Another option in this circumstance is to bolster the "*do not disclose to LO*" rule with a supplementary tactic—disclose to someone else. This could be a trusted friend, mentor, coach, counselor, therapist, or possibly even a spouse or partner. The benefit of this tactic is that it removes plausible deniability.

Once you have shared your predicament with someone else, especially someone whose good opinion you care about, you can no longer maintain the façade of friendship with the LO. If you know that someone else is aware of the situation, and will notice if you start to behave inappropriately with your LO, it is a powerful check on the temptation to give in to limerent impulses and suspend your principles to get some limerence sugar. Social accountability is a potent force. Deploy it deliberately to help keep yourself honest.

Finally, as well as the fear of judgment, if you choose your confidante wisely, they will be someone who has your best interests at heart. They are not just an accountability partner, they can also be a champion—someone who helps you, encourages you, and celebrates your successes.

Perhaps the highest stakes approach is to disclose your limerent struggles to your existing partner. This requires great sensitivity, but it can prove transformative for your chances of success. First, it will be less damaging to their trust in you if you freely admit to the situation, rather than being found out (or directly lying to them). Second, it sets up a narrative of "us against the problem," which can be a powerful way of repairing the pair bond. Third, they are likely to be your greatest champion, as they are obviously highly motivated to help you free yourself of the destructive obsession.

For all those benefits, though, there are risks. Obviously, disclosure of this sort is going to be painful for them to hear. You have to take responsibility for allowing the limerence to escalate, but make it clear that you want it to end. You need to disclose enough to convey the seriousness of the situation, while making clear that you remain fully committed to your partner. Withholding information that your partner wants to know is duplicitous and, whatever you do, don't fall into the trap of obsessively talking about your LO with them. Disclosure is not a free pass to now spend all your time ruminating out loud about your infatuation and seeking support through the emotional ups and downs of your limerence from the person it is harming most.

> Last night I fully disclosed (unvarnished, non-sugar-coated disclosure, God it was hard!) to my significant other and I am still waiting for the dust to settle after that bombshell. He's not angry (yet) and not overly surprised and has been very supportive, but it's early days so let's see. I had to do it, it's the only way I can be free from this limerence episode. The only good thing out of this mess is that I never had an affair. —LA

The guiding principle of all these tactics is to deliberately remove sources of uncertainty, and clarify your decisions. Anything that helps dispel the gray fog of ambiguity that limerence loves to hide in is a good step.

Ways to limit contact

As previously mentioned, contact with an LO feeds the addiction. You'll need to wean yourself off this dependency if you are ever going to relate to them in a healthy way. The most reliable way of limiting contact is to adopt the "staged withdrawal" strategy introduced in Chapter 18, where you gradually reduce exposure over time, so as to not cause abrupt shocks to yourself or your LO. The starting point is to review how much contact you have currently with your LO, and think about how you could gradually taper this off over time. Remember to include all four channels of contact—direct, indirect, passive, and imagined. It may be impossible to control in-person contact for social or professional reasons, but it's advisable to limit as many of the channels as you can.

In practice, implementing staged withdrawal would look something like this: I have lunch with my LO every day at work, and we text in the evenings, and I browse their social media whenever I'm bored. Starting from next week, I'm going to skip one lunch date by bringing a sandwich and working through the lunchbreak. If LO asks about it, I'll say I need to focus on work for a while. The next week, I will skip two lunch breaks, and start to plan for an alternative way for me to spend my lunch hours in the future. Similarly, for the texting habit, instead of responding to their every text as quickly as I can, I'll begin to be less responsive. I will set my phone to "do not disturb" for an hour each night. I will also be less proactive in my own texting behavior, and when I'm bursting to share a new post or meme, I'll skip every second temptation. As time goes on, the goal is to progressively transition to new routines that restrict contact with the LO.

How you explain this change to your LO will depend on the basis of your relationship at the outset. They may accept your behavioral shift without much comment, or they might react more negatively, possibly becoming upset or thinking they have offended you somehow. You'll have to use your judgment as to how frank you can be about your reasons, particularly if you have personal or professional constraints that mean you cannot responsibly be open about your feelings.

Be methodical, be systematic, work in stages. Use tools to help you succeed—mute their social media, divert their number to voicemail, set up autoreplies on email. Gradually escalate the strictness of your limits. This analytical approach helps to make your executive brain the driving force behind the plan and protects you from the instinctive drives that reinforce limerence. Occasional steps backward are fine as long as you are going in the right general direction of reducing overall limerent supply. The idea is to try and facilitate the normal petering out of friendship, rather than breaking it off abruptly in a dramatic severance.

If this plan strikes you as callous, calculated, and manipulative, remind yourself of a sobering truth—you are pretending to be their friend when you are actually hopelessly infatuated. It is in everyone's best interest for you to detach. If circumstances allow, you could rip off the Band-Aid in one pull and go No Contact immediately, after explaining to them why you have to do it. This might be a more honest strategy, in a blunt kind of way, but staged withdrawal is like slowly peeling the Band-Aid off in an attempt to get used to the gradual detachment and minimize the pain.

Either way, though, the wound needs to breathe before it can heal.

Self-talk

Habits are an autopilot mode for the brain. Once you've made the decision to reverse your limerent programming, you'll need to regularly remind your lazy brain about your choice. One effective way of doing this is through the use of self-talk or mantras.[2] This can involve using specific emotionally charged phrases, but it also includes a broader reimagining of your limerence experience. When you feel limerent desire, coach yourself. Review the costs: the countless hours of thought and energy devoted to a one-sided obsession, other good people overlooked, opportunities missed, dreams delayed, productive days squandered. Concentrate on how life will be better when you are free.

The primary benefit of this mental technique is that it terminates rumination quickly and efficiently. Mantras focus the mind onto a keystone principle, cutting through doubt and abruptly derailing old patterns of obsessive thought. We touched on this principle in Chapter 18—when you notice yourself falling into one of the limerent habits, engage your executive and execute a new script. Intervene with a positive message:

- Limerence isn't helping me.
- I'm in charge now.
- Time to take control.
- I choose freedom.
- I'm done with limerence.

Mantras are most effective when they are tailored to your personality and your own motivators. If you find yourself assaulted by a limerent craving, you know better than anyone else what is likely to help most—do you respond better to praise or criticism, optimism or sternness? Find a phrase or saying that moves and inspires you, and use it as a mental shield against the limerent impulses that bubble up from the subconscious. Eventually, if a mantra is repeated enough, it becomes the new autopilot response and replaces the old limerence-reinforcing mental loops.

Another useful application of self-talk is counteracting the uncertainty that worsens in the early stages of withdrawal. No Contact is a path to freedom, undoubtedly, but it does have an inescapable feature: You don't know what's going on anymore. What is LO doing? What do they think of you? Are they depressed? Even worse, are they happy? Argh! It's agony.

It's easy to talk yourself into a quick Facebook stalk, just to find out for sure. After all, if they don't know about it, it doesn't really count as contact, does it? Whenever this fear of missing out kicks in, try the following mantra:

I don't know, and that's OK.

Train yourself into accepting uncertainty you can't control, and you'll be much more resilient to the challenges of limerence.

Antirewards

The next batch of limerence deprogramming tactics focus on the issue of spoiling rewards. The guiding principle is that you ruin the reward-seeking habits that you developed during the early stages of limerence. You use punishment to accelerate the overwriting of memories linking LO to reward, so that you can more rapidly reverse the limerent programming that you accidentally implemented. There are three specific tactics that work well.

Negative immersion involves deliberately exposing yourself to evidence that limerence can lead to terrible outcomes. Good examples of this are reading books and articles about the consequences of infidelity on spouses and children. Browse affair recovery sites and contemplate the generational damage that can be caused by family breakdown after adultery. Put yourself in the role of the person who caused their children to develop stress-related mental health disorders. Read about the pathology of stalking, and imagine what your LO might feel if they saw you as their stalker. Instead of researching the evidence for whether monogamy is a natural state for humans, read accounts of how some experiments in open marriage have ended in disaster.³ Immerse yourself in the worst outcomes that you can dream up. Catastrophize.

Your goal here is not to come to a balanced, objective view of marriage, parenthood, or social conventions. That's a lofty ideal that can wait until you are back in your right mind. For now, you need to get out of the addictive spiral that you're caught in by deliberately and willfully feeding your mind negative data. It's an intentional, time-limited tactic to retrain your brain by exclusively focusing on the toxic consequences of limerence for a while, so that the habit of reverie becomes less attractive.

The second tactic is similar, but more personal.

The daymare strategy involves methodically spoiling the pleasant fantasies you used to indulge in—taking your romantic daydreams and changing the ending so they turn into nightmares. Invent new outcomes to your favorite fantasies so you can turn your sweet, rewarding reverie into a sour punishment.

Let's say you have a daydream about driving off into the sunset with your LO. Now you need to vividly imagine LO suddenly shouting "I've made a terrible mistake! Stop the car! I have to leave! I don't know what I was thinking! I never want to see you again!" (include all the exclamation marks). Or perhaps you have a sexy fantasy about seducing your boss in his office? Change the ending to include his wife walking in on you, and you having to flee in a state of undress while your coworkers point and laugh. The key thing is to make your old heartwarming daydreams punishing. When you fantasize about having a new life with your LO, turn it into a nightmare of rows, regrets, misunderstandings, and emotional devastation. Reimagine the scenario into such a train wreck of humiliation that you never want to reenter that dreamworld again.

Identifying the anchor memories of your limerent experience is the final, related tactic. These are real-world encounters that were especially powerful, especially potent, and which lingered in your memory. Often, limerents revisit those moments in times of stress and uncertainty. Let's say your LO has just cancelled an appointment at short notice or sent a cruel text that has pushed you into a spiral of doubt and embarrassment. A way of soothing that discomfort is to recall an anchor memory of a time that gave you glorious hope: *Remember that time when I bumped into her in town, and she smiled the biggest, happiest, most natural smile I have even seen? And then we hung out at the coffee shop for two hours, and she just gazed into my eyes and laughed and talked and flirted. There's no way she was faking that. That was real. I'll just dwell on that vividly until the pain goes away.*

Most limerents collect these anchor memories as comforting hints of reciprocation. Equally, though, we also tend to accumulate memories of times when things went very wrong: *Remember that time when I spent hours on a handmade card for his birthday and he laughed and said, "Don't give up the day job!"*

You can't rewrite the past in the same way that you can rewrite daydreams, but you can choose to focus on the negative anchor memories and dismiss the positive ones. Anytime you feel yourself giving in to rumination, avoid the happy memories and remind yourself of the negative ones. Think *"that is the truth of our 'relationship' and I need to let it go."* Concentrate on the negative encounters to change your perception of LO from a source of comfort to a source of discomfort.

> *Guess it's been a busy week when he's told me how he's so attracted to me in many ways while he's also started dating a different person. Busy lad. I didn't misinterpret anything. But I have learned that he's truly not for me. He's untrustworthy and inconsistent and I deserve more. Ick. Onward, somehow. —H*

Emerge from the darkness

Several of these tactics for reversing the mental programming of limerence are intentionally demoralizing. They work as countervailing forces against the overactive reward-seeking that leads into person addiction. They aren't going to make you feel good, so they should be used in moderation. Limiting contact may give you some positive relief as you gain space and clarity, and positive self-talk will help you see the situation from a more constructive perspective, but the antirewarding corrections are, by definition, unpleasant. Consequently, a critical last step in getting over a specific person is to only use those dispiriting tactics for awhile, and to exercise extra caution if you are already suffering with anxiety or depression.

A way to tell if they are beginning to work is if the appeal of daydreaming about your LO wears off and you no longer feel the same rush of excitement when the intrusive thoughts force LO into your mind. If you are starting to feel an aversion to rumination, the negative reprogramming is working—at that point it is wise to ease off the punishment and focus on the more positive tactics. You want to deprogram yourself out of a state of limerence, not drive yourself into a state of depression.

Once the combination of methods begins to recalibrate your emotional response to the LO (and you no longer feel such positive emotions when you contemplate them), it is time to move into the last stage of recovery: understanding why you were vulnerable to them in the first place, and how to protect yourself against unwanted limerence in the future. The ultimate solution, the best-case scenario, is to emerge from the darkness of person addiction with a much better understanding of yourself, a clearer view of the forces that shaped you, and a positive, inspiring view of how you want your life to be going forward.

For that, we need to move away from short-term psychological tactics that can shunt you out of an altered state of mind, and into the slower, deeper work of understanding who you really are, what you really want, and how to make purposeful changes to your life that can turn the disruption of limerence into lasting personal growth.

CHAPTER 20
THERAPY FOR LIMERENCE
What works and what doesn't

We are all shaped by our unique pasts. Brains are learning machines, but what they learn depends on the experiences we have, and the environments we grow up in. Our brains give us the capacity to experience limerence, but our personal history is what programs our "limerence circuits" to respond to particular people and situations.

The limerence recovery strategy has so far focused on behavioral techniques for deprogramming yourself out of the altered state of mind of limerence. That intervention deals with the immediate issue: how to stabilize your emotions and bring some order to the psychological chaos that limerence can cause. Regaining mental composure is essential for halting the runaway limerence locomotive before it causes any more damage, but the next stage of recovery is more personal and open-ended—working on understanding yourself better.

If resources allow for it, personal therapy during limerence recovery can be highly beneficial. The psychological tactics we've already covered overlap with the principles of cognitive behavior therapy—become more aware of your thought processes, identify mistaken beliefs that are causing negative outcomes, reframe the situation from a more objective viewpoint, and take action to improve outcomes. These principles all contribute to the goal of learning to construe events in the most constructive way.

Having an expert CBT therapist guide you through this "deprogramming" process can be valuable. As you make progress, they can help you clarify what works for you personally, and what doesn't, and how to adapt and improve your recovery plan. A good therapist can also act as confidante, champion, and accountability partner, all of which is helpful for keeping you on track.

Therapy has broader goals, though. If applied well, individual counseling or coaching can help you understand the origin of your own unique limerence vulnerabilities. You can get to the root of where your beliefs came from, the formative impacts on your romantic sensibilities, and why certain people hold such particular power for you. Therapy can be a route to self-knowledge that will help you understand the full context of your personal limerence experience.

The goals of therapy

In the deepest sense, therapy seeks an understanding of the individual across their life span. In the present moment, therapeutic intervention is intended to manage distress—to develop self-awareness and find coping strategies that can help recover your peace of mind. That distress is usually the immediate trigger for someone seeking therapy in the first place—they recognize that they need help to manage their thoughts, feelings, or behaviors to improve their quality of life. People often don't seek support until they are desperate, and finding relief is understandably their immediate priority. For clients suffering with person addiction, addressing the negative symptoms of intrusive thoughts, unstable moods, and emotional anguish will be the first order of business when consulting a therapist.

To achieve this aim, therapy often looks back to the past. Memory is mined for origin stories, seeking out the causes of maladaptive beliefs, recalling formative events that shaped self-image, and how first relationships with childhood caregivers may have influenced the formation of adult relationships. The therapist seeks to help the client understand their life history, to assess how they have ended up where they are in the present. For limerence, this is likely to involve identifying patterns of behavior in past romantic relationships, what the limerent object represents for you, and why you might have developed the specific emotional vulnerability that is so potent at driving you into a state of infatuation. This is a process of self-discovery, guided by a trusted adviser.

Finally, therapy also looks to the future. The ultimate aim is to help the client achieve the insights and personal growth that are needed for them to transform their lives for the better—to develop the knowledge, skills, and confidence to recover from setbacks; be resilient to future stresses; and thrive in all the key areas of life.

This process is rarely quick or easy. The therapist needs to be skilled enough to provide a safe environment with appropriate boundaries that encourages the client to be totally open, and share (possibly for the first time) the most sensitive and private experiences of their lives. Progress often depends on breaking down the emotional barriers and ego-preserving defenses that the client has built up over the years of improvised coping strategies, without causing excessive additional distress. Clients must confront the protective excuses and rationalizations that mask uncomfortable truths, which are holding them back, but also believe that it is leading to a positive outcome. That work can be painful—confrontational, even—and emotionally destabilizing. Once you start rooting around in the dark recesses of the psyche you can discover monsters.

Good therapy is holistic in this sense of effectively integrating past, present, and future. For a client suffering with person addiction, success would mean uncovering romantic vulnerabilities from the past, recovering peace of mind in the present, and developing fortitude against unwelcome limerence in the future. Excellent aspirations.

Unfortunately, it doesn't always go well.

The risks of therapy

Perhaps the biggest risk associated with managing limerence through therapy is that the concept of limerence (and its neuroscientific basis) is not widely known in academic or clinical circles. Consequently, when encountering the idea for the first time, therapists can react with skepticism. Limerents seeking support can find their experiences dismissed, or explained in terms of an alternative disorder.

> *I have never been able to share [my limerence] with anyone. I tried last week with my therapist who I've been seeing for years and I thought I can trust her so I dared to go ahead ... and I received one of the most invalidating comments ever in my life. —K*

> *Today I had a first talk with a therapist, that was a disaster. I told her I was a limerent, she had never heard of it and reacted very skeptical, hostile almost. She told me I more likely have an attachment problem, which I'm not sure of. I doubt that to be honest, she told me I was not open for therapy and I left unfinished business. —M*

It's understandable that busy professionals would be wary of accepting what looks, at a cursory glance, like a new fad or pop-psychology buzzword. As a rule of thumb, being skeptical of an unfamiliar concept makes sense in evidence-based care. Unfortunately, misinterpreting limerence symptoms as manifestations of some other condition—such as an attachment disorder—can lead to very bad outcomes.

Dorothy Tennov devoted a section of her book, *Love and Limerence*, to psychotherapy, and it is fair to say that she was antagonistic to the point of hostility about psychoanalysis and its impact on limerents:

> *Now that the haze is being lifted from both of these phenomena, it is evident that limerence and psychotherapy have combined to produce untold suffering.... It is essential that the profession be called to task for irresponsibility.*[1]

Before *Love and Limerence*, Tennov published *Psychotherapy: The Hazardous Cure*, detailing the damage caused by "erotic transference" to the well-being of many female patients.[2] Transference is the concept that a client can transfer the emotional dynamic of previous relationships onto their interactions with the therapist as a surrogate parental or romantic figure.[3] Transference can be seen as positive progress in psychoanalytic therapy if it allows the client's suppressed emotions about the past to be reanimated and worked through in the present.

From Tennov's perspective, transference instead represented a critical risk for interpersonal therapy for limerents—they could become limerent for their therapist, and this would be encouraged as part of the healing process. In practice, this misreading of the situation can prove destructive.

> *When I told my therapist about my limerence [for her], she didn't really take the term seriously, but she seemed shocked because I confessed how intense it was. I asked for an honest answer from her part. She said that she had no other feelings for me other than being my therapist. At first, she wanted to end the therapy, but then she went into case review with her colleagues and they must've encouraged her to go on with me and so I stayed with her for more than another year. Long story short ... I suffered very much during that year. It felt so humiliating being so dependent. Every time having to leave after those goddamn 50 minutes. —J*

Psychoanalysis has obviously evolved significantly since Tennov's critique in the 1970s, but the danger of limerence developing for a therapist clearly remains. Many of the reinforcing elements of limerence are present in the therapeutic setting. The therapist is caring, supportive, and patient, and helps the client uncover new insights about their personality and history. Highly arousing thoughts and feelings are unearthed. Bonds of intimacy and trust form. Combined with that are the unavoidably impersonal elements to the relationship—therapists are guarded about their own feelings, close down the conversation after a fixed period of time, have lots of other clients, and take payment for their services. There is a combination of hope, uncertainty, and social barriers. For a limerent client, it would be amazing if limerence didn't develop for their therapist if they felt any hint of the glimmer. Even worse, therapy provides an irreproachable excuse for regular contact, allowing the client to enthusiastically reinforce their limerent connection—often to the point of crisis.

> *Before each appointment I had butterflies in my tummy, after every appointment I felt disoriented and I couldn't concentrate for the rest of the day. Outside of therapy I would fantasize about my therapist teaching me to cope with and manage my anxious thoughts. I'd close my eyes and imagine how I'd thank him for helping me become better.... For hours at a time. He told me it was transference and it was normal. [But, when he found out that my husband looked like him] he used the "No Contact" technique with me. He referred me to dialectical behavior therapy and told me to never contact him again and if I did he said he would take the matter up the chain.... I responded with a psychotic break.* —CA[4]

Therapists are not themselves immune to this problem, of course. "Countertransference" is often discussed as a professional risk in psychotherapy, where therapists develop erotic or romantic desire for their clients. Mutual attraction is a perennial risk in such an intimate setting.[5] A good rule of thumb when seeking a therapist for limerence is to pick someone who is very unlikely to be a potential LO.

Another risk in therapy is that limerence can be incorrectly interpreted through one of the better established therapeutic "lenses." Limerents frequently report being diagnosed as codependent, or having anxious attachments, or "pure-O" obsessive compulsive disorder.[6] At the benign end of the scale this might only mean a weakening of the limerent's confidence in their therapist, but the situation can become more serious if a treatment plan that works for a related condition makes limerence worse.

> *My therapist told me "You have created a fantasy out of him. You need to see him for who he really is." She advised me to spend more time with him to shatter the illusion.* —T

Obsessive, irrational fears can be effectively managed by progressive exposure techniques, behavioral addictions cannot.[7]

How to find the right therapist for you

There is a quip in scientific circles that if you ask two statisticians how to analyze a dataset, you'll get three different answers. A similar principle seems to hold in psychotherapy. There are countless schools of therapy that vary in their focus, philosophy, treatment strategy, and evidence base. There are even more informal sources of support, with faith-based communities, support groups, and coaches offering their own perspectives and solutions. All approaches have their advocates.

This variety can be bewildering. How would a limerent in distress go about identifying the right therapist and making sound decisions about the best approach to treatment? Finding a therapist who is familiar with the concept of limerence (and its psychological significance) is going to be a big advantage, of course, but beyond that, finding a therapist who also helps you in the larger project of limerence recovery through self-development is a daunting task. As a starting point, there are a couple of therapeutic approaches that have particular relevance for limerence, given what we know about its origins and impact on behavior.

Attachment theory is the first approach. If the results of the survey outlined in Chapter 6 can be safely extrapolated to the wider population, it seems that around 50 percent of individuals with secure attachments have experienced limerence. For people with anxious attachment styles, that number rises to 79 percent. Anxious attachment can't be the cause of limerence (as plenty of non-anxious people experience it), but it undoubtedly correlates with it. For anyone with the double whammy of anxious attachment and limerence, understanding the roots of your attachment style is likely to be essential to fully understanding your "limerence avatar" and how your familial relationships have shaped your adult romantic vulnerabilities. Childhood bonding traumas cast long shadows and are likely to result in patterns of limerence that mirror old patterns of insecurity—both in terms of the sorts of people who trigger the glimmer and the type of behavior that triggers bonding panic and insecurity. Clearly, working with a therapist who specializes in this area would be highly advisable.

In contrast, for limerents who have secure attachments, the parental-bonding perspective on therapy will likely prove frustrating and unsatisfying. Trying to fit an explanation of limerence into a framework of past attachment anxiety will diminish trust between the secure client and their therapist, as well as providing limited insight into the true origins of their vulnerabilities.

> *Therapists have had a field day figuring out what my mother must have done wrong to make me this way, but honestly, it feels like part of my temperament.* —GM

Developing an understanding of your own attachment style is valuable work, of course, but is not in itself likely to explain limerence as a phenomenon.

Couples therapy is a second potentially important specialism for recovery from limerence—specifically when limerence is disrupting an established long-term relationship.[8] Couples therapy will not directly help with unearthing the root causes of individual limerent tendencies, but it is a valuable supplement to any individual therapy that the limerent may be undertaking in parallel. When limerence is stress-testing a relationship there are two problems that need to be solved at once: the limerent recovering mental control and the partnership fixing problems that were hindering unity. Couples counseling can help identify causes of poor communication and misalignments in beliefs or goals between the partners. It can stop the downward spiral of devaluation and rewriting of history that limerents can be prone to. It provides a valuable counterforce against the slow deterioration of connection caused by instinctively crossing the "tipping points" that lead into a limerent affair. Combining individual therapy with couples therapy is a powerful way to both understand yourself and reenergize your existing bond, allowing you to recover from intrusive limerence and improve your relationship.

> LO is still very much in my head, but I am trying to ensure I communicate better with my husband so that if I need emotional support, he has a fair chance to provide it. Me disclosing about LO has been a massive wake up call, and with the support of our therapist we are making progress. —S

Personal compatibility

These two forms of therapy are particularly noteworthy for limerence recovery, but in fact, the wide range of other schools and approaches that exist could be seen as a cause for encouragement. Several reviews of a wide variety of talking therapies have found that one of the most important factors for a successful therapeutic outcome is the rapport between client and therapist.[9] Part of the reason why so many therapeutic theories exist is because they each resonate with different people, different personalities, different worldviews. Good therapy is a bespoke service.

> I remember talking to my therapist about my LO, saying something about how I thought I was in love with him, and she asked, "But where is the love?"' The question hit me like a ton of bricks. —M

> With the help of my therapist we peeled away at it and as soon as we got to the subject of my parents, the bricks started to fall. My Co-dependent Mother and my Narcissistic Father. BINGO! . . . I remember the last thing my therapist said last week: "We are going to start working on you beginning to love yourself and we will go from there." —A

> My therapist was really good at connecting things I was going through now to my childhood and early adulthood. I think I discovered a lot about myself through therapy and I found it to be a positive experience. —SW

Selecting a therapist who has compatible values and builds understanding between you both is the surest way of finding the champion you need to explore your past, present, and future. Regardless of the method they adopt or the school they adhere to, a good therapist is one who earns your trust. Someone who can help you see the full sweep of your life clearly, who is open to your ideas, does not try to force you into a therapeutic box, and acts as a trusted adviser. Someone who helps you come to enlightenment, and supports you as you work your way to self-determination.

That work can uncover how your personal history has shaped your emotional landscape and programmed your limerence circuits. It can help you to identify the triggers that kindle the glimmer in you, recognize the sort of people who you respond to, and anticipate when you may be vulnerable in the future. Gaining self-awareness about the emotional foundations to your personality will help guide your decisions. Once you learn who you are and why you are that way, you can make much better-informed choices about how to improve your life. It's the ultimate solution to limerence: Transform your life for the better, and you will not only be wise enough to avoid drifting unthinkingly into unhealthy infatuations, but they will no longer have the same escapist appeal. It's lasting freedom. When you are living with purpose, you seek healthy rewards, build meaningful relationships, and live in alignment with your principles.

It's the final step in the journey to recovery.

CHAPTER 21
LASTING FREEDOM
Reshaping your future and moving on

This book has laid out a store of knowledge about limerence—what it is, how it develops, how it's reinforced by instinctive behavior, how it causes mismatched expectations about love, and how it can be resisted and reversed when it's unwelcome. All that knowledge is valuable, of course, but to be truly useful, knowledge must be put into action. It should be used to improve your life in a meaningful way.

The practical deprogramming techniques outlined in Chapters 18 and 19 can help with short-term recovery from limerence. They can be effective for jolting you out of the altered state of mind that defines addictive infatuation—like jogging the needle on a record that is stuck endlessly repeating one line from a love song. The process of "extinction" is effective for breaking the old training that limerence is rewarding, but you can't just relentlessly punish yourself—you need to replace the old, misguided rewards with new, healthier rewards. The promise of a better life is needed if you are going to fully recover.

Similarly, personal therapy can help uncover the deep causes of emotional vulnerability that make you limerent for particular people at particular times. It can also uncover new insights into why you act the way you do, but just understanding those influences isn't enough. You cannot undo the past that shaped you. The best you can hope for is to use the insights from your personal history to imagine a better future—one that you can sincerely look forward to.

Ultimately, simply comprehending the intricacies of the neuroscience, or the psychological roots of your own limerence, does not actually solve the problem. While deeper understanding of how our brains work and what has led us to the point of destructive infatuation is undeniably necessary and beneficial, the blunt question that still needs to be answered at the end of all that learning is: *Now what?*

To get lasting freedom from limerence you need to apply these lessons to a higher-level goal—a new direction for life that can give you a sense of optimism. The foundation of long-term rehabilitation is creating a positive vision for the future. The ultimate protection against limerence disrupting your life again is to focus your energy on making your life more *purposeful*.

The hazards of drifting through life

Many of us drift through life. After school we go to university, start a trade, or sign up for public service of some sort, and then find ourselves carried into a job that seems like a sensible choice from the options available. Along the way, we hope to meet someone special who is drifting in basically the same direction—like two sailboats that could be hitched together as the currents and winds carry you down the river of life. This isn't to say that people don't work hard to succeed in life, it's just that it's rare that we are truly intentional about our choices. More commonly, we absorb lessons from family and friends and the stories that our culture immerses us in and then act on instinct.

Drifting is easy. It's a way of life where you concentrate on keeping the metaphorical boat afloat, avoiding the obvious whirlpools and rapids, but letting the flow of the river do the work of determining your direction and your destination. Many of us can be carried all the way to midlife in this way—it is, after all, a life that can be secure, satisfying, and successful by most sensible measures. Eventually, though, the river is going to catch us out with an unwelcome surprise—such as an unexpected gust of limerence that capsizes the boat.

At the risk of overdoing the metaphor, there are two big ways that drifting through life can make us more vulnerable to limerence. First, if we are coasting along in a complacent manner, we tend to be less vigilant about hazards along the way. Second, when we do capsize and scrabble back into our boat, we can be completely disoriented about what happened, what it means, and where to go next.

These life hazards can take different forms. A common one is drifting for so long that you lose touch with yourself. Perhaps you have fallen into the habit of prioritizing the needs of others or avoiding conflict by always being the one to compromise. Maybe you never had a clear sense of what you wanted to do with your life and so allowed other people (with stronger opinions) to influence your choices. Maybe obligations weigh heavy on you and you act more often out of duty than from free choice.

It's not that being selfless is bad, but inattention to your own emotional needs builds a vulnerability that you are unaware of until it's triggered. You get caught out by limerence. Perhaps you meet someone new who inspires you to live for yourself, awakening old dreams or ambitions that you had suppressed for too long, and you cling to them for the energy they kindle in you. Perhaps you know deep down that your partner is domineering but had desensitized yourself enough to tolerate it—until someone else shows you a crumb of compassion and you fall hopelessly into limerence for them.

The reason the emotional storm of limerence erupts so powerfully under these conditions is that there is a wellspring of frustration in your subconscious that's been silently building a head of pressure for so long that when it's finally released, it blows the roof off your life.

Another common hazard of drifting through life is benign neglect. This most frequently comes from ignoring the romantic aspect of life while you are preoccupied with other priorities. Perhaps you've given up on love after too many disappointments, or your marriage has become more about family responsibilities and companionship than romance. Again, this is not irresponsible, or a dereliction of duty, it's just an everyday oversight of a hidden hazard. Maybe you didn't realize that you would be vulnerable to flattery from an attractive LO because you'd suppressed your need to feel desired. You thought that taking a content and stable marriage for granted would be OK, not realizing that someone else showing romantic interest could upend your world and smash your moral compass. Ignoring the problem—or assuming you could deal with it sometime in the future when life was less hectic—was storing up trouble. Subconscious issues tend to quietly worsen if they are not confronted.

A final hazard is that life is full of stresses and, revealingly, limerence often flares up at those times.

> *I do find limerence changes with my mood—if I'm anxious it'll go round my head in a desperate loop. If I'm depressed all seems hopeless and that he's the only one who can rescue me. If I'm relaxed it's just there as a background disappointment. —S*

Bereavement, financial crisis, redundancy, illness—there are a distressingly plentiful number of trials that can arise. It's natural to crave escape from hardship, and limerence offers a source of intense reward at times when other sources of reward are hard to come by. This psychological vulnerability is another manifestation of drifting through life. If your daily life is not fulfilling, the overwhelming excitement, motivation, and exhilaration of limerence is like a golden promise. A dream to pursue. A way to escape the miserable status quo.

Drifting makes us overlook all these hidden hazards. We may dodge them for years by the grace of good fortune, but eventually our luck runs out. At that point, we discover the other consequence of a directionless life: we don't know how to recover. Once our little boat of life has been overturned and dunked us in the water, it can be the first time that many of us ask whether we were on the right course. An eruption of limerence causes us to look around and finally wonder if the course we'd been following for so long was really taking us where we wanted to go. We begin to notice the people who made different choices.

When life is unplanned, a shock makes you realize how little thought you gave to the early years. You marvel at how powerful the feeling of limerence is—how flat you had previously felt, how little exhilaration your life had involved, how risk averse you had been. Existential doubt like that is hugely destabilizing, which is bad enough, but it also makes it hard to act. When limerence has made you doubt your old certainties, when you're no longer sure what you want, you can become paralyzed by indecision. A major cost of drifting through life is that you are poorly prepared to cope with an emergency because you find yourself having to simultaneously deal with the emotional assault of limerence and an identity crisis at the same time. When you don't know where you are going it's hard to get back on course.

Purposeful living

The way to avoid the psychological vulnerabilities that are created by drifting through life is to take a more active approach to decision-making and be more mindful about where you are going and why. You are most at risk of succumbing to limerence when you are blind to your true needs and reflexively reacting to confusing emotions as they bubble up from the subconscious.

If you live with purpose, you can neutralize those risks. Purposeful living means living in a way that is more fulfilling, more meaningful, and more self-directed; making active decisions on the basis that they will help you achieve your life's goals; being more conscious of the consequences of your actions; being deliberate in your choices, and not just reacting impulsively to circumstances. Fundamentally, it means understanding yourself—knowing yourself as you truly are, and beginning the work of unlearning the limiting beliefs and received wisdom that may have constrained your life previously.

This is an old idea. The philosophical maxim, "Know thyself," was inscribed on the Temple of Apollo in ancient Delphi, but thousands of years later it remains hard to put into practice.[1] Life has a way of alienating us from our true natures—not in an exploitative or oppressive way, necessarily, but just in the normal tension between our desires and our responsibilities; in the conflict between individual wants and societal expectations. It's in this gray fog that we can lose track of ourselves as we struggle to answer difficult questions. How much should we compromise for the sake of harmony? Is the fear we feel a protective instinct that saves us from harm, or a limiting belief born of insecurity? Is giving up on an impractical dream good sense or self-negation?

It's very difficult to navigate these complex choices without a clear sense of our own identity and purpose. We do have impulses that are destructive and should be curbed. We have emotional fears that stop us from realizing our potential. Persuasive people can influence us into making choices that aren't in our best interests. The critical distinction between living with purpose and drifting through life is that purposeful people make choices from a position of self-knowledge. They have learned what they need, emotionally and practically, to help themselves thrive. They have prioritized goals so that they focus more on the things that really matter in all the key areas of life—health, relationships, work, and community. With that clarity of purpose, decision-making is simplified. If an obligation is taken on consciously, it is much less likely to be resented later. If an opportunity is passed up because it isn't going to help achieve your primary aims in life (no matter how superficially attractive), there won't be that awful pang of "fear of missing out" that besieges those who are unsure of their purpose.

> *Now, the focus has shifted from LO to myself, what was/is going on in myself to cause this limerence, why this LO? The last months have been a journey of introspection, analyzing my upbringing, where I fit in on attachment theories, etc. So to me, what started as a crazy love addiction has turned into a psychology class on myself! —R*

Purposeful living begins with examining the relationship you have with yourself and with the world. It requires a kind of painstaking sifting through the past that can be discomforting, but empowering.

Limerence often forces this self-examination upon us, so it only makes sense to capitalize on the disruption and use it as a starting point to permanently improve your life.

How to live with purpose

Let's get practical. If you want to be more purposeful, how do you begin?

There are seven key principles that define a purposeful life—seven attitudes of mind and core behaviors that define someone who is focused on transforming their life for the better. Adopting these behaviors is the best way to navigate your life toward more purpose.

1. Honesty

Most importantly, you have to be honest with yourself, but also with others. Honesty is the only way to successfully align your life with your true beliefs, principles, and values. If you deny your true feelings and instead try to live in a way that you think others will approve of, you open yourself up to temptations (like limerence) that arouse the desires you've suppressed.

2. Self-awareness

Being true to yourself is difficult if you are estranged from your own feelings and nature. We are forged from the combined influences of genetics and environment, and many of us grow up in an environment that punishes us for our inherent traits (like shyness, boldness, doubt, nonconformity, sensitivity, curiosity). Rediscovery of our intrinsic personality traits, and how they have been influenced by outside forces, is an essential step toward knowing thyself.

3. Openness to renewal

To transform a life for the better, we need to imagine an alternative mode of living. Our attitudes toward fundamental aspects of life—family, romance, money, work, society—are founded on a set of beliefs that are so deeply embedded that we rarely examine where they came from or how we developed them. An openness to rewriting some of those narratives is necessary for telling yourself a new story about how life can be.

4. The courage to face discomfort

Renewal is a nice way of saying change, and change often comes with discomfort built in. Change requires courage, but it is the courage to face short-term trials for long-term prizes. In fact, many self-development gurus point out that humans actually thrive on discomfort, because it stimulates growth (of strength, resilience, and stamina—both mental and physical).[2] Getting comfortable with discomfort is a keystone skill.

5. An internal locus of control

Part of the recovery mindset (see Chapter 17) is adopting the belief that you have the power to influence your fate. There are many practical constraints that limit our ability to take action— not enough time, money, freedom, or opportunity—but if you want your life to be better, you need to plan within the world as it is, not lament the fact that it isn't how you would like it to be. Practical problem-solving is the best approach to improving your life on your own terms.

6. Decisiveness

Uncertainty is the rocket fuel of limerence. Using your purposeful mindset to end uncertainty about your own situation is an incredibly powerful step in limerence recovery, but its value goes far beyond that short-term benefit. Indecision is usually caused by fear of loss, not by prudent risk management. Purpose comes from making decisive choices, not from keeping all your options open in the hope that worrying about them for long enough will improve your odds of making the right choice. You will undoubtedly make wrong choices. The solution is to correct them once you know for sure, not to indefinitely put off the decision. Impulsive choices are risky, but so is chronic uncertainty.

7. Action orientation

Finally, the personal transformation needed to live with more purpose isn't just about internal shifts in mindset. You also have to pursue meaningful goals, and that means taking action. To benefit from knowledge you have to implement it. Even more importantly, you learn new things by taking action that you could never have anticipated during the scheming and dreaming phase of life planning. Until you start actively transforming your life, your purpose will remain unfulfilled.

The benefits of a purposeful life

This switch in perspective from living reactively to living with purpose can fundamentally transform your life. Maybe you want to launch a new business, improve your relationships with your family and friends, travel the world, achieve financial independence, found a charity, run for political office, or improve your community. Anything that is worthwhile requires purpose and drive, and all the worthwhile things in the world around us were made by people being purposeful. It changes you, and it changes how you contribute to the world.

The benefits of purposeful living also radiate out into the future, compounding as they go. For the immediate short-term challenge of dealing with a limerence emergency, adopting a purposeful mindset can help get the appropriate perspective on your predicament. More usefully, though, purposeful living solves one of the most difficult problems of overcoming limerence: it offers new rewards that are similar in scope to the thrill of limerence.

Pursuing purposeful goals can be profoundly stimulating and rewarding, and so dispel the illusion that limerence is a unique source of emotional fulfillment. Instead of daydreaming about being with a limerent object, you can daydream about your ideal future life. What could life be like if you were free of the limerent obsession and instead exerting your energy and will to attaining your life's goals? If you're going to daydream, you might as well dream big, and there are fewer sources of optimism bigger than liberating yourself from your unnecessary burdens and seeking happiness—not the cheap thrills of pleasure-seeking, but the deep gratification of a life well lived.

The other big benefit of adopting purposeful living as a new reward is that it is limitless. Life is always moving, there are always new goals to pursue, new dreams to try and bring to life, new relationships to nurture (with full self-awareness about glimmer-chasing, naturally). You can start small and work on something modest—perhaps picking up a paint brush for the first time in years, or learning a new language, or taking singing lessons—but then increase your ambitions as you start to get the hang of self-improvement. Living with purpose is about building, it's about creating things that give you joy, whether it's as simple as a new hobby or as aspirational as launching a new business. If you are doing something purposeful, you are building something worthwhile and can take natural and healthy pride in that achievement—with the added benefit of also building self-esteem.[3] Creative work helps you find meaning and hope, and those are inexhaustible resources.

Beyond these immediate benefits for well-being and limerence recovery, there is a longer-term benefit too. Purposeful living makes you more emotionally resilient and future-proofs you against unwanted limerence disrupting your life again. When you are living in an aimless way, limerence can be a very stimulating diversion. When you are living with purpose, limerence is an unwelcome distraction from your good life.

If life is fulfilling, you are acting with purpose and pursuing meaningful goals, the blandishments of limerence are far less appealing than if you are drifting in discontent. People who are purposefully engaged in meaningful work and healthy relationships are far less likely to see limerence as an attractive escape. Limerence can still happen, of course, if you meet the right sort of person who sets off the glimmer, but that experience will not be such a revelation, such a welcome injection of euphoria. It might still be gratifying, but can also be understood as a potentially disruptive risk to happiness. Armed with an understanding of what limerence is and how it develops, you can make more deliberate decisions about whether getting closer to a potential LO is going to help or hinder you in your purposeful endeavors.

> I am pleased to say that I am now able to concentrate on other things like my job, career, finances, family life, social life and education without limerent ruminations destroying my concentration. I am also able to refocus my thoughts much more successfully when I set my mind to it. I am again thinking about some of the personal goals I had set or was thinking of setting prior to limerence taking hold of me. —VL

Ultimately, the best way to reduce your psychological vulnerability to limerence is to make your life better.

The first steps to freedom

For some people, finding purpose is easy. They may have a long-nurtured but neglected ambition that presents itself when they ask the "What if?" questions of contemplating an alternative life.

Others encounter an immediate stumbling block: *Where do I start?* They are so estranged from themselves that they don't know what they want, or they've never had any burning passions or secret dreams that they can excavate and reexamine. Fortunately, there is a helpful starting point for finding purpose if you get stuck in this way:

Your purposeful goal is to understand yourself better.

Focus a good portion of your time and energy onto the project of self-discovery. Practice honesty. Ask yourself some arousing questions: What do you want out of life, how could you get it, what would be the first step you could take? What gives you energy? What do you not like about yourself? What big problem have you been ignoring for too long that hangs like a black cloud over your life? Be alert to ego-protecting rationalizations. Build self-awareness—it's the foundation for good decision-making.

Everyone benefits if you understand yourself better.

♡

Limerence is a lifequake. While it can be very destructive, it can also be used as an opportunity for renewal. The process of rebuilding will be faster and easier if you are excited about the new life that you could create from the rubble—the shock can be an epiphany that can be steered into a personal renaissance. If you want to be free of the addiction of limerence, it really helps to have a positive future to escape to.

If you have been reading this book to help overcome a bad bout of limerence in yourself, purposeful living is the best solution I know. It's the surest path to freedom.

If you have instead been reading to try and understand how limerence has made someone you love apparently lose their mind, or if you are just trying to understand why past relationships haven't worked out, living with purpose is also a powerfully effective remedy for creating a better future. Purposeful living works for both limerents and non-limerents, and is likely to help them come to mutual understanding and learn how to thrive together.

There's no real downside.

ABOUT THE AUTHOR

Tom Bellamy, PhD, is a neuroscientist and honorary associate professor at the University of Nottingham. He received a PhD in neuroscience from UCL in 2001 and held a personal fellowship at the Babraham Institute in Cambridge from 2004 to 2010. For the next fourteen years he lectured and researched at the University of Nottingham before leaving to pursue an independent career in 2024. He has published more than forty scientific papers, abstracts, and book chapters on esoteric aspects of neurophysiology, but now writes about how fundamental neuroscience can help us understand human behavior. He started the blog *Living with Limerence* in 2017 and continues to write about the causes and consequences of intense infatuation.

ACKNOWLEDGMENTS

I'd like to thank the four groups of people who made this book possible.

First, my agents at Blake Friedmann. Thanks to Sam Hodder who got things started, saw potential in the project, and was willing to take a chance on a new author. Thanks for also suggesting the title, which I immediately liked for the double meaning of both being besotted and being hit by a powerful blow.

Many thanks to Juliet Pickering, who took the book forward after Sam moved on, and found publishers who shared our vision for the project. While that success might be the most obvious benefit for an author, I'm also immensely grateful for her good humor, steady hand, and patient advice—the best champion I could have hoped for.

Second, I'd like to thank my publishers. At Watkins, thanks to Lucy Carroll and Sophie Blackman for shepherding the book from concept to first draft and through the revisions to the final version. Thanks, too, to Jodie Gaudet, Brittany Willis, and Fiona Robertson who oversaw all the elements that needed to come together.

At St. Martin's, thanks to Anna deVries for taking the book to a new audience and for valuable feedback at critical stages of its development. It was a huge relief to have things run so smoothly across two continents.

Third, I am truly grateful for the great community at livingwithlimerence.com. When I first started blogging about limerence, I was writing into the void. Over time, readers arrived, began to comment, share their own stories, and then everything snowballed. The site is now a thriving community and an invaluable store of knowledge about limerence, with nearly six million words of personal testimony having been added over the years. The lessons shared have shaped all our understandings of limerence, and some of the comments that illustrate key principles particularly well are quoted in the book. Thanks to everyone who has contributed to the collective wisdom.

Fourth, the biggest thanks go to my family. To my wife Teika, for unwavering support, guidance, editorial expertise, and all-round excellence. To my children Rebecca and Jerome, my brother, Matthew, and Mum, Patricia—thank you for all the encouragement and the many years of happiness. Finally, thanks to my dad, Laurence, for everything you taught me. I hope you would have been proud of my book, and I wish you could have been here to read it.

NOTES

1. What is limerence?
1. Throughout the book, I will be quoting from the experiences of limerents who have visited the livingwithlimerence.com website or emailed me directly. Comments are attributed by initials to preserve anonymity.
2. "Ecstatic union" is from *The Second Sex* by Simone de Beauvoir and was quoted approvingly by Dorothy Tennov in her first description of limerence. The quote is, "A desire for the complete destruction of the self, abolishing the boundaries that separate her from the beloved. There is no question here of masochism, but of a dream of ecstatic union." De Beauvoir, S, *The Second Sex*, Jonathan Cape, 1957, p.615.
3. The importance of attentional bias is well-illustrated by the power of cues related to addiction to capture attention and trigger drug-seeking cravings—a point that will become relevant to limerence later. See: Anderson, B, "What is abnormal about addiction-related attentional biases?" *Drug and Alcohol Dependence*, 167, 2016, pp.8–14.
4. This quote is from De Munck, V, ed., *Romantic Love and Sexual Behavior*, Praeger, 1998, p.5.
5. See: Meloy, J, ed., *The Psychology of Stalking*, Academic Press, 1998.

2. The phases of limerence
1. See: Tennov, D, *Love and Limerence: The Experience of Being in Love*, Scarborough House, 1998, p.142.

3. The neuroscience of limerence
1. See the chapter entitled "Love Madness" in *A Scientist Looks at Romantic Love and Calls It Limerence: The Collected Later Works of Dorothy Tennov*. ebook. www.gramps.org.
2. The concept of human universals was introduced by Donald Brown in his book of the same name (New York, McGraw-Hill, 1991). It defines aspects of human existence that "comprise those features of culture, society, language, behavior and psyche for which there are no known exception."
3. See the chapter entitled "The Birth of Limerence Theory" in *A Scientist Looks at Romantic Love and Calls It Limerence: The Collected Later Works of Dorothy Tennov*. ebook. www.gramps.org.

4. Ibid.
5. The idea that the basal ganglia represented a "reptilian complex" originated with the neuroscientist Paul MacLean in the 1960s. It was an attempt to link evolutionary development of the brain to the comparative anatomy of different species, but is now viewed as a metaphor rather than a meaningful description of subcortical brain regions in humans.
6. For a good review of the latest research on reward prediction errors, see: Schultz, W, "Neuronal Reward and Decision Signals: From Theories to Data," *Physiological Reviews*, 95(3), 2015, pp.853–951.
7. See the chapter entitled "The Individual Experience of Limerence" in Tennov, D, *Love and Limerence: The Experience of Being in Love*, Scarborough House, 1998.
8. For a review of the actions of oxytocin in birth and lactation, see: Gimpl, G, Fahrenholz, F, "The oxytocin receptor system: Structure, function, and regulation," *Physiological Reviews*, 81(2), 2001, pp.629–83.
9. For a recent review on the impact of vasopressin on water regulation, see: Bankir, L, Bichet, D, Morgenthaler, N, "Vasopressin: Physiology, assessment and osmosensation," *Journal of Internal Medicine*, 282(4), 2017, pp.284–97.
10. These projections can act as a "gain" signal for the core circuits. See: Grinevich, V, Ludwig, M, "The multiple faces of the oxytocin and vasopressin systems in the brain," *Journal of Neuroendocrinology*, 33(11), 2021, p.e13004.
11. Rilling, J, Young, L, "The Biology of Mammalian Parenting and its Effect on Offspring Social Development," *Science*, 345(6198), 2014, pp.771–6.
12. Kosfeld, M, et al., "Oxytocin increases trust in humans," *Nature*, 435(7042), 2005, pp.673–6. For an overview of the evidence in humans, see for example: Marsh, N, Marsh, A, Lee, M, Hurlemann, R, "Oxytocin and the Neurobiology of Prosocial Behavior," *Neuroscientist*, 27(6), 2021, pp.604–19; Kendrick, K, Guastella, A, Becker, B, "Overview of Human Oxytocin Research," *Current Topics in Behavioral Neuroscience*, 35, 2018, pp.321–48.
13. Carmichael, M, Humbert, R, Dixen, J, Palmisano, G, Greenleaf, W, Davidson, J, "Plasma oxytocin increases in the human sexual response," *Journal of Clinical Endocrinology and Metabolism*, 64(1), 1987, pp.27–31.
14. Kleiman, D, "Monogamy in Mammals," *The Quarterly Review of Biology*, 52:1, 1977, pp.39–69.
15. Winslow, J, Hastings, N, Carter, C, Harbaugh, C, Insel, T, "A role for central vasopressin in pair bonding in monogamous prairie voles," *Nature*, 365(6446), 1993, pp.545–8.
16. Putnam, P, Young, L, Gothard, K, "Bridging the gap between rodents and humans: The role of non-human primates in oxytocin research,"

American Journal of Primatology, 80(10), 2018, p.e22756; Gavrilets, S, "Human origins and the transition from promiscuity to pair bonding," Proceedings of the National Academy of Sciences USA, 109(25), 2012, pp.9923–28.
17. Boccia, M, Petrusz, P, Suzuki, K, Marson, L, Pedersen, C, "Immunohistochemical localization of oxytocin receptors in human brain," *Neuroscience*, 253, 2013, pp.155–64.

4. Person addiction

1. Broadly, incentive salience is the relative importance attached to a desire, or how much you want something. See, for example: Olney, J, Warlow, S, Naffziger, E, Berridge K, "Current perspectives on incentive salience and applications to clinical disorders," *Current Opinion in Behavioral Sciences*, 22, 2018, pp.59–69.
2. For a good discussion of the role of reward prediction errors in guiding behavior, see: Schultz, W, "Dopamine reward prediction error coding," *Dialogues in Clinical Neuroscience*, 18, 2016, pp.23–32.
3. This is the reason why drug users can have detectible release of dopamine in response to images of drug use, or drug paraphernalia. See: Maas, L, et al., "Functional magnetic resonance imaging of human brain activation during cue-induced cocaine craving," *American Journal of Psychiatry*, 155(1), 1998, pp.124–6.
4. For a review of the latest research on wanting versus liking, see: Berridge, K, Kringelbach, M, "Pleasure systems in the brain," *Neuron*, 86, 2015, pp.646–64.
5. For a good summary of the evidence for "hedonic hotspots" see: Peciña, S, Smith, K, Berridge, K, "Hedonic hot spots in the brain," *Neuroscientist*, 12(6), 2006, pp.500–11.
6. In humans, another brain region known as the *orbitofrontal cortex* appears to be central to integrating all these influences on the experience of pleasure—the connection to wanting, how quickly the pleasure can fade, and the range of different stimuli that are enjoyed. It seems to be a central hub for processing "liking." See: Kringelbach, M, "The orbitofrontal cortex: Linking reward to hedonic experience," *Nature Reviews Neuroscience*, 6, 2005, pp.691–702.
7. Habituation of responses has again been most commonly studied in pleasurable tastes and food. See, for example: De Luca, M, "Habituation of the responsiveness of mesolimbic and mesocortical dopamine transmission to taste stimuli," *Frontiers in Integrative Neuroscience*, 8, 2014, p.21.
8. I came across this neat concept of certain social media apps acting as "infinity pools" of limitless entertainment in the book *Make Time* by

Jake Knapp and John Zeratsky. Bantam Press, London, 2018.
9. The evidence for direct sensitization is reviewed here: Samaha, A, Khoo, S, Ferrario, C, Robinson, T, "Dopamine 'ups and downs' in addiction revisited," *Trends in Neurosciences*, 44(7), 2021, pp.516–26.
10. Sensitization of wanting as a basis for addiction is discussed in depth here: Berridge, K, Robinson, T, "Liking, wanting, and the incentive-sensitization theory of addiction," *The American Psychologist*, 71(8), 2016, pp.670–9.
11. American Psychiatric Association, *Diagnostic and Statistical Manual of Mental Disorders* (5th ed), 2022.
12. For a good article on this topic, see: www.forbes.com/sites/davidschwartz/2018/06/04/how-casinos-use-math-to-make-money-when-you-play-the-slots/ [Accessed Apr 2024].
13. The classic work that describes how reinforcement schedule affects the intensity and persistence of reward learning was the 1957 book *Schedules of Reinforcement* by CB Ferster and BF Skinner. The principle of intermittent reinforcement being especially powerful has been reestablished in multiple contexts, including human behavior. See, for example: Clark, L, Zack, M, "Engineered highs: Reward variability and frequency as potential prerequisites of behavioral addiction," *Addictive Behaviors*, 140, 2023, p.107626.
14. For a good discussion of the commonalities of different addictions, see: Robinson, M, et al., "Roles of 'Wanting' and 'Liking' in Motivating Behavior: Gambling, Food, and Drug Addictions," *Current Topics in Behavioral Neuroscience*, 27, 2016, pp.105–36.

5. Is limerence a mental illness?
1. For the World Health Organization definition, see: www.who.int/news-room/fact-sheets/detail/mental-disorders [Accessed Apr 2024].
2. As a common principle, reference to one of these authorities is a simple way of deciding whether a condition is strictly defined as a mental health disorder, but many well-known conditions are not listed (such as Asperger's syndrome and sex addiction) and there is considerable debate about what should be added or removed when the guides are periodically revised.
3. For an overview of obsessive compulsive disorder, see: www.nimh.nih.gov/health/topics/obsessive-compulsive-disorder-ocd [Accessed Apr 2024].
4. The Wakin-Vo model of limerence is explained in: Wakin, A, and Vo, DB, "Love-variant: The Wakin-Vo I. D. R. model of limerence," Inter-Disciplinary–Net. 2nd Global Conference; Challenging Intimate Boundaries, 2008.

5. Like all neurobiology, there is still a lot of uncertainty in the details and nuances of OCD and how the circuits involved gives rise to key symptoms. A good review of the current evidence is here: Robbins, T, Vaghi, M, Banca, P, "Obsessive-Compulsive Disorder: Puzzles and Prospects," *Neuron*, 102(1), 2019, pp.27–47.
6. For an overview of bipolar disorder, see: www.nimh.nih.gov/health/topics/bipolar-disorder [Accessed Apr 2024].
7. For a recent review of the evidence, see: Kloiber, S, Rosenblat, J, Husain, M, Ortiz, A, Berk M, Quevedo, J, Vieta, E, Maes, M, Birmaher, B, Soares, J, Carvalho, A, "Neurodevelopmental pathways in bipolar disorder," *Neuroscience and Biobehavioral Reviews*, 112, 2020, pp.213–26.
8. Reports of erotomania as a romantic delusion go back to antiquity, with Hippocrates describing the condition. A detailed review on the history and symptoms of erotomania can be found here: Kelly, BD, "Love as delusion, delusions of love: Erotomania, narcissism and shame," *Medical Humanities*, 44, 2018, pp.15–19.
9. See Jordan, HW, Lockert, EW, Johnson-Warren, M, Cabell, C, Cooke, T, Greer, W, Howe, G, "Erotomania revisited: Thirty-four years later," *Journal of the National Medical Association*, 98(5), 2006, pp.787–93.
10. See, for example: Kelly, BD, "Erotomania," *CNS Drugs* 19, 2005, pp. 657–69.
11. For the authoritative text, see: Bowlby, J, *Attachment: Attachment and loss*. Basic Books, New York, 1969. For a good popular account of attachment theory see: Levine, A and Heller, R, *Attached*, Bluebird, London, 2019.
12. See, for example: Perlini, C, Bellani, M, Rossetti, MG, Zovetti, N, Rossin, G, Bressi, C, Brambilla, P, "Disentangle the neural correlates of attachment style in healthy individuals," *Epidemiology and Psychiatric Sciences*, 28(4), 2019, pp.371–5.
13. These classic experiments were carried out by Harry Harlow and colleagues, and show how crucial the need for maternal contact is for primate development. Monkeys separated from their mother would favor cloth models to cuddle over wire models that provided food. The original reports were published in: Harlow, HF, Dodsworth, RO, and Harlow, MK, "Total social isolation in monkeys," *Proceedings of the National Academy of Sciences USA*, 54, 1965, pp.90–7. Reports of the mental health catastrophe among institutionalized children in the orphanages of Ceausescu's communist regime began to emerge in the late eighties. For an account of the conditions of the institutions and the children see: www.npr.org/sections/health-shots/2014/02/20/280237833/orphans-lonely-beginnings-reveal-how-parents-shape-a-childs-brain [Accessed Apr 2024].
14. Other terms are sometimes used for attachment styles to discriminate

between different forms, including anxious-avoidant, anxious-preoccupied, fearful-avoidant, ambivalent, and disorganized.
15. See: Feeney, JA, and Noller, P, "Attachment style as a predictor of adult romantic relationships," *Journal of Personality and Social Psychology*, 58(2), 1990, pp.281–91.
16. See: Grunze, H, Schaefer, M, Scherk, H, Born, C, Preuss, UW, "Comorbid Bipolar and Alcohol Use Disorder—A Therapeutic Challenge," *Frontiers in Psychiatry*, 12, 2021, p.357.

6. Who becomes limerent?

1. For some classic reviews on how sample selection and thresholding (especially in statistical tests) can distort results, see: Berk, R, "An Introduction to Sample Selection Bias in Sociological Data," *American Sociological Review*, 48(3), 1983, pp.386–98; and Nickerson, R, "Null hypothesis significance testing: A review of an old and continuing controversy," *Psychological Methods*, 5(2), 2000, pp.241–301.
2. Wakin, A, Vo, D, "Love-variant: The Wakin-Vo I. D. R. model of limerence," Inter-Disciplinary-Net. 2nd Global Conference; Challenging Intimate Boundaries, 2008.
3. For a good review, see: Hatfield, E, Bensman, L, Rapson, R, "A brief history of social scientists' attempts to measure passionate love," *Journal of Social and Personal Relationships*, 29(2), 2012, pp.143–64.
4. All the data for the quiz and survey can be found at livingwithlimerence.com/how-common-is-limerence-the-numbers/.
5. Also known as a "normal" or "Gaussian" distribution, the bell-shaped curve is a symmetrical graph that looks like the cross section of a bell. It is what is expected for any measurement that varies randomly around an average value—for example, the height of all people in a population or exam scores in standardized tests. This suggests that the intensity of limerence symptoms vary randomly on either side of an average among the people who took the quiz.
6. The completion rate of a survey is another source of bias. For our survey, only 20.1 percent of people who started it ended up answering all the questions. A lot of people gave up along the way for unknown reasons, excluding themselves from the results.
7. Our survey was carried out using Pollfish.com, which uses incentives to encourage survey completion, rather than simple financial rewards. Typically, the survey is presented to people browsing a website and delivers a targeted perk or offer of some sort if the survey is completed. For full details of the methodology, see: livingwithlimerence.com/how-common-is-limerence-the-numbers/.

8. For a couple of good reviews, see: Regan, P, Levin, L, Sprecher, S, Christopher, F, Gate, R, "Partner Preferences: What Characteristics Do Men and Women Desire In Their Short-Term Sexual and Long-Term Romantic Partners?," *Journal of Psychology & Human Sexuality*, 12(3), 2000, pp.1–21; and Schmitt, D, Shackelford, T, Buss, D, "Are men really more 'oriented' toward short-term mating than women? A critical review of theory and research," *Psychology, Evolution & Gender*, 3(3), 2001, pp.211–39.
9. See, for example: Goldenberg, T, Stephenson, R, Bauermeister, J, "Cognitive and Emotional Factors Associated with Sexual Risk-Taking Behaviors Among Young Men Who Have Sex with Men," *Archives of Sexual Behavior*, 48(4), 2019, pp.1127–36.
10. Census data was obtained from this site: www.census.gov/library/visualizations/interactive/sexual-orientation-and-gender-identity.html [Accessed Apr 2024].
11. For a comprehensive analysis of the Big Five dimensions, see: Goldberg, L, "An alternative 'description of personality:' The Big-Five factor structure," *Journal of Personality and Social Psychology*, 59(6), 1990, pp.1216–29.
12. The application of the Myers-Briggs test in practice is overseen by the Myers Brigg Foundation (myersbriggs.org). For a review of the evidence for the test, see: Randall, K, Isaacson, M, Ciro, C, "Validity and Reliability of the Myers-Briggs Personality Type Indicator: A Systematic Review and Meta-analysis," *Journal of Best Practices in Health Professions Diversity*, 10 (1), 2017, pp.1–27.
13. The data from this online poll can be found at neurosparkle.com/infatuation-mbti/ [Accessed Apr 2024].
14. The idea of a second adolescence at midlife has appeal, but it's more a popular conceit than an established principle. See, for example: www.theguardian.com/lifeandstyle/2016/jul/17/going-through-your-second-adolescence-aka-the-middlepause.
15. There isn't universal agreement about what ages constitute "midlife," but it can be broken into early (age thirty-five to forty-four) and late (age forty-five to sixty-four) stages. See, for example: Medley, M, "Life satisfaction across four stages of adult life," *International Journal of Aging and Human Development*, 11(3), 1980, pp.193–209.
16. In principle, because the survey question asked "Have you *ever* experienced this altered state of mind" the percentage of people answering yes should just increase with age. The peak at midlife probably reflects what's known as an "immediacy bias" when recent experiences come to mind more easily that past experiences. See Van Boven, L, White, K, Huber, M, "Immediacy bias in emotion perception: Current emotions seem more intense than previous

emotions," *Journal of Experimental Psychology. General*, 138(3), 2009, pp.368–82.
17. For a good analysis of attachment style in US adults, see today.yougov.com/society/articles/45827-what-do-americans-say-about-their-attachment-style.

7. Why does limerence exist?

1. One of the best popular accounts for this principle is Dawkins, R, *The Blind Watchmaker: Why the Evidence of Evolution Reveals a Universe without Design*, Norton and Company, New York, 1986.
2. For a thorough review of the elements of sexual arousal and learning and how they can be discriminated see: Georgiadis, J, Kringelbach, M, Pfaus, J, "Sex for fun: A synthesis of human and animal neurobiology," *Nature Reviews Urology*, 9, 2012, pp.486–98.
3. The background to Tinbergen's interest in ethology and the classic experiments that established the concept of supernormal stimuli is well summarized in his Nobel Prize acceptance speech: www.nobelprize.org/prizes/medicine/1973/tinbergen/biographical/.
4. Barrett, D, *Supernormal Stimuli: How Primal Urges Overran Their Evolutionary Purpose*, Norton and Company, New York, 2010.
5. For a good overview, see: Kappeler, P, "Male Reproductive Strategies," *Nature Education Knowledge* 3(10), 2012, p.82.
6. Buss, D, "The Evolution of Love in Humans," *The New Psychology of Love*, second edition, Cambridge University Press, Cambridge, 2019.
7. The principle of kin selection was formalized in Maynard Smith, J, "Group selection and kin selection," *Nature*, 201, 1964, pp.1145–47. Although well validated and widely accepted, it does have its critics: Birch, J, Okasha, S, "Kin Selection and Its Critics," *BioScience*, 65(1), 2015, pp.22–32.
8. Cowden, C, "Game Theory, Evolutionary Stable Strategies and the Evolution of Biological Interactions," *Nature Education Knowledge*, 3(10), 2012, p.6.
9. For a recent review of the evidence and controversies around sexual selection in evolution, see: Petrie, M, "Evolution by Sexual Selection," *Frontiers in Ecology and Evolution*, 9, 2021, p.e786868.
10. The Handicap Principle was introduced by Amotz Zahavi and has been refined over the years: Zahavi, A, Zahavi, A, *The Handicap Principle: A Missing Piece of Darwin's Puzzle*, Oxford University Press, Oxford, 1999. As with much evolutionary theory, there are ongoing disputes as to the interpretation of the evidence: Penn, D, Számadó, S, "The Handicap Principle: How an erroneous hypothesis became a scientific principle," *Biological Reviews*, 95, 2020, pp.267–90.

8. Social and cultural forces

1. The full quote is: "We are the storytelling ape, and we are incredibly good at it. As soon as we are old enough to want to understand what is happening around us, we begin to live in a world of stories. We think in narrative. We do it so automatically that we don't think we do it. And we have told ourselves stories vast enough to live in." Pratchett, T, Stewart, I, Cohen, J, *The Science of Discworld II*, Ebury Press, London, 2002.
2. For more on the development of tribal psychology see: McDonald, M, Navarrete, C, Van Vugt, M, "Evolution and the psychology of intergroup conflict: The male warrior hypothesis," *Philosophical Transactions of the Royal Society B*, 367(1589), 2012, pp.670–9.
3. For good insights into how important storytelling is to interpersonal skills development see: Smith, D, et al., "Cooperation and the evolution of hunter-gatherer storytelling," *Nature Communications*, 8, 2017, p.1853, and Garcia-Pelegrin, E, Wilkins, C, Clayton, N, "The Ape That Lived to Tell the Tale. The Evolution of the Art of Storytelling and Its Relationship to Mental Time Travel and Theory of Mind," *Frontiers in Psychology*, 12, 2021, p.e755783.
4. For an authoritative argument in support of this concept see: Booker, C, *The Seven Basic Plots: Why We Tell Stories*, Continuum, London, 2005.
5. Prophet, E, *Soul Mates and Twin Flames: The Spiritual Dimension of Love and Relationships*, Summit University Press, Corwin Springs, 1999. Jungian psychoanalysis is an extremely rich vein for ideas about why we connect to individuals who mirror our anima/animus personae. A satisfying summary that links Jungian theory to mythical storytelling can be found in Johnson, R, *We: Understanding the Psychology of Romantic Love*, Bravo Ltd, London, 1998.

9. Why do they seem so special?

1. This field is a lively area of debate, but a good summary of the case for universal markers of attraction can be found in these reviews: Rhodes, G, "The evolutionary psychology of facial beauty," *Annual Review of Psychology*, 57, 2006, pp.199–226; Langlois, J, et al., "Maxims or myths of beauty? A meta-analytic and theoretical review," *Psychological Bulletin*, 126, 2000, pp.390–423. It is worth noting that these claims are contested—for a popular account of the disputes and social downsides that can result see: Wolf, N, *The Beauty Myth*, Chatto and Windus, London, 1990.
2. Little, A, Jones, B, DeBruine, L, "Facial attractiveness: Evolutionary based research," *Philosophical Transactions of the Royal Society B*, 366(1571), 2011, pp.1638–59.
3. Wedekind, C, Seebeck, T, Bettens, F, Paepke, A, "MHC-dependent mate

preferences in humans," *Proceedings of the Royal Society B: Biological Sciences*, 260(1359), 1995, pp.245–9.
4. DeBruine, L, "Trustworthy but not lust-worthy: Context-specific effects of facial resemblance," *Proceedings of the Royal Society B: Biological Sciences*, 272, 2005, pp.919–22.
5. Bereczkei, T, Gyuris, P, Weisfeld, G, "Sexual imprinting in human mate choice," *Proceedings of the Royal Society B: Biological Sciences*, 271(1544), 2004, pp.1129–34; Marcinkowska, U, Rantala, M, "Sexual imprinting on facial traits of opposite-sex parents in humans," *Evolutionary Psychology*, 10(3), 2012, pp.621–30.
6. Park, Y, MacDonald, G, "Consistency between individuals' past and current romantic partners' own reports of their personalities," *Proceedings of the National Academy of Sciences of the United States of America*, 116(26), 2019, pp.12793–97.
7. Morton, H, Gorzalka, B, "Role of Partner Novelty in Sexual Functioning: A Review," *Journal of Sex and Marital Therapy*, 41(6), 2015, pp.593–609.
8. Chapman, G, *The Five Love Languages: How to Express Heartfelt Commitment to Your Mate*, Manjul Publishing House Pvt Ltd, Bhopal, 2009.
9. Little, A, Burt, D, Penton-Voak, I, Perrett, D, "Self-perceived attractiveness influences human female preferences for sexual dimorphism and symmetry in male faces," *Proceedings of the Royal Society B: Biological Sciences*, 268(1462), 2001, pp.39–44.
10. Curiously, this effect seems to also depend on whether the participant in the study considered themselves as having a romantic nature. Mutual gaze had little impact on the more even-tempered participants. See: Williams, G, Kleinke, C, "Effects of Mutual Gaze and Touch on Attraction, Mood, and Cardiovascular Reactivity," *Journal of Research in Personality*, 27(2), 1993, pp.170–83.
11. Quotes are from Tennov, D, *Love and Limerence: The Experience of Being in Love*, Scarborough House, New York, 1998.

10. Why are some people so addictive?

1. Misinterpretation of sexual interest is an apparently stable variable in psychological studies. Numerous studies have found a significant tendency for men to overestimate sexual interest from women and women to underestimate male sexual interest. See: Abbey, A, "Sex differences in attributions for friendly behavior: Do males misperceive females' friendliness?," *Journal of Personality and Social Psychology*, 42, 1982, pp.830–8; Haselton, M, "The sexual overperception bias: Evidence of a systematic bias in men from a survey of naturally occurring events," *Journal of Research in Personality*, 37, 2003, pp.34–47; Perilloux, C,

and Kurzban, R, "Do Men Overperceive Women's Sexual Interest?," *Psychological Science*, 26, 2015, pp.70–7. More recently, a study that was skeptical of the evolutionary psychology hypotheses to explain this sex difference found that estimates for the sexual interest of partners correlated with their own perceived attractiveness and desire for casual sex: Lee, A, et al., "Sex Differences in Misperceptions of Sexual Interest Can Be Explained by Sociosexual Orientation and Men Projecting Their Own Interest Onto Women," *Psychological Science*, 31, 2020, pp.184–92.
2. For a popular definition of love bombing see: www.psychologytoday.com/gb/basics/love-bombing.
3. The tendency to use manipulation as a mate retention strategy correlates with different personality types and is prevalent among those who have the "dark triad" of personality traits (narcissism, Machiavellianism, and psychopathy). For a good overview see: Holden, C, Zeigler-Hill, V, Pham, M, Shackelford, T, "Personality features and mate retention strategies: Honesty–humility and the willingness to manipulate, deceive, and exploit romantic partners," *Personality and Individual Differences*, 57, 2014, pp.31–6.
4. As a curious aside, there is evidence for an increase in narcissistic behavior in Western societies, so maybe the last scoundrel that wronged you really was trouble. Twenge, J, Campbell, W, *The Narcissism Epidemic: Living in the Age of Entitlement*. Simon and Schuster, New York, 2009.

11. Dating while limerent

1. See: Rosenfeld, M, Reuben, J, Thomas, J, Hausen, S, "How Couples Meet and Stay Together," 2017-2020-2022 combined dataset [Computer files], Stanford University Libraries, Stanford, CA, 2023.
2. The emergence of dating apps has been a particular benefit for LGBTQ communities. Having your search limited to a subculture within an already small local population was challenging enough, but when you add the risks of a bad reaction from someone whose sexuality you weren't sure of... well, having a big database of people who have already confirmed their preferences is a massive benefit. For heterosexual men and women, the dominance of online connections has had a strange impact on the supply-and-demand forces of dating. An infamous 2009 survey by one of the big online dating companies, OKCupid, revealed some startling asymmetries in the swiping habits of men and women (this post is no longer live, but can be accessed via the internet Wayback machine:http://blog.okcupid.com/index.php/2009/11/17/your-looks-and-online-dating/). The emergence of large databases of easy-access and low-stakes dating options has introduced a lot of skewed

expectations into an already complex situation. And, if this all feels like a horrible, reductive way to look at romance, well, I guess that is one of the downsides of turning dating into a literal market.
3. For those not familiar with the term, "catfishing" refers to the use of a fake online identity to try and lure others into a scam of some sort, usually romantic and/or financial. It comes from a 2010 film directed by Henry Joost and Ariel Schulman, which chronicles the experience of Schulman's brother forming an online relationship with someone who turned out to be middle-aged woman using a fake Facebook profile.
4. There is a wide abundance of articles about the pros and cons of hook-up culture out there. Predictably, the pro articles tend to predominantly be in publications that skew young in readership, such as: www.womenshealthmag.com/uk/health/a41410832/situationship/www.vice.com/en/article/pkpegz/catching-feelings-from-hook-up-advice, www.teenvogue.com/story/how-to-be-an-ethical-hook-up [Accessed Feb 2024]. For an evolutionary view of how modern dating culture maps onto reproductive strategies, see: Ponseti, J, Diehl, K, Stirn, A, "Is Dating Behavior in Digital Contexts Driven by Evolutionary Programs? A Selective Review," *Frontiers in Psychology*, 13, 2022, pp.678439.
5. The neurophysiology of bonding and limerence was covered in Chapter 3, but the most relevant factor in this context is how the combination of simultaneously activating both the dopamine reward circuits and the oxytocin and vasopressin bonding system is the mechanism that associates the extreme rewards of limerence with a specific person.
6. From time to time, somebody leaves a comment on the *Living with Limerence* site to suggest the creation of a "limerents only" dating app. While it seems like a nice idea, I always have the sinking feeling that it would also be a rich hunting ground for predatory or narcissistic characters who want to ensnare a devoted limerent into their schemes.
7. From: Tennov, D, *Love and Limerence: The Experience of Being in Love*, Scarborough House, 1998, p.16.

12. Social media

1. Analyzing the social impact of social media has become a virtual industry. For a recent academic review of some of the key concerns, see: Rosen, D, *The Social Media Debate: Unpacking the Social, Psychological, and Cultural Effects of Social Media*, Routledge, London, 2022. For a review of some of the most influential popular books, see: www.theguardian.com/books/2020/sep/23/top-10-books-about-social-media-viral-matthew-sperling [Accessed Feb 2024].
2. Mirroring, or behavioral mimicry, is widely observed among

primates in multiple contexts. It appears to be an important aspect of social bonding in general, not specifically romantic relationships. For a recent review of the literature, see: Chartrand, T, Lakin, J, "The antecedents and consequences of human behavioral mimicry," *Annual Review of Psychology*, 64, 2013, pp.285–308. At the neuroscience level, mirroring has a basis in literal "mirror neurons" that fire in response to observed changes in the emotional state of others. For an overview of this discovery, see: Bonini, L, Rotunno, C, Arcuri, E, Gallese, V, "Mirror neurons 30 years later: Implications and applications," *Trends in Cognitive Sciences*, 26, 2022, pp.767–81.

3. For an engaging overview of how digital worlds amplify inherent drives toward tribalism, see: Cavanagh, S, *Hivemind: The New Science of Tribalism in Our Divided World*, Orion Spring, London, 2019.
4. This isn't always reliable. One horrified limerent emailed me after discovering that LinkedIn could inform people when their profile had been accessed by another user. Her multiple daily visits to gaze at her LO's profile picture must have given him a bit of a clue that she was unusually invested!
5. Social media addiction falls into that same contentious gray area as other behavioral addictions, at least from a strictly clinical definition. However, most users have personal experience of how compulsive it can be. How deliberate the actions of the social media companies have been is the subject of an ongoing lawsuit brought by the attorney generals of forty-one states and the District of Columbia against Meta, the owner of Instagram and Facebook. See: www.nytimes.com/2023/10/25/health/social-media-addiction.html for more [Accessed Mar 2024].
6. Opening up to a stranger versus a friend is exemplified by the "Reddit effect," where people will be more honest on anonymous sites than on public social media. An in-depth analysis of the phenomenon was carried out by Professor Mario Small at Columbia and published in his book, *Someone To Talk To: How Networks Matter in Practice*, Oxford University Press, Oxford, 2017.

13. Can't we just be friends?

1. Aristotle's view of friendship was laid out in the *Nicomachean Ethics*. For a summary of the ideas in the context of a broader discussion of philosophical perspectives on friendship, see: Bennett, H, "Friendship," *The Stanford Encyclopedia of Philosophy* Zalta, EN, and Nodelman, N, (eds.), Fall 2023.

14. Limerence and long-term love

1. The idea of obsessive or passionate love—in some sense synonyms for limerence—is frequently analyzed in contrast to healthy or mature love. For a review of this perspective, see for example: Sussman, S, "Love Addiction: Definition, Etiology, Treatment," *Sexual Addiction & Compulsivity: The Journal of Treatment and Prevention*, 17, 2010, pp.31–45.
2. The color wheel theory of love was introduced by Canadian psychologist John Alan Lee in *Colors of Love: An Exploration of the Ways of Loving*, New Press, Toronto, 1973. As previously mentioned, the concept of five love languages was introduced by Chapman, G, *The Five Love Languages: How to Express Heartfelt Commitment to Your Mate*, Manjul Publishing House, Bhopal, 2009.
3. Helen Fisher has published many books outlining the progression of love, monogamy, and infidelity. Perhaps the most authoritative is: Fisher, H, *Anatomy of Love: A Natural History of Mating, Marriage, and Why We Stray*, W. W. Norton & Company, New York, 2016. For an accessible overview of the idea of love progressing in three stages, see: www.psychologytoday.com/us/blog/the-mindful-self-express/201603/the-science-love-and-attachment [Accessed Mar 2024].
4. I've always preferred this formulation of the adage. Many commentators argue that the tension between erotic and philia love is at the heart of marriage problems. Perhaps the most influential recent example is Esther Perel's book *Mating in Captivity*, Hodder & Stoughton, New York, 2007.
5. For a good review of the associations between sexual expectations and relationship satisfaction (and how this has been changing under the influence of marketing campaigns in Western nations), see: Schwartz, P, Young, L, "Sexual satisfaction in committed relationships," *Sexual Research & Social Policy*, 6, 2009, pp.1–17.
6. For a comprehensive overview of the literature on marital stability, see: Karimi, R, Bakhtiyari, M, Masjedi, A, "Protective factors of marital stability in long-term marriage globally: A systematic review," *Epidemiology and Health*, 41, 2019, pp.e2019023.

15. Limerence and infidelity

1. Perhaps the ultimate example of this sort of slow neglect leading to limerence vulnerability is the sexless marriage. A common scenario in the correspondence I receive at Living with Limerence is a limerent who has grudgingly accepted continual sexual rejection by their spouse, internalizing the lesson that even the person who once declared their love for them to the world cannot muster enough desire to touch them. Every romantic overture is rebuffed. Eventually the dam breaks

and they become limerent for someone new, multiplying the marital problems further.
2. The theory of cognitive dissonance as a source of distress in response to contradictory beliefs was proposed in the 1950s by Leon Festinger. It is now a well-established principle of psychology. For a definitive guide see: Harmon-Jones, E (ed.), *Cognitive Dissonance: Reexamining a Pivotal Theory in Psychology*, American Psychological Association, 2019.
3. For a thorough analysis of how infidelity can lead to relationship breakdown see: Grøntvedt, T, Kennair, L, Bendixen, M, "Breakup Likelihood Following Hypothetical Sexual or Emotional Infidelity: Perceived Threat, Blame, and Forgiveness," *Journal of Relationships Research*, 11, 2020, p.e7.
4. To quote psychotherapist Matt Lundquist as a (randomly chosen) example of this alternative mindset: "[An emotional affair] is another disease invented out of nonsense and is emotional policing under the auspices of fidelity." See: tribecatherapy.com/5292/an-argument-for-emotional-infidelity/ [Accessed Apr 2024].
5. Some notable contributions to the perspective that changing cultural expectations of romance, marriage, sex, and companionship have converged on making a single person into the source of all emotional nourishment include: Giddens, A, *The Transformation of Intimacy: Sexuality, Love and Eroticism in Modern Societies*, Stanford University Press, 1992; Mitchell, S, *Can Love Last: The Fate of Romance over Time*, W. W. Norton & Co., 2002; Coontz, S, *Marriage, a History: From Obedience to Intimacy or How Love Conquered Marriage*, Viking, 2005; Perel, E, *Mating in Captivity: Reconciling the Erotic and the Domestic*, HarperCollins, 2006.
6. See, for example: Cano, A., & O'Leary, K, "Infidelity and separations precipitate major depressive episodes and symptoms of nonspecific depression and anxiety," *Journal of Consulting and Clinical Psychology*, 68, 2000, pp.774–81; Rachman, S, "Betrayal: A psychological analysis," *Behavior Research and Therapy*, 48, 2010, pp.304–11.

16. Finding balance
1. Research into the effects of long-term relationships on well-being tend to focus on marriage, for which there is a large body of evidence showing a strong association between marital quality, health, and happiness. For recent reviews see: Proulx, C, Helms, H, Buehler, C, "Marital Quality and Personal Well-Being: A Meta-Analysis," *Journal of Marriage and Family*, 69, 2007, pp.576–93 and Robles, T, Slatcher, R, Trombello, J, McGinn, M, "Marital quality and health: A meta-analytic review," *Psychological Bulletin*, 140, 2014, pp.140–87. There is also growing

evidence that these benefits are greater in monogamous marriage, see: Al-Krenawi, A, Graham, J, "A Comparison of Family Functioning, Life and Marital Satisfaction, and Mental Health of Women in Polygamous and Monogamous Marriages," *International Journal of Social Psychiatry*, 52, 2006, pp.5–17.

17. How to get rid of limerence

1. For a history of the development of cognitive behavioral therapy, see: Beck, A, "A 60-year evolution of cognitive theory and therapy," *Perspectives on Psychological Science*, 14, 2019, pp.16–20. The definitive textbook is Beck, J, *Cognitive Behavior Therapy, Third Edition: Basics and Beyond*, Guilford Press, New York, 2020.
2. A good overview of the study of locus of control in psychology is Nowicki, S, *Choice or Chance: Understanding Your Locus of Control and Why It Matters*, Prometheus, New York, 2016.
3. An internal locus of control predicts success in multiple domains of life. See, for example, Ng, T, Sorensen, K, Eby, L, "Locus of control at work: A meta-analysis," *Journal of Organizational Behavior*, 27, 2006, pp.1057–87; Findley, M, Cooper, H, "Locus of control and academic achievement: A literature review," *Journal of Personality and Social Psychology*, 44(2), 1983, pp.419–27; Yu X, Fan, G, "Direct and indirect relationship between locus of control and depression," *Journal of Health Psychology*, 21(7), 2016, pp.1293–98.
4. A classic psychological case study is the patient "Elliot" who suffered a brain tumor that damaged the link between subcortical (emotional) systems and cortical (executive) systems. Instead of becoming a purely logical thinker, Elliot was instead unable to make seemingly trivial decisions—such as what to have for lunch, or whether to use a blue or black pen. Our emotions and intellect are in constant dialogue, sending messages back and forth from the lower to higher brain centers, shaping each other and trying to arrive at a decision on how to act. Understanding this dance between feeling and thinking is critical to understanding limerence. For a good overview of the principle, see: Damasio, A, *Descartes' Error: Emotion, Reason and the Human Brain*, Vintage, New York, 2006.
5. Two highly influential and popular books on this topic are Kahneman, D, *Thinking, Fast and Slow*, Penguin, New York, 2012 and Duhigg, C, *The Power of Habit: Why We Do What We Do, and How to Change*, Random House, New York, 2013.

18. Breaking the limerence habit

1. For a good review of the latest research on how the different regions of the striatum are interconnected and feed forward and backward to the cortex, see: Haber, S, "Corticostriatal circuitry," *Dialogues in Clinical Neuroscience*, 18(1), 2016, pp.7–21.
2. For a deeper understanding of how cortical feedback to the basal ganglia can become compromised in addiction, see: Goldstein, R, Volkow, N, "Dysfunction of the prefrontal cortex in addiction: Neuroimaging findings and clinical implications," *Nature Reviews Neuroscience*, 12, 2011, pp.652–69.
3. Physical withdrawal symptoms reflect the fact that drugs of abuse pharmacologically disrupt physiology (unlike behavioral addictions). The body adapts to the presence of the drug, leading to physical dependence. Sudden elimination of the drug can therefore cause a withdrawal syndrome that can cause serious risks—for some classes of drug, including alcohol, opioids, and benzodiazepines, cold turkey withdrawal can even be lethal.
4. If you feel a twinge of excitement at the possibility of reconnecting with your LO in the future, then you are not ready to attempt it yet!
5. This sort of approach has been called a "Ulysses pact" or contract, after the episode in *The Odyssey* where Ulysses instructed his men to plug their ears with wax and tie him to the ship's mast before they passed the island of the sirens—knowing they would be helpless if they heard the irresistible song. For a popular perspective on how this can be useful in life, see: www.psychologytoday.com/gb/blog/the-carpe-diem-project/201709/writing-your-own-ulysses-contract.
6. Metacognition is a function of the prefrontal cortex. It's a clear psychological sign that the "executive brain" is becoming dominant. For a good review, see: Badre, D, "Cognitive control, hierarchy, and the rostro–caudal organization of the frontal lobes," *Trends in Cognitive Sciences*, 12(5), 2008, pp.193–200.
7. For a recent review on extinction in the context of addiction, see Chesworth, R, Corbit L, "Recent developments in the behavioral and pharmacological enhancement of extinction of drug seeking," *Addiction Biology*, 22(1), 2017, pp.3–43.
8. Strictly speaking, many behavioral scientists would class punishment as a different phenomenon to extinction, but they have the same consequence of updating the learned association rather than erasing the original lesson and a similar vulnerability to relapse. For a discussion of the nuances, see: Bouton, M, "Why behavior change is difficult to sustain," *Preventative Medicine*, 68, 2014, pp. 29–36.

19. Getting over limerence for a specific person

1. From the Latin, *de-* "off" plus *-caedere* "to cut."
2. Mantras have obviously been part of ancient religious traditions for centuries, and more recently popularized as part of the mindfulness movement. Mindfulness practice has been increasingly integrated into cognitive behavior therapy approaches to managing addiction. For a summary, see: Hsu, S, Grow, J, Alan Marlatt, G, "Mindfulness and Addiction," *Recent Developments in Alcoholism*, 18, Kaskutas, L, Galanter, M (eds.), Springer, New York, 2008.
3. A good case study is the philosopher Bertrand Russell. In 1929, he published a book titled *Marriage and Morals*, which was a blistering attack on Victorian attitudes to monogamous sex and marriage. In 1921, he married Dora Black (his second wife), a writer and philosopher who also advocated free love. Things started to unravel for the Russells when Dora became pregnant by her live-in lover, an American journalist, Griffin Barry. With Barry, she had two children, Harriet and Roderick. Bertrand initially tried to accept the situation and even registered Harriet as his child, but ultimately, he abandoned them all for another woman who became his third wife, and with whom he had another child. He divorced and married for a fourth time and continued to have extramarital affairs throughout these later marriages. The Russell home was described by Harriet as a complex, difficult, extended family. Her father, Griffin Barry died "a poor, lonely and disappointed man" according to her account in *A Man of Small Importance: My Father Griffin Barry*. Dormouse Books, Suffolk, 2003.

20. Therapy for limerence

1. See Chapter 5 in Tennov, D, *Love and Limerence: The Experience of Being in Love*. Scarborough House, Maryland, 1998.
2. Tennov, D, *Psychotherapy: The Hazardous Cure*, Abelard-Schuman, New York, 1975.
3. For more on the theory and history of transference, see Handley, N, "The Concept of Transference: A Critique," *British Journal of Psychotherapy*, 12, 1995, pp.49–59. For a personal reflection on how attitudes toward transference have evolved over the years, see: Gold, J, "Events in the Life of the Therapist: The Effect on Transference and Countertransference," *Harvard Review of Psychiatry*, 6(5), 1999, pp.263–9.
4. On a more positive note, CA ultimately found dialectical behavior therapy helpful: "Therapy helped me become aware of my limerence and I'm grateful. Now I can be more proactive about dealing with it."
5. See, for example: Gelso, C, Pérez Rojas, A, Marmarosh, C, "Love and

sexuality in the therapeutic relationship," *Journal of Clinical Psychology*, 70(2), 2014, pp.123–34.
6. Although it is not recognized as a separate condition in the *Diagnostic and Statistical Manual of Mental Disorders*, intrusive thoughts without behavioral compulsions can be interpreted as a form of "pure obsessional" or "primarily obsessional" obsessive compulsive disorder. For a review of the evidence, see Williams, M, Farris, S, Turkheimer E, et al., "Myth of the pure obsessional type in obsessive-compulsive disorder," *Depression and Anxiety*, 28(6), 2011, pp.495–500.
7. For clinical practice guidelines for conditions in which exposure therapy is recommended, see: www.apa.org/ptsd-guideline/patients-and-families/exposure-therapy.pdf.
8. For an influential review of the value of couples therapy, see: Baucom, D, Shoham, V, Mueser, K, Daiuto A, Stickle, T, "Empirically supported couple and family interventions for marital distress and adult mental health problems," *Journal of Consulting and Clinical Psychology*, 66(1), 1998, pp.53–88.
9. For a review of the evidence, see: Flückiger C, Del Re A, Wampold, B et al., "How central is the alliance in psychotherapy? A multilevel longitudinal meta-analysis," *Journal of Counseling Psychology*, 59(1), 2012, pp.10-17.

21. Lasting freedom

1. The second Delphic maxim—*nothing in excess*—is also relevant. The sweet spot for purposeful living is to be honest with yourself about your intrinsic temperament, but also gain an understanding of where your limiting fears come from. If you try to force yourself to live in conflict with your nature you'll never find peace. If you let fear constrain your choices, you will never reach your potential. It's all about balance.
2. Two recent popular books that make a good case for how trials make us stronger are Holiday, R, *The Obstacle Is the Way*, Portfolio, London, 2014 and Taleb, N, *Antifragile*, Penguin, New York, 2013.
3. For a deep dive into the factors that contribute to self-esteem, see: Branden, N, *Six Pillars of Self-Esteem*, Random House, New York, 1995.

INDEX

A
abuse 20, 114
addiction 47–62, 209–10
  alcoholism 73, 209
  drug addiction 47, 51, 56
  gambling addiction 56–8, 150
  person addiction 6, 47–60, 200
adrenal glands 40
adrenaline 40
affairs 23, 31–2, 84–5, 176–86, 227
  emotional affairs 178, 181–2
agape 17, 168
age differences 84–5
alcohol 56
alcohol addiction *see alcoholism*
alcoholism 73, 209
American Psychological Association 56, 63
amphetamines 56
anchor memories 228–9
ancient Greece 16–17, 161, 167
Anna Karenina 107
antirewards 227–9
anxiety 11, 15, 27, 31, 39, 61, 65, 74, 76, 79, 92, 160, 188, 191, 193, 230
anxious attachment 69–73, 86, 236–7
Aristotle 161–2

arousal system 39–40, 44, 48, 56–8, 67, 150, 200
Arthurian legend 104
art *see creativity*
ascending reticular activating system 39
asexuality 16, 88
associative learning 207
associative mating 112–13
attachment styles 68–72, 85–6
  anxious attachment 69–73, 86, 236–7
  avoidant attachment 69–72
  disorganized attachment 69–70
  fearful-avoidant attachment *see disorganized attachment*
  secure attachment 69, 71, 237–8
attachment theory 68–72, 85–6, 237–8
avoidant attachment 69–72

B
Bain, Lucy 83
barriers 22–3, 31, 154–5, 179, 221
basal ganglia 44, 49
beau ideal 20
Beauty and the Beast 103
Beck, Aaron 197–8
behavioral change 207–19

bereavement 66
Big Five personality types 83–4
bipolar disorder 63, 66–7, 73
bisexuality 81–3, 87
bonding system 42–6, 48, 105, 200
bonobos 92
Bowlby, John 68–9
breastfeeding 43
Brokeback Mountain 104
butterflies 91

C

casual dating 137–9
CBT *see cognitive behavioral therapy*
celebrities 20
cheating *see affairs*
childbirth 43–4
childhood abuse 114
childhood bonding 44, 68–9, 112–15, 237–8
childhood neglect 114
Cinderella 103
classic love 17
clinical psychology 56
closure 211–12
cocaine 56
coercive control 20
coffee 50–1
cognitive behavior therapy 197–8, 216–17, 231
cognitive dissonance 179–80, 200–1
cold turkey 215
countertransference 236

couples counseling *see couples therapy*
couples therapy 238–9
creativity 191–2
cuckoos 91

D

Dante 104
dating 133–43
dating apps *see online dating*
daymares 228–9
de Beauvoir, Simone 1, 11
deceit 29, 61, 176–86
de Clérambault's Syndrome *see erotomania*
De Munck, Victor 17
depression 31, 63, 66–7, 199, 230
deprogramming (from limerence) 196–206, 220–30
desperation phase 30–2
Diagnostic and Statistical Manual of Mental Disorders 56, 63
disclosure 31, 123–4, 158, 178, 221–4
disorganized attachment 69–70
Divine Comedy, The 104
divorce 23
dopamine 41–2, 49–60, 105, 123, 138, 218–19
drifting 242–5
drug addiction 47, 51, 56
Dr. Zhivago 106

E

ecstatic union 11
emotional affairs 178, 181–2

endocannabinoids 51
endorphins 51, 54
Enduring Love 20
erratic behavior 31–2
eros 167–8
erotic desire *see sexual desire*
erotomania 20, 67–8
Eugene Onegin 103
euphoria phase 26–8, 190–2, 202
evolution 37–8, 88–97, 111
executive system 67, 173, 200–1, 207–8, 216–17
extramarital affairs *see affairs*
extinction process 217–19
eye contact 115, 118–19

F
Facebook 147–9, 227
fairy tales 103
false dawn 213–14
fearful-avoidant attachment *see disorganized attachment*
fear system 65
fight or flight response 40
Fisher, Helen 168
fitness interdependence 93, 95
flirting 11, 19, 25, 89, 115, 121–3, 159, 177–8
Forster, EM 104
Frankenstein 183
friendship 145–64, 203
friends with benefits *see casual dating*

G
gambling addiction 56–8, 150
game theory 95–6
gender differences *see sex differences*
ghosting 215
Goethe 1

H
habituation 52–3, 55–6, 217–19
Hamlet 197
handicap signaling 96
hedonic hotspots 51–2, 55–6
heroin 53–4, 56
herring gulls 91
hippocampus 49
HIV 82
homosexuality 95
hook-up culture 138–9
Human Universals 35
hyperarousal 40, 46
hypothalamus 44

I
incentive salience 48–50, 55, 58
infidelity *see affairs*
initiation phase 25–6
insomnia 66, 193
Instagram 25, 145, 149
International Classification of Diseases 11th Revision (ICD-11) 63
intrusive thoughts 3, 73, 208, 210, 217
Irish elk 95

J

Jane Eyre 106
Jekyll and Hyde 107
Jung, Carl 106

L

limerence limbo 188
limerent–limerent relationships 140
limerent–non-limerent object relationships 141–2
limerent–non-limerent relationships 140–1
Living with Limerence 5, 8, 33, 75–7, 79–81, 84, 117, 189
lizard brain 37–8
locus coeruleus 40
locus of control 199, 248
Lost in Translation 104
Love and Limerence: The Experience of Being in Love 2, 4, 234
love bombing 123–5
love languages 114
ludus 16–17, 167
lust *see sexual desire*

M

MacBeth 107
Madame Bovary 107
major depressive disorder 63
mania 31, 66–7
mania (obsessive love) 167–8
manipulation 128–9
mantras 226–7
maternal bonding 44, 68–9, 112

Maurice 104
McEwan, Ian 20
mental illness 20, 60–74
metacognition 216–17
mice 51
Microtus ochrogaster see prairie vole
midlife crises 84–5, 177
mixed messages 125–7, 220–1
mood regulation 202, 217
mood swings 31
monogamy 45, 92–7, 176–86
motor output 207
Myers-Brigg Type Indicator 83–4

N

natural selection 89–90
negative immersion 227–8
neuroanatomy 36
neuropeptides 43–6
neuroscience 34–60, 65, 105, 200
Nobel Prize 91
no contact 214–16, 225
noradrenaline 40
nucleus accumbens 36, 49

O

obsessive compulsive disorder 62–4, 73, 236
  pure-O 236
OCD *see obsessive compulsive disorder*
OCEAN framework *see Big Five personality types*
Odyssey, The 107
online dating 134–6, 144

open marriage 227–8
orbitofrontal cortex 65
orgasm 44, 52, 54, 90
Ovid 1
oxytocin 43–6, 90, 105

P
pair bonding 92–7, 138, 165–75, 181, 194–5, 200
paranoid schizophrenia 68
passionate love scale 77
Payne, Helen 1–2
peacocks 95–6
person addiction 6, 47–60, 200
personality disorders 128
personality types 83–4
Phantom of the Opera, The 107
phases of limerence 24–34
    desperation 30–2
    euphoria 26–8, 190–2, 202
    initiation 25–6
    psychological fixation 28–30
    recovery 32–3
phenotype matching 111–13
philia 167–8
philautia 167
Picture of Dorian Gray, The 107
pituitary gland 43
pragma 167
Plato 1
powerlessness 198–9
prairie vole 45
Pratchett, Terry 100
prefrontal cortex 36, 42, 49
Pretty Woman 104
Pride and Prejudice 103

Prophet, Elizabeth Clare 106
psychiatric conditions 20
psychological fixation phase 28–30
psychometric tests 6–8, 77–81
Psychotherapy: The Hazardous Cure 234
punishment 218–19, 227–9
pure-O 236
purposeful living 245–52

R
Rapunzel 103
Relationship obsessive compulsive disorder 65–6
recovery mindset 32–3, 196–206
recovery phase 32–3
reproduction 88–97, 111, 166
reproductive fitness 89
reward prediction 49–57
reward prediction error 49–51, 57, 218–19
reward system 41–2, 48–60, 67, 105, 146, 156, 200, 207, 209–10, 217–19
risk taking 31–2
risky sexual behavior 82
Robin Hood 107
RODC *see relationship obsessive compulsive disorder*
Romanian orphan study 69
romantic archetypes 129–32
romantic monomania 94
Romeo and Juliet 103

rumination 20, 32, 73, 83, 125, 136, 143–5, 149, 160, 178–9, 209–10, 226, 229–30

S

salience bias 12, 29
same-sex couples 88
sampling bias 77–8
schizophrenia 63, 67–8
secure attachment 69, 71, 237–8
selection bias 78–9
self-improvement 192–4
self-report bias 77
self-sacrificing altruism 95
self-talk 226–7
Sense and Sensibility 106
sensitization 567
sex 14–16, 44, 81–3, 89–92, 137–8, 178
sex differences 81–3
sexting 178
sexual desire 14–16, 40, 42, 89–90, 177
sexual harassment 122
sexuality 81–3
Shakespeare, William 197
silverback gorillas 92
Sleeping Beauty 103
sleep-wake transition 39
social barriers *see barriers*
social media 25, 28, 145–53, 209, 216
  Facebook 147–9, 227
  Instagram 25, 145, 149
  X 25, 145
social media addiction 150–2

spiders 95
spiritual narratives 105–6
stable love 165–75
staged withdrawal 215–16, 224–5
stalking 20, 25, 227
Stanford University *see University of Stanford*
Stendhal 1
stickleback fish 91
storge 167–8
storytelling 100–8
striatum 41, 49–50, 54, 65, 207
substance abuse 66
supernormal stimuli 91–2, 96–7
superstition 57
sympathetic nervous system 40

T

Temple of Apollo 245
Tennov, Dorothy 1–5, 8, 10, 33–6, 42–3, 46, 64, 76, 80–1, 116, 142, 234–5
texting 209, 216
  sexting 178
thalamus 65
therapy 193–4, 197–8, 210, 231–40
threat detection 65
Tinbergen, Niko 91
transference 234–7
triggers 121–132
Truly, Madly, Deeply 106
Twin Flames 106
Twitter *see X*

U
University of Stanford 134

V
vasopressin 43–6, 90, 105
ventral tegmental area 36, 41
Vo, Duyen 64

W
Wakin, Albert 64
Wakin-Vo model 64–5, 76, 78, 80–1

WhatsApp 149, 209
When Harry Met Sally 104
withdrawal 59–60, 215
World Health Organization 63
Wuthering Heights 107

X
X (social media platform) 25, 145